AF477810

Nationalism and Its Logical Foundations

NATIONALISM AND ITS LOGICAL FOUNDATIONS

Amílcar Antonio Barreto

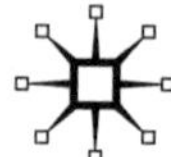

NATIONALISM AND ITS LOGICAL FOUNDATIONS
Copyright © Amílcar Antonio Barreto, 2009.

First published in 2009 by PALGRAVE MACMILLAN® in the United States—a division of St. Martin's Press LLC, 175 Fifth Avenue, New York, NY 10010.

Where this book is distributed in the UK, Europe and the rest of the world, this is by Palgrave Macmillan, a division of Macmillan Publishers Limited, registered in England, company number 785998, of Houndmills, Basingstoke, Hampshire RG21 6XS.

Palgrave Macmillan is the global academic imprint of the above companies and has companies and representatives throughout the world.

Palgrave® and Macmillan® are registered trademarks in the United States, the United Kingdom, Europe and other countries.

ISBN: 978-0-230-61864-0

Library of Congress Cataloging-in-Publication Data is available from the Library of Congress.

A catalogue record of the book is available from the British Library.

Design by Scribe Inc.

First edition: October 2009

10 9 8 7 6 5 4 3 2 1

Printed in the United States of America.

I dedicate this book to James R. Stellar

CONTENTS

ACKNOWLEDGMENTS

The seeds for this project were sown soon after I moved to Boston in 1996. Although I was a new Assistant Professor, I was already interested in tackling this topic at some future date. Many of my peers would have been enticed to jump headfirst into a new project. The fashion conscious—or *fashionistas*, according to some of my friends—wait with gleeful anticipation for the latest trends; they are first in line to gleefully don the most recent craze. Like some of the individuals discussed in this book, they blissfully submit to their innermost and fervent passions. Many academics do likewise. They can be tempted to stop what they were doing, or shelve their current research agenda, in order to jump into an exciting and novel line of inquiry. Despite temptation I heeded the wise counsel of many who warned me that junior faculty needed to focus their efforts on a narrow topic and wait until they were tenured before leaping into new adventures. Indeed, over the years, I saw one to many brilliant academics enticed, like Icarus, to fly too close to the sun. Painful as it was I heeded their counsel.

Without institutional support I could not have completed this project in a timely manner. From my home department, I deeply appreciate the help I received from my chairman, John Portz. To our dedicated staff, especially Barbara Chin and Janet-Louise Joseph, all I can do is quote Tina Turner and say, "*Simply the Best!*" I appreciate the support of my Dean, Bruce Ronkin, and his staff. I researched a portion of this project while on a Visiting Fellowship at the Chaim Herzog Center for Middle East Studies and Diplomacy at Ben Gurion University in 2005. There I was introduced to a remarkable group of scholars who were gladly willing to share their insights. I am profoundly indebted to my host at Ben Gurion, Yoram Meital, and his outstanding assistants—particularly Dvorah Kramer and Aliza Uzen-Swisa—for making that fellowship a possibility and a delight.

This project would never have been possible without the input of many friends and colleagues. Through casual chats, conversations, and quite a few arguments, their poignant questions forced me to reconsider and refine some of my core assumptions. Over the years I benefited from incredible, and sometimes heated, exchanges with Silvia Álvarez Curbelo, Christopher Bosso, Karla Cunningham, Vesna Danilović, Mila Dragojević, Ronald Hedlund, Nadia Kim, Michael Kuczkowski, Michelle Lee, Michael Handel, Matthew Hunt, and Dov Shinar. But in the ideas department, I owe a special round of thanks to two people in particular—Sam Kaplan and Yoram Meital. Since 2005, Sam Kaplan and I have had several disagreements over the basic premise of this book. His suggestions were not meant to transform me into a cultural anthropologist; they were simply meant to make me a better scholar. For his friendship and his incredible insights, I say many thanks. Intellectually, if Sam challenged me on one front, Yoram struck back from another angle. My friendship and delightful arguments with Yoram Meital go back many years. As a historian, Yoram was trained to see social phenomena in a different context. Despite our diverse disciplinary approaches—perhaps because of them—his criticisms have been extremely useful. Along the same lines I am profoundly grateful for the valuable feedback offered by an anonymous reviewer who took the time to go through a couple of drafts. *My thanks!*

One should never underestimate the importance of moral support, particularly while working on a multiyear project. I am grateful to my parents, Eloína and Amílcar Barreto, who remain devoted supporters through thick and thin. I would also like to acknowledge a few wondrous relatives— my sister Lisa Barreto, my aunt Olga Iris Barreto, and my cousin Vilma González—whose uplifting encouragement was a true blessing while working on this project. Encouragement from many colleagues and friends helped me to get through many rough patches. I would like to express my gratitude to Joyce and Otto Berliner, Oscar Blanco-Franco, Holly Carter, Robin Chandler, Maud Duquella, Denise García, Robert Gilbert, Denise Horn, Amy Killeen, Luis Falcón, Richard O'Bryant, Antonio Ocampo-Guzmán, Maurizio Marroni, Juan Carlos Negrón, Rachel Nezer, Ana Y. Ramos-Zayas, Kirsten Rodine-Hardy, Bette Siegal, Itır Toksöz, Michael Travaglini, and Lauren Wise. My academic life changed significantly in 2008 when I became involved in my university's nascent Humanities Center. Serving as the center's associate director has been a true labor of love. I would like to take a moment and salute our fantastic staff and young scholars in the making—Nakeisha Cody and Jennifer Sopchockchai. But I would be absolutely reckless for not recognizing an amazing source of personal and intellectual inspiration from my friend and our founding Humanities Center director, Carla Kaplan. It goes without saying that I owe a very deep, personal and special order of thanks to Phillip McMullen for his support throughout this long process.

I dedicate this book to a dear friend, a great mentor, a true humanitarian, and my former College dean, James R. Stellar. Over the years I have discovered, sadly, that this phenomenal combination of attributes is exceedingly rare in the administrative halls of higher education. At first glance, someone might ask what a political scientist and a psychological biologist might have in common. True, we shared a fondness for great food. As the son of a physician, I was unfazed by conversations centered on biological issues, including detailed discussions of neurological processes. But there was more to our exchanges than just culinary delights or human anatomy. A while back, I traveled with him and other officials from my institution to meet with our counterparts at the Río Piedras campus of the University of Puerto Rico. After our morning meetings we took a lunch break at a well-known restaurant—*El Hipopótamo*—on Luis Muñoz Rivera Avenue. As our discussion meandered, I began discussing my book project with him. Although he was not from my field, I was pleasantly surprised to hear his genuine enthusiasm for my research questions. I was shocked when he presented me with a suggested reading list. Over the following months and years, we discussed those readings as if he were my academic advisor. I heeded his advice and kept an open mind with regard to how different disciplines approach the debate over the interplay between emotions and rationality. Let us just say that I have not been the same scholar since that conversation in a blazing hot San Juan parking lot all those years ago. Little could I have imaged that at that time I unexpectedly acquired a mentor. With great joy I dedicate this book to him. *¡Gracias Jim!*

INTRODUCTION

dulce et decorum est pro patria mori.
mors et fugacem persequitur virum,
nec parcit imbellis iuventae
poplitibus timidove tergo.

[Honorable and sweet to die for one's country,
Since death doesn't spare the deserter either
Nor the boy without a warrior's instinct
Who goes down with his back and tendons slashed.][1]

FIDELITY TO A *NATION* IS A POTENT feeling that often evokes the poignant imagery of courageous throngs fighting side by side, engaged in a common struggle. It also invokes images of the lone hero who shepherds his forces and stands above the multitudes. Passionate responses from ordinary individuals should not surprise us. After all, on behalf of their nation, leaders proclaim that their mission is a sacred duty and justify their actions as a necessary means to defend an immense extended family. Safeguarding the nation is an extension of protecting citizens' homes, their kin, and their community. Such potent sentiments are frequently displayed in believers' resolve to stand in long lines in order to cast their votes. Exercising one's franchise can be an act of patriotic affirmation or an actor of national defiance. Displays of nationalist pride appear in the multitudes, marching, parading, or engaging in a strike. In more extreme cases a sense of communal obligation leads individuals to join their brethren in a call to arms. This sentiment may even lead to martyrdom. A compulsion to join the group and carry out the leaders' bidding starts within. Here it lies nestled in the deepest recesses of someone's soul. For the truly devout, this fervor is utterly incomplete until the sentiment is incarnate through direct action. Like a musical composition, their passions remains inert until the notes on paper are performed in a public venue; and these performers yearn to play.

Among the multitudes that joined the struggle, a handful are singled out and honored in special ways. This meritocracy reveres only the superlatives. The cherished few find their names inscribed on special markers signifying their rightful place among the roster of national heroes. Schools, government buildings, town squares, and major thoroughfares are named after the honored dead. Images of the gallant appear on coins, stamps, and statues erected in a public square. Public art, in the hands of nationalist leaders, is less about aesthetics than conveying a message of patriotic responsibility. Teachers recount stories of the champions' valor. These legends are echoed in theatrical productions, film, and television. While the deeds that earned them special recognition often occur outside the limelight, their commemoration is out in the open. Memorializing the brave and dutiful is an exceedingly public affair.

Monuments such as tombs of the unknown illustrate that we do not have to individually identify our defenders in order to extol their exploits. In the words of Benedict Anderson, "No more arresting emblems of the modern culture of nationalism exist than cenotaphs and tombs of Unknown Soldiers."[2] Just outside the District of Columbia, on the grounds of a plantation previously owned by Confederate General Robert E. Lee, lie the remains of four Americans in a special vault. Each one was killed in a different war. Throughout the day, visitors amass in front of the Tomb of the Unknowns in Arlington National Cemetery to watch the voiceless march of a military honor guard pacing back and forth in front of the sarcophagi, signaling that the nameless fighters buried here deserve the country's utmost praise and admiration. Nameless and faceless, their crypts present the public with a blank slate where admirers and visitors can sketch out the prototypical national.[3]

The social standing, educational achievements, ancestral origins, and former financial assets of these entombed anonymous veterans are all washed away, leaving us only with the message of national pride and responsibility. In their anonymity, they have been transformed into generic and paradigmatic nationals. The public remembrance takes on a truly national aura when the country's president lays flowers at this marker on Memorial Day. A clear message from this and other such rituals is that a sense of duty reaches its climax when transformed into a deed. Martyrdom, sacrificing one's life for a cause, usually stands at the apex of nationally extolled acts. Interestingly, this represents an extreme. The vast majority of all collective activities are modest in scale though resolute in their conviction.

A nameless cenotaph glorifies the nation in its most abstract form. But this is not what young *would-be* soldiers aspire to when they think about their own possible legacy. Glory and fame are celebrated out in the open. They want their exploits to be remembered. Recognition like this is inseparable from a proper moniker tied to a specific face. If their mortal remains are going to be deposited in a crypt for the honored dead, they want the vault with their names clearly inscribed for all to see. Glory seekers do not aspire to a tomb of the unknown. Rather, they admire Kennedy's tomb at Arlington National Cemetery with its eternal flame, or Lenin's imposing mausoleum in Moscow's Red Square, or Anıtkabir—Atatürk's immense sepulcher in Ankara. The tombs of kings and queens are quite impressive but rarely are these monarchs people of humble origin. Few princes stem from the good earth. They were not ordinary beings who achieved greatness via great deeds and not their family pedigree. No, impressionable adolescents look to monuments such as the Alamo in San Antonio. Unlike tombs of the unknown, the names of the Texas insurrectionists are known.

Joseph Trumpeldor is remembered in Israel. His memorial celebrates an ordinary fighter who was transformed into a legend. Within his society, Trumpeldor's exploits reached the pinnacle of nationalistic heroism. In the northern Galilee lies a memorial commemorating him and seven other Zionist pioneers who died at Tel Hai in February 1920.[4] Although this was not the first armed encounter between Jewish immigrants and local Arab inhabitants, the Battle of Tel Hai became legendary in Zionist folklore.[5] A former soldier in the czarist army, Trumpeldor was one of the few early Jewish immigrants in British Palestine with a military background. He was mortally wounded in an armed encounter with local Arab villagers. On his deathbed, a physician asked this man from Russia how he felt. Purportedly, Trumpeldor said, "*ein davar, kedai lamut be'ad ha'aretz*"—"never mind, it is worth dying for the country."[6] In time, this skirmish became the stuff of legends for a generation of Jewish settlers. Years later, a monument commemorating that event was erected on the battle site. Its centerpiece is a roaring brawny white stone lion. Inscribed on the tall pedestal below this lion's paws we find a nationalistic adaptation of Trumpeldor's last words; it reads "*tov lamut be'ad artsenu*"—"it is good to die for our country."[7]

This monument commemorated an ordinary person undergoing extraordinary circumstances. Its central message is crystal clear. Our hero was willing to surrender his life if it significantly enhanced the greater good. The value of this precious sacrifice was reinforced by the very existence of the monument. Like a flag fluttering in front of an important building, this memorial's presence signifies that *we* were victorious. In a reticent response, an appreciative nation erects this petrean testimonial to *our* fallen paladin. The nation's glory is exalted in stone, as is the name of the one who made that sacrifice. A memorial like the one at Tel Hai inspires future warriors far more than the crypts of kings.

Stories of great personal sacrifices in the name of national glory have left many academics baffled. A host of social sciences have argued whether it conforms to predictable behavior. For decades, scholars interested in nationalism have intensely debated the most appropriate manner to approach this topic, and they still quarrel over what motivates ordinary citizens to take risks and engage in collective action. Academics have referred to this conundrum as the *free-rider paradox.* We have a much easier time explaining the thinking behind nationalist leaders than the logic of their rank and file. For advocating home rule, Mahatma Gandhi was imprisoned by the British authorities. The same fate befell Pedro Albizu Campos and Éamon de Valera for insisting on Puerto Rico's independence from the United States and Ireland's freedom from the United Kingdom, respectively. Father Miguel Hidalgo was executed for promoting Mexico's independence from Spain. Indeed, leaders may pay a handsome price for their activities, and some may forfeit their lives in the quest to fulfill their aspirations. Yet many survive. If they do, the nationalist movement leaders stand to make great gains. They take great risks, but if their gamble pays off, they are slated to accrue significant rewards. Successful nationalist elites will be well positioned to reap a series of sizeable benefits. Explaining elite motivation behind nationalist causes is nowhere near as problematic as elucidating the behavior of their followers.

Commonplace nationalist activities span an incredibly wide gamut. Casting a ballot is not, generally speaking, an onerous burden. Still, it requires voters to take time out of their busy schedules to first register with electoral officials and then subsequently line up at a polling station. The cost of voting for the nationalist cause escalates dramatically in cases of political violence. Many states ban nationalist parties. Catalan and Basque nationalist parties freely operate in Spain, as is the case with Québécois. But Kurdish parties in Turkey and Palestinian parties in Israel are banned. Thus, depending on the level of suppression supporting our preferred party and its standard bearers could cost us an unwanted visit by the police, the threat of being beaten, the loss of our jobs, or even imprisonment. Other forms of nationalist mobilization only add to the cost of engaging in nationalist activities. Given these potential sacrifices it is a wonder that any movement launches off the ground. Many movements do just that—they wither on the vine.

Elite motivations are not in question. Long ago, observers and scientists pointed to the vast array of benefits they received for leading the movement. Their contributions are rewarded with the choicest posts and the highest honors. Instead, the debate has centered on the role of ordinary citizens—the throngs of thousands or millions who cooperate out of the limelight. Their numbers are too great for leaders to reward their rank and file individually and selectively for their individual contribution. As a result, some have suggested that nationalism, as is the case with any other large-scale collective endeavor, adheres to rules outside of logic's parameters.

This book contends that there is a fundamental logic to engaging in nationalist activities. We cannot understand the true nature of nationalist movements, or any other large-scale social or political campaign, until we take into account that we cherish different kinds of benefits from our endeavors. But in order to understand this form of strategic thinking, we must cast aside the standard myopia that restricts strategic thinking to the pursuit of tangible goods. Nonelite participation seems illogical until we are willing to examine the emotive side of collective action. In the following pages we will explore those contentious debates and suggest that social scientists need to reexamine some of their underlying assumptions.

The first chapter delves into the contentious theoretical and methodological debate within political science over the best approach to studying nationalism. Rather than agree on one central paradigm, comparative political studies increasingly center on one of three main approaches—political culture, structuralism, and rational choice. Within the political culture school, some suggest that nationalism is like a primordial urge that instinctually bubbles up from the deepest recesses of our genetic makeup. Cultural variation, they suggest, triggers both intragroup cooperative behavior and intergroup conflict. Structuralism sees nationalism differently. It does not blame our DNA or cultural idiosyncrasies but insists that this phenomenon is the result of marked disparities between national groupings such as degrees of modernity or levels of economic development. Methodologically, both political culture and structuralism approach nationalism at a macro level. Rational choice attacks the problem from another angle. Scholars who employ this approach propose that individuals partake in the nationalist mission because of their self-interest. As of yet, there is no consensus on how best to study nationalism or how to tackle one of the most pressing questions in the field—the motivation of the commonplace participant. None of the three existing paradigms adequately accounts for one of the most perplexing issues in this field—namely, explaining why ordinary group members partake in nationalist collective action rather than simply stay home and take a *free ride* on the backs of others.

The second chapter examines how social scientists have assessed strategic behavior. Under the influence of economics, the discipline introducing this approach to the other social sciences, and Christian theologians, emotions were cast out of logic's Edenic terrain. As a result, mainstream scholars limited rationality's parameters to the pursuit of tangible goods and avoidance of material losses. However, a new generation of intellectuals challenge that premise and ask us to revisit the classic scholarship in this field. These readings suggest that human beings strategically pursue both material and social rewards. We tactically pursue honor and prestige among our peers as we hunt for wealth and high-quality professions. This being the case, our notions of rationality need to be readjusted in order to accommodate the full breadth of purposeful behavior.

Chapter 3 lays out our basic model, which takes into account our pursuit of more than one kind of reward. Our lust for emotional satisfaction, our desire for material objects, and our sense of solidarity with our community all combine to sway our actions in one direction or another. We do not participate in the collective struggles of every group—only those for which we have a strong emotive attachment. Not surprisingly, nationalist elites expend a great deal of effort generating and propagating stories of common ancestry in order to promote this ethnic solidarity. Self-esteem is a private sensation. Glory and honor cannot be born from within; they must be bestowed by outsiders. Generating collective action will not be possible without an array of grassroots norm enforcers who keep vigil over our membership, reward cooperators, and punish deviants. This chapter also discusses how these norm enforcers are themselves compensated for their adjudicating duties.

The next two chapters look at several examples of grassroots mobilization on behalf of a nationalist cause. Chapter 4 concentrates on the most common forms of nationalist collective action. As a set, these displays of nationalism are modest and premeditated. Engaging in these behaviors generates a tremendous amount of pride and personal satisfaction. Some of these solidarity-driven individuals pay a material penalty for their gestures. This category would encompass those who vote for a national party, participate in a demonstration, or partake in a public patriotic ritual. National performance could be a matter of words. Beyond the selection of one word versus another, national identities can be presented by opting to employ one language versus another or using different dialects. In one case, parading one's identity can be a matter of flaunting modernity and secularism. A couple of cases will examine how nationalism can be demonstrated via choosing where to live. As a group, these examples highlight that most nationalists perform their identities through carefully measured activities.

Chapter 5 assesses the most extreme forms of nationalist action. These individuals have such an elevated sense of group solidarity that they are willing to risk, or intentionally sacrifice, their lives in order to pursue their objectives. Their sacrifices or risk-taking were not random acts or the actions of irrational beings. Nationalist diehards and zealots knowingly and willingly pursue their objections via performing their identities in the most extreme manner. Without question, their feats are extreme; still, these are not the actions of the mentally unstable. They are aware of the risks they are taking and the material costs they must endure. Pressured by society and driven by their internalized code of honor, they are driven to give the collective their utmost. A true altruist would never expect any compensation. This is not the case here. Our heroes fully expect a handsome return on their investment. They expect to be immortalized and cherished as national champions.

CHAPTER 1

NATIONALISM FROM THREE DIRECTIONS

APPRENTICES ARE TRAINED IN THE MANNER OF their masters. Ancient craftsmen established guilds to judge their novices' work and determine at what point they could partake in the profession without immediate supervision. As an educational system and guardian of cultural transmission, guilds established the guidelines for what they deemed quality goods. Interestingly, colleges and universities—particularly those generating future academics—share many attributes with this deep-rooted system. Young scholars are instructed to scrutinize the works of established thinkers before plunging into their own analysis. Earlier scholarship sets the standard, supposedly, for how particular phenomena are supposed to be studied, how data should to be collected, and aided in understanding the most appropriate way to evaluate one's research findings. Employing the language of political ideologies, scientific inquiry is a kind of *geritocracy*.

Learning from one's elders is an easy concept to grasp. Complying with this mandate is problematic when established scholars fundamentally disagree on the most appropriate approach toward studying a topic. As a field of academic study, nationalism suffers from a lack of scholarly consensus. What impacts this subfield affects the larger discipline in much the same manner. Sadly, theoretical and methodological heterogeneity are among the most recognized features of comparative political studies. Rather than leading to a melodic chorus, the output from this field is notorious for resonating like cacophonous dissonance. One upshot of this rancorous deliberation in this particular branch of political science is a growing coalescence around three major approaches: political culture, structuralism, and rational choice.

Political culture focuses on nationalism's assumed primordial nature. Like a primal urge, it unconsciously calls upon its membership to join in a nationalist campaign. Adherents to this school insist that the emotive nature of this phenomenon excludes it from strategic analysis. Not all scholars buy this argument. There are those who insist that underlying societal structures foment nationalism. Although a few Marxists addressed this issue a century ago, most structural analyses of nationalism emerged half a century ago, paralleling other studies of modernization and its disruptive impact on traditional societies. These structuralists claim that nationalism is either a byproduct of modernization or a consequence of a core region's economic exploitation of a culturally distinct periphery. Some reject both the culturalist and structuralist points of view, preferring, instead, to follow an alternative path. These critics shift the spotlight from societal features to strategizing by individuals. Research employing a rational choice framework, whether explicitly or implicitly, have concentrated on the fabrication of national identities and the generation of excludible goods by ethnic entrepreneurs for the elite stratum. Even this approach has had tremendous difficulty accounting for the participation of the ordinary citizen.

This chapter will examine some of the most significant attributes and pressing weaknesses of these three major research paradigms. One of the most pressing challenges to the study of nationalism, or indeed any large-scale collective action, is explaining why nonelites join such movements. Individual participation is swayed by recompense and punishments. But do movements have the resources to employ sentinels, watch over the group's entire membership, and punish deviant behavior? These forms of sanctions and rewards, we shall argue, are ultimately meaningless without exploring an individual's sense of solidarity with the group in question. The debates presented here will serve as a launching point for a larger discussion about human nature and the role played by different kinds of rewards and sanctions upon our collective behavior.

POLITICAL CULTURE

As a formal approach, political culture debuted in an article written by Gabriel Almond in 1956.[1] The discipline needed to move away from its standard dependence on traditional typologies, he contended. Some in the field focused on differentiating two-party regimes from their multi-party counterparts. Alternatively, others described the disparities between parliamentary democracies, presidential systems, and varieties of authoritarian regimes. Almond insisted that these features failed to explain the underlying political character of most countries. Two countries with presidential systems could exhibit dissimilar voter turnout rates, degrees of political stability, or susceptibility to military takeovers. Formal mechanisms and limitations on power found in statutes, regulations, and constitutions help to explain some aspects of the political process. Still, such instruments neglect critical aspects of the informal elements of political life. Instead, Almond suggested that the discipline needed to gravitate toward culture as the main feature describing a polity and the key independent variable typifying a society's political orientation.[2]

Although Almond's conceptualization of political culture is related to a society's general culture, the two are not the same thing. A political culture represented a "particular distribution of patterns of orientation toward political objects among the members of the nation."[3] It does not precisely coincide with any one society or political system.[4] Aside political culture stands the much broader concept of culture. Most adherents to the political culture approach begin with Clifford Geertz's definition.[5] He described culture as "an historically transmitted pattern of meanings embodied in symbols, a system of inherited conceptions expressed in symbolic forms by means of which men communicate, perpetuate, and develop their knowledge about and attitudes toward life."[6] Culture represents the fundamental framework individuals rely upon to run their day-to-day affairs. It sets the basic parameters for ordinary interactions with one's acquaintances, kin, foes and strangers. Beyond its role in guiding mundane affairs, adherents to this school of thought insisted that culture also represented the foundation for individuals' social and political identification.[7] There are various types of political cultures, but the apogee was the *civic culture*—a variety Almond associated with Anglo-American democracies.[8]

Geertz's notion of culture was not limited to intergenerational social transmission. It also claimed roots in evolutionary biology. Natural selection favored individuals with beneficial traits—such as those who were effective, resourceful, and persistent hunters.[9] Survival in a hostile environment was not a game for the clichéd rugged individual. Evolutionary success was contingent upon individual cooperation with others. As a result, cooperators were more likely to survive than pure egoists. In this process of natural selection, individuals with a proclivity toward strong bonds of social solidarity passed on their collectively oriented traits to succeeding generations. Over the eons this selectivity produced increased proportions of cooperators in the general population—high enough to tolerate some selfish individuals.[10] With whom should one cooperate? Collaboration was easier to foment among one's kin than outsiders.

Fidelity to one's family was not just a positive social trait; ultimately, it was a quality necessary for human survival.

According to these thinkers, primordial ties—the links that can be traced back thousands of generations—remain the building blocks of our modern society.[11] Adherents to this line of reasoning claim that our partiality for our fellow ethnic group members originated in an innate attachments toward our near relations.[12] A predisposition favoring coethnics over outgroup members derived, ultimately, from kin selection.[13] In the study of nationalism, the presumption that national and ethnic identities are hardwired is often referred to as *primordialism*. For primordialists, the participation of ordinary individuals in a nationalist campaign is derived from a deep-seated, genetically wired impulse to safeguard kin.

From the political culture perspective, primordial sentiments are not only deep, they are also exclusive. For Sam Huntington, cultures are exclusory, they are nested within larger macrocultural units, and they resist infiltration. What was at the heart of American identity? Given the country's diverse immigration history, some might suggest that cultural diversity or ethnic pluralism was at least part of the answer. Huntington rejected the notion that it had anything to do with multiculturalism. He insisted, instead, that this national identity was Anglo-Protestant at its core. Protestant colonists from the Anglo-Irish isles established the first European beachhead on the eastern shores of North America. Their vernacular became the country's *lingua franca*, their cultural norms represented the very essence of American identity, and their institutions were the ones entrenched into the Articles of Confederation and the Constitution of 1789. The United States was planned as a Protestant state in much the same way Israel and Pakistan were created as states for Jews and colonial India's Muslims, respectively.[14] Huntington proposed that national sentiments were indivisible and nested within a larger macrocultural structure. He subsumed national sentiments within larger identity blocs—civilizations.[15] In this scheme, the United States belonged within the Western bloc. His categorization partially overlaps with Almond's *civic culture* classification. Although far from explicit, Huntington suggested that there is an inverse relationship between civilizational and national conflicts, on the one hand, and boundary or border security, on the other.[16]

Another scholar in the culturalist camp, Jean Laponce, did not embrace Huntington's premise that national identities were subsets of larger civilizational clusters. Still, Laponce accepted the assumption that these identities were exclusive and resisted permeation. While bilingualism and multilingualism were common, people innately think in one only language. People were inherently unilingual and identified with their language. Language communities have a territorial imperative, and linguistic stability is best preserved in recognized geographic niches.[17] Although Laponce, Huntington, and Almond approached cultural politics from different perspectives, they shared an assumption that contact between culturally distinct peoples precipitated conflict. Such a conjecture would certainly justify government-led assimilationist policies in the name of safeguarding public security and social stability. Although few come right out to admit it, many nationalist activists espouse rhetoric that buys into the culturalist assumptions of the inevitability of the innate incompatibility of cultures.

Detractors criticized the culturalist approach on a number of grounds, starting with the vagueness of the concept of itself. Huntington's macrocultural units—civilizations—were defined on the basis of both objective elements—e.g., history, institutions, language, religion—and subjective self-identification.[18] This characterization shares many of the same attributes found in Stalin's classic depiction of a nation as "a historically evolved, stable community of language, territory, economic life, and psychological make-up manifested in a community of culture."[19] Even by Huntington's own admission civilizations, his fundamental units of analysis do not have "clear-cut boundaries and no precise beginnings and endings."[20] The differentiation between two national identities is sometimes based on one trait, such as language, but in other instances, it is classified on the basis of others such as religion, physical features, folk customs, or a historic narrative. In any scientific endeavor it is important to select observable concepts. Ambiguous notions such as culture may be constructive at the initial stages of research, such as theory formation. But they become an impediment to a theory's empirical evaluation unless they can somehow be measured or clearly observed.[21] The ambiguity of culture as a unit of analysis represents a substantial challenge even to the approach's advocates.[22] Beyond issues of observation and measurement, there are also questions about its applicability to the study of nationalism.

Ethnic identities—beliefs that group members share a common ancestry—are quite old. While nationalism begins with ethnicity, it does not end there. Nationalists advocate the correspondence of cultural and political boundaries.[23] While its agenda is justified on an ethnic basis, ultimately, nationalism is a political ideology. Nationalism is a phenomenon that emerged in the late eighteenth century. Therefore, this novel form of politicized ethnicity cannot be a primordial phenomenon. Patrick Geary's work elucidated that ancient peoples indeed had specific political loyalties. Nevertheless, our contemporary nationalist orientations were not direct derivatives of their counterparts from the Middle Ages or earlier epochs.[24] Nationalist ideologies posit that prince and pauper share a common, albeit distant, ancestry. Yet in Medieval Europe, town and countryside were often inhabited by distinct peoples.[25] Nationalists borrow labels from the ancient past—labels we now assign to *ethnic* categories. But these labels have been applied in a discontinuous manner.[26] The people today who lovingly brandish these age-old labels are not descended, in most cases, from the ancient peoples who were described with the same term.

Benedict Anderson's famous tome *Imagined Communities* concurs that our contemporary political orientations favoring coethnics was not a feature of previous eras where leaders emphasized common religious ties linking sovereign and subject rather than a shared ancestral past.[27] Such popular political principles from the prenationalist era allowed Austrian Hapsburgs to rule over Catholic Spain, and a Dutch aristocrat, William of Orange, to reign over a Protestant British empire, and Turkish Sultans to govern Kurds and Arab Muslims.[28] Ironically, the power of religious convictions impeded Greek nationalism. As late as the eighteenth century, most Balkan Christians centered their identities on a common Orthodox faith.[29] Approaching from the West like a fiery tempest, ideals from the Enlightenment and the new nationalism born out of the French Revolution increasingly influenced Greek intellectuals.[30] These Greek elites then sketched a new account of ancient past whereby modern Greece was declared the natural, undisputed, and unquestionably legitimate heir of ancient Hellas.[31] Greek nationalists sought to animate society's rank and file with stories of a glorious past and an inalienable birthright in a bid to end Ottoman rule. In so doing, their status changed from that of a subjugated community to the heirs of the wellspring of Western civilization. Without a shared myth of ancestry binding sovereign and subject, there is no shared national identity.

Decades before Anderson's research, the legendary Leon Trotsky articulated the thesis that national identities were artificial constructs. At the crossroads of the Balkan and Anatolian peninsulas, he and Arne Swabeck, a leader in the American Communist movement, met on the Turkish island of Büyükada[32] in 1933 to discuss the "Negro question" in the United States.[33] They debated whether African Americans were destined to become an integral part of the workers' movement in the United States or whether they were ordained to create a black homeland of some kind.[34] The future of African Americans depended on their status. Did black

Americans comprise a distinct nation? He suggested that black Americans represented a *race* but not a *nation.* Trotsky said, "We of course do not obligate the Negroes to become a nation; whether they are is a question of their consciousness, that is, what they desire and what they strive for."[35] They were not a nation, Trotsky contended, because African Americans had yet to *will* it into existence. As opposed to natural phenomena, one that was organically determined, Trotsky insisted that nationhood was a conscious act.

Despite vociferous assertions of antiquity, one must be careful in uncritically accepting the presumption that modern national principles are contemporary manifestations of ancient belief systems. As Thomas Eriksen noted, "An important aim of nationalist ideology is thus to recreate a sentiment of wholeness and continuity with the past; to transcend that alienation or rupture between individual and society that modernity has brought about."[36] The previous example focused on Greece. But modern Greek nationalism is far from the only prominent example of a novel movement that has been portrayed as a primordial national compulsion. Another national identity in the eastern Mediterranean claims an even older pedigree.

A distinctive Jewish identity is well documented in the Torah.[37] Jacob was notified that he was destined to become the father of his people and he was promised the land belonging to Abraham and Isaac.[38] The biblical narrative reports that the land of Canaan—the country "flowing with milk and honey"—was divinely promised to Moses and his heirs.[39] Over time, the borders of earlier Jewish polities in the eastern Mediterranean fluctuated considerably. For a period, there were two distinct Jewish states—the southern Kingdom of Judah and the northern Kingdom of Israel. Still, Zionists pointed to the Jewish scriptures as the source of a celestially ordained bond between a people and a land their forebears once inhabited.[40] The sacred nature of the narrative's source infused this nationalist movement with a unique attribute—divine sanction.[41]

While Jewish identity is indeed ancient, the Zionist dream of establishing a Jewish polity in Palestine is historically modern. The concept of a Jewish homecoming to the land of Israel was explicitly expressed in the seventeenth century.[42] But at that time it was more a contemplation or idyllic aspiration than a political manifesto or plan of action. Scholars have pointed to three nineteenth-century notables in their directory of the first proto-Zionists—Rabbi Yehudah Alkalai, Rabbi Zvi Hirsch Kalischer, and Moses Hess.[43] Born in Sarajevo in 1798, Alkalai lived in Serbia at a time when Serbian nationalists were advocating their independence from the Ottomans.[44] Alkalai's appeal for Jews to return to the land their forebears was an act of spiritual devotion and was regarded a precondition for the Messiah's arrival.[45] Born in Posen three years before Alkalai, Kalischer spent his early years in the buffer zone between Poles and Russians. A return to the Holy Land represented, in his view, an important step toward fulfilling spiritual redemption and attaining economic salvation.[46] As John Klier suggested, "It should not be overlooked that the Messianic element was as much—if not more—plagiarized from Russian Populism as from the Jewish Messianic tradition. The new pretender had no difficulty in putting on the clothes of the religious Messiah, however. Thus, when Theodor Herzl launched political Zionism, there were refurbished myths ready at hand which could easily be reactivated."[47]

In contrast to Alkalai and Kalischer, Moses Hess held rather secular political beliefs. Born in Bonn in 1812, Hess was quite active in European politics and collaborated with both Karl Marx and Friedrich Engels.[48] The persecution of Jews in Damascus—the same 1840 event that roused Alkalai's interest in establishing a Jewish haven—was the calamity precipitating Hess's return to his faith.[49] Given the persuasive state of anti-Semitism throughout the Diaspora, the creation of a separate state was described as a necessary step for communal emancipation.[50] This generation of spiritual and political activists laid the groundwork for their late nineteenth-and early twentieth-century Zionist successors.

The ideological heirs to Alkalai, Kalischer and Hess turned to the *Holy Land*—the only space that retained a common meaning to Jews.[51] This was the only real estate that could successfully conjure vibrant images of a Jewish "golden age"—a common strategy by nationalist elites.[52] Setting sights on a particular parcel of land is critical for the fulfillment of nationalist aspirations. After all, "national identity, moreover, required a 'territorial ideology,' the fusing of spatial knowledge with nationalistic conviction. Space is politics, politics is space."[53] Indeed, nationalist obsession over territoriality has long been problematic for ethnic mythmakers—particularly in cases where the ethnic group in question does not numerically overwhelm the land in question. Demography notwithstanding, nationalist elites are more than willing to draw boundaries that appeal to the popular imagination regardless of whether those lines correspond to current realities or realistic prospects. As Bogdan Denitch commented, "When convenient, nationalists insist not on those boundaries that reflect the political choices of the present inhabitants, but rather on historical boundaries, meaning those boundaries from that part of the historical past that would support a claim to a disputed territory. Of course in other cases where the historical argument is weak or nonexistent but the ethnic composition of the population is favorable, the plebiscitary (the will of the people) argument is used. Where neither historical not ethnographic arguments exist, the argument of strategic necessity is used."[54]

Theodor Herzl, one of the leading figures in late nineteenth-century Zionism, explicitly stated that his objective was nothing less than the "restoration of the Jewish State."[55] Intrinsically, the word *restoration* calls for a return to the *status quo ante*, or something approximating the old order. In 1940, David Ben Gurion, the future founder of the modern Israeli state, asserted that "Zionism is the greatest venture in Jewish history since the destruction of the Temple."[56] The destruction of the temple took place over 1,800 years before he uttered those words. Symbolically, Ben Gurion attempted to graft present-day events onto the biblical past.

Ultimately, nationalism rests its legitimacy on a pseudo *geritocracy*—the older a claim to primordial origin the greater the legitimacy of the nationalist claims. This modern phenomenon wraps itself in an out-of-date and folkloric cloak in a bid to obscure its novelty. Addressing the romanticization of Spain in literary and political spheres, José Ortega y Gasset said, "Spain—land of ancestors! Therefore, not ours, not the free property of present-day Spaniards. Those who have gone before continue to rule us and form an oligarchy of the dead, which oppresses us."[57] Referring to Oliver Cromwell and Martin Luther, Karl Marx commented, "Thus the awakening of the dead in those revolutions served the purpose of glorifying the new struggles, not of parodying the old; of magnifying the given task in imagination, not of fleeing from its solution in reality; of finding once more the spirit of revolution, not of making its ghost walk about again."[58] The dearly departed are resurrected. But unlike Mexico's *Day of the Dead*, their spirits are not expected to visit those of us among the living. Instead, the deceased are selectively put to work validating the present and justifying future actions.

The prior examination of the modern origins of Zionism undermines the assertion that nationalism is an old phenomenon. This critique is based on the assessment of an array of scholars whose work is centered in history and the social sciences. Such an evaluation cannot directly assess the primordalist contention that nationalist sentiments are hard-wired at the genetic level. For this purpose, we should return to the Balkans, the region where Rabbi Yehudah Alkalai was born and served as a cleric. Yugoslavia's disintegration provided the backdrop for Goetze and Patrick's examination of genetics and political violence.[59] That violence, they claimed, was directly linked to instincts passed down through the generations. When threatened, individuals coalesced around their group for the collective's survival. Contemporary national and ethnic communities in this region derived from smaller religious associations, which themselves were built atop clan connections.[60] Their suppositions seemed to correspond with the claims of nationalists.[61] Goetze and Patrick's work would seem to substantiate Geertz's speculation that there was a genetic origin to our contemporary cultural identities.

Frank Harvey disputed the idea that nationalism had a genetic foundation and his critique centered on the Balkans. He pointed out four fundamental flaws to primordialist analyses of recent conflicts in this region.[62] Due to high rates of intermarriage, it is virtually impossible for anyone in the Balkans to accurately trace their ethnic lineage. Indeed, genealogical studies in this area show a great diversity of ancestral connections crossing today's confessional and linguistic cleavages. Second, while ethnic differences were constant—objectified in terms of religious identification and language—the levels of interethnic political violence varied considerably in this region over the course of centuries. Third, equivalent ethnic and racial differences exist in many parts of the world without producing ethnically defined civil wars or genocide. Finally, differences in vernaculars and religious creeds did not trigger the collapse of Yugoslavia, he contended. It was the collapse of this federated state that manufactured and magnified such divisions and animosities. José Ortega y Gasset commented, "neither blood nor language gives birth to the national State, rather it is the national State which levels down the differences arising from the red globule and the articulated sound."[63] In sum, we cannot blame DNA for generating or antagonizing differences in language, religious beliefs, or national identity.

STRUCTURALISM

Rather than deliberate over the role of culture as an explanatory variable, structuralists looked to underlying economic conditions and elements of the bureaucratic-organizational environment to explain politics. Structuralism, as an approach to the study of politics and society, traces its intellectual heritage to Marx and Weber in the latter part of the nineteenth century.[64] Of these two thinkers, theories founded on Marxist assumptions had the most significant impact on the study of nationalism, particularly in the 1970s and early 1980s. But the first wave of structuralist studies of nationalism emerged two decades earlier; these were inspired by an analytic trend called *modernization*, which found its inspiration in Weber's work.

The years following World War II represented an unprecedented epoch in the historical development of sovereign states. Within three decades of the war's conclusion, the vast majority of the world's overseas territorial dependencies became sovereign states. Some achieved independence via the ballot box; other former colonies secured it through blood-strewn battlefields. By the end of the twentieth century, the membership of the United Nations more than tripled. With the dissolution of these formal colonial bonds, metropolitan policies regulating everything from the day-to-day management of the bureaucratic apparatus to medium of instruction in the public school system in their far-flung colonial wards slowly eroded. In their place emerged a host of new state policies, some of which triggered, rather than diminished, interethnic tensions.

For instance, English was the language of the colonial administration in Sri Lanka. This colonial policy forced both Sinhala and Tamil speakers to learn and conduct business in an outside language. Exogenous colonial languages placed the linguistically heterogeneous colonial wards on an equal footing vis-à-vis each other. They were, in other words, equally handicapped. English was not the mother tongue of either its Sinhala majority or Tamil minority. Yet the percentage of English-trained Tamils was higher than their proportion of the country's population—a condition that generally leads to interethnic resentment. Following independence, these tensions swelled after the Sinhala majority adopted its language as the medium of bureaucratic administration—a move that marginalized the country's Tamil-speaking minority.[65] Rhetoric aside, the adoption of a local language as the official medium of governmental operations was often a first step toward the elevation of one ethnic group over others.[66] A dominant ethnic group—the *staatvolk*—will habitually regard policies favoring its particular community in ethnically neutral terms.[67] As Uradyn Bulag noted, "A majority is not just a matter of numerical supremacy. It has the clearly ideological connotation of signifying the right track on which the people is advancing. Likewise, the mainstream majority is by extension, a standardization, against which all others are to be measured."[68]

The first wave of structuralist analyses of nationalism bought into modernizationist assumptions. These theorists assumed that Western liberal democratic states represented the paragon of political, economic, and social development.[69] Modernization was characterized by the following four characteristics: a government structure with differentiated political roles and institutions, an increased centralization of political authority, a dissemination of political power to adult citizens, and the enfeeblement of traditional sources of power.[70] In newly independent states, modernization was synonymous with the desire to establish a liberal democratic regime led by Westernized secular elites.[71] North American and West European modes of development were showcased as the model that all developing societies should follow, and modernization was perceived to be a linear process.[72] Western modernity contrasted with the traditionalism of clerics, local chieftains, and aristocratic families.[73] These elites upheld the belief that the lot of one's descendants would be similar to those of one's ancestors, or "long-run fatalism."[74] For modernization to take place, this old order had to be sidestepped.

In a political system where everyone knew *their place*, traditional authority figures were confident in their own long-term prospects. Rather than foment forward progress, these rival political elites were viewed as obstacles undermining the infancy of the budding secular state.[75] Instead of embracing an identity defined in terms of the newly established state, these elites articulated a justification for creating a new configuration of sovereign polities that should coincide with ethnic boundaries. Rustow put it bluntly: "Nationalism—and all that goes with it in terms of human sentiment and public policy—is a hangover from the world of traditional societies."[76] Seemingly, modern societies had already surpassed this stage of political development. Borrowing a metaphor from medicine, these scholars expected that nationalism was simply one of the growing pains associated with modernization. As had been the case in Western societies, peoples in former colonial societies were expected to shake off their attachments to ethnic and other traditional identities in favor of newly created states.

Modernization studies began to loose their luster by the early 1970s. They could not surpass a significant challenge; they remained a "loose collection of assumptions, generalizations, and hypotheses."[77] The emergence of numerous anomalous cases cast serious doubts on this framework's credibility. For example, modernizationists expected so see the emergence of nationalist movements in Indonesia's Aceh region, India's Punjab, or Biafran succession in Nigeria. These societies were, after all, former colonies undergoing the anticipated challenges associated with becoming modern. They were still engrossed in a state-consolidation phase. But modernizationists were perplexed with the emergence and persistence of nationalist movements in advanced industrial states.

Clearly, the United States was not completely vaccinated from the scourge of nationalism. Since the Spanish-American War of 1898, the United States has ruled Puerto Rico. In the wake of the island's rapid industrialization following World War II, support for independence parties subsided. But by the 1970s, it was apparent that a separatist movement, although much smaller than its partisan rivals, continued to endure. Its bedrock was not traditional centers of political power, such as clerics or local notables, but the island's intelligentsia. Furthermore, nonseparatists continued to embrace unmistakably nationalist sentiments.[78]

Exceptions do not forge new rules, and one might argue that a colonial society in the Caribbean might still retain traditional attitudes despite decades of American rule. Puerto Rico was—and remains—a territorial dependency of the United States, and it is not an integral part of the American federation in political or cultural terms despite its incorporation into the U.S. economy. But such a justification could not hold any validity in the United Kingdom, Spain, Belgium, or Canada. The advent of the *Troubles* in Ulster during the 1960s was a sign that anti-British nationalist tensions remained even after Ireland's independence decades earlier. Then again, its emergence could also be a sign revealing anti-Catholic sentiments in Northern Ireland's Protestant community. Like the United States vis-à-vis Puerto Rico, perhaps Northern Ireland remains a significant outlier. Ulster anomalies could not explain the electoral victories, modest as they were, of Plaid Cymru, Wales' nationalist party, and the Scottish National Party in the 1960s.[79] Basque nationalism also exploded onto the Spanish political scene in the 1960s. Franco's death in the mid-1970s did not eradicate nationalism in Euskadi (the Basque lands) or in Catalonia. Nationalist tensions delineated in linguistic and cultural terms in Spain also described a critical aspect of Belgium's political reality. Belgium remained a country divided by loyalties to its Flemish- and French-speaking communities. The 1960s also witnessed the emergence of the Parti Québécois (PQ). In less than a decade, the PQ took the reins of Quebec's government. Anomalies such as these led many structuralists to question their modernizationist premises.[80]

The eroding popularity of modernization as an explanatory framework for nationalism did not mean the decline of structuralist attempts to explain nationalism. Instead, some structuralists turned to Marxist-inspired analyses that centered on conflicting interclass relations.[81] Michael Hechter's *Internal Colonialism* thesis represented the zenith of this new structuralist hypothesis.[82] He analogized classes to nations. If classes could be differentiated in terms of their relationship to the means of production, so could national groupings. Class conflict turned into a clash of rival national identities as two regions took on increasingly class-like attributes. Hechter posited that British industrial development led its English industrial core to seek out new sources of raw materials and additional markets for its finished products. English industrialists fulfilled that quest with their overseas colonies. They also satisfied that pursuit internally—in Britain's Celtic periphery.

The metropolitan state's penetration of its periphery's economy was not nearly as damaging to domestic peripherals as it was to its overseas colonial wards. Economic penetration of new markets could, in time, improve the economic lot of segments of the periphery's populace— particularly the coastal and urban petit bourgeoisie. Yet even when the periphery witnessed economic development in absolute terms, it did so in a dependent fashion vis-à-vis the core. In cases where they are culturally distinct, the core's ascendancy over the hinterland generated a "cultural division of labor." Bitterness toward its subordinate status encouraged its subjects out in the periphery to envision themselves as a distinct national community and pursue independence.[83] The ethnically defined division of labor that emerged in Great Britain's overseas empire had an internal counterpart—one pitting England against its Celtic periphery. In his syllogism, ethnic tensions were clear-cut derivatives of interclass feuds.

Internal colonialism ran into major obstacles when applied to other cases. In Canada, for instance, comparative interprovincial economic development served as a poor explanatory device for explaining the rise of Québécois nationalism in the second half of the twentieth century. Economic development and *per capita* income in this province were on par with the other industrialized, English-speaking Canadian provinces. Comparatively speaking, this was not an economically oppressed region. Quebec, particularly the greater Montreal metropolitan area, was a fundamental part of Central Canada's industrial base. Quebec's French speakers turned to nationalism in response to their socioeconomic marginalization vis-à-vis the local and economically dominant Anglophone minority. What, to some, appeared to be an interprovincial cultural division of labor turned out to be an intraprovincial socioeconomic hierarchy.[84] Within Quebec, as nationalists insisted, the Francophone majority was relegated to a status of "hewers of wood and drawers of water."[85]

Two turbulent events laid the groundwork for the labor force schism typifying two centuries of Quebec's history—Britain's 1763 conquest of New France and the American Revolution fourteen years later. The first episode precipitated the French Crown's departure. The exodus of Paris' civil servants, the colony's appointed political elite, left Roman Catholic priests at the bedrock of the Francophone patrician society in this quadrant of North America by default.[86] The British government looked disparagingly upon this link between the French-speaking *Canadien* peasantry and the church. And yet government officials in London also acknowledged that this deference to ecclesiastical authorities helped maintain British rule.[87] Thus, the British discarded their early policy of culturally assimilating the *Canadiens* with the tacit understanding that Catholic authorities would assist them in maintaining order, particularly during the American insurrection.[88] Rome's church set itself up as intermediary between the British colonial state and these French-speaking subjects.[89] Logically, the ethnic identification sanctioned implicitly by the Catholic Church would be socially conservative and antiseparatist.

The second incident, the American rebellion, triggered a mass exodus of British loyalists to Upper and Lower Canada. This demographic surge inundated Upper Canada's engendering today's English-speaking dominance in Ontario. Anglophone migration to Lower Canada was numerically less significant; but as a cohort, these newcomers rose to Quebec's commercial upper stratum. Markets in the Anglo-Irish isles replaced French markets for Canadian goods, opening numerous economic opportunities for the post-1776 Anglophone migrants.[90] Twentieth-century industrialization did not change that division of labor. Until the last quarter of that century, English Canadian and American enterprises were responsible for almost 80 percent of Quebec's manufacturing output.[91] Even taking into account comparable levels of formal education, English speakers were still favored over French speakers for the same positions.[92]

The nationalist upheaval of the 1960s, Quebec's *Révolution Tranquille* (Quiet Revolution), was triggered by the formation of a new and aggravated class of well-educated Francophones.[93] Their frustration came as they found the aperture to upward mobility severely restricted under the best of circumstances. This cohort exhorted to become *maîtres chez nous*— masters in our own house. Quebec's government succeeded at employing some of these newly minted college graduates in newly nationalized public corporations.[94] Throughout the 1960s and 1970s, the government in Quebec City amended its language laws with the goal of creating more spaces in the public and private sectors for a new French-speaking middle class.[95] In time, the Quebec provincial government substituted the Catholic Church as the epicenter of Francophone power.[96]

Nationalism in post-Franco Catalonia flourished despite the fact that this region was among the most prosperous and industrialized parts of

Spain. Unlike Quebec, the Catalan majority was not economically subordinate to speakers of the state's dominant language—Castillian, or Spanish. To the contrary, the nationalistic Catalans represented the dominant group vis-à-vis Castillian-speaking migrants from the south—particularly from Andalusia.[97] Economic conditions may exacerbate ethnic tensions but they do not engender them.[98] Indeed, echoing Benedict Anderson's sentiments, Yoshiko Herrera claimed that economic advantage and disadvantage are just as *imagined* as national identities.[99] The economic environment is not irrelevant; rather, Herrera claimed that "the meaning of the economy is socially constructed by actors and their social and institutional contexts."[100] Less critical than an objective comparison of the economic potency of two groups is the subjective articulation of grievances. These alleged wrongs or injustices may be conveyed in terms of economic exploitation. Moreover, these inequalities may be championed by society's dominant ethnic groups as well as by any subaltern community.

These criticisms cast serious doubts on the future of the *cultural division of labor* thesis in nationalist studies. Where does this leave scholars who approach nationalism in structural terms? Michael Hechter himself offered a solution. The study of ethnic phenomena, he insisted, could benefit from applying other theoretical models. Which ones? He clamed that "rational choice best hope of arriving at a higher degree of theoretical consensus in the field."[101] The author of the most popular structuralist model of nationalism advocated gravitating toward the third framework discussed in this work.

RATIONAL CHOICE

The first two approaches examined in this chapter presumed that nationalism was a macro-level phenomenon. Nationalists claim, after all, that theirs is a movement of the entire populace. In nationalism, there is no first-person singular, only the first-person plural. One approach contended that a society's culture was itself the driving force behind nationalism while the other approach looked to various socioeconomic variables to explain this manifestation of ethnicized politics. Rational choice theories start from a different premise. They shift the level of analysis down to the individual person. Hypotheses employing this approach center their studies on individual decision-making processes. A rational individual is not guaranteed a particular outcome. Indeed, a political actor could make a decision based on incomplete or erroneous information. But a core assumption of this approach is that decision makers pursue their ends in a strategic manner. Their means are inextricably tied to their ultimate ends. Rodney Barker commented, "One of the contributions of rational choice theory within political science has been a reassertion of the importance of individual agency, even if it has at the same time been insufficiently sensitive to the individuality of individuals."[102]

In the study of nationalism, there are many who reject this approach out of hand. For example, Eric Hobsbawm claimed that nationalism is neither subjective nor objective.[103] Its mutability leaves it an inappropriate phenomenon to assess in terms of strategic calculation. Nationalism is publicly articulated on the basis of cultural traits. Therefore, it must be irrational, said John Edwards, since national identities are based on defining groups in terms of objective cultural traits that cannot, *ipso facto*, maintain these group boundaries.[104] In a way, these cultural traits are important, and yet, they are not. Inconsistency is a sign, he would contend, that nationalism is a nonlogical phenomenon. Other researchers described nationalism as a variety of false consciousness. Prevalent among these critics of the rational choice school are Marxists who discount the logic of expending resources in a national struggle led by rival factions of the bourgeoisie or petite bourgeoisie. "The workingmen have no country," insisted Karl Marx and Frederick Engels in *The Communist Manifesto*.[105] It is illogical for workers and peasants to champion the causes that primarily benefit the capitalist classes.

What, exactly, do scholars in this school of thought mean when they claim that individuals are rational? Popular notions hinge on the premise that a rational person is a *reasonable* being. Of course, reasonableness is a popular election open to a mass franchise. This judgment is susceptible to the public's ethical norms and personal values. This sense of the term is *substantive* rationality. Scholars who conduct research employing a theory within the rational choice approach focus not on this sense of the term but on *utilitarian* or *instrumental* rationality. For these analysts, a rational being is someone who can discern between different alternatives, is capable of ranking those choices, orders those options transitively, selects from them the alternatives that maximizes this individual's preferences, and if faced with the same opportunities and circumstances a rational actor would make the same decision over again.[106] This version of rationality incorporates an implicit notion that rational beings check their emotions at the door. Dispassionate computation is presumed to be the standard operating procedure. By boiling things down to the lone individual—a person devoid of cultural trappings—supporters of this approach aspire to lay the groundwork for universal and testable theories.[107]

Scholars who conduct research within a rational choice framework often list the writings of Niccolò Machiavelli and Jeremy Bentham as foundational works. The fifteenth century's Machiavelli broke with an earlier philosophical tradition emphasizing the ideal state or the state obsessed with promoting the general welfare. More than two thousand years ago, Aristotle wrote in *The Politics* that the state's ultimate goal was to foment the public good.[108] Machiavelli dismissed this premise. This Florentine writer counseled his prince that a ruler's tenure in office could not be secured by committing to the public good.[109] Such a virtuous ruler could not survive in a sea teaming with unscrupulous political players. A successful sovereign, Machiavelli insisted, is one who would have to learn that cruelty was a necessary tool of political staying power.[110] The eighteenth century's Jeremy Bentham said that individuals aspire to maximize their pleasure and minimize their pain, and he clarified that political actors were no exception to that rule.[111] At the heart of the ruler's strategic thinking was not the greater good but the best interest of the ruler.

It is important to note that inquiries explicitly employing a rational choice framework represent the smallest proportion of all three major approaches used to analyze nationalism. This should not be surprising. A considerable number of area specialists and those oriented toward descriptive and historic investigations are often unreceptive, if not hostile, to an approach charged with a derisory appreciation for the unique social, cultural, political, and historic characteristics of cases.[112] Such scholars are adamant that the only way to conduct research in the social sciences is to immerse oneself in the unique details and minutia of that phenomenon. Still, many studies implicitly buy into rational choice assumptions without declaring it as such.

While *primordialists* profess that contemporary national identities emerged from premodern identities, *constructivists* posit that national identities are artificial constructs.[113] The most noteworthy work within the constructivist camp is Anderson's *Imagined Communities*.[114] Nations are not innate; they are not natural. Anderson insisted that they are man-made constructs. Gellner concurred; he stated that nations are "artefacts of men's convictions and loyalties and solidarities."[115] Constructivists reject the culturalist's thesis of primeval origin to national identities.[116] Russell Hardin goes one step further; he insisted that no conviction or ideology could be primordial.[117]

If national identities are constructed, the question remains, who assembles them? Constructivists highlight the role of a small set of pivotal individuals—the intelligentsia.[118] Ordinary citizens have their own beliefs and principles. But the mobilization of large groups depends upon the articulation of a more complex ideology or theory that the intelligentsia can provide.[119] Intellectuals possess a more extensive formal education that provides these elites with particular strategic advantages in generating and disseminating nationalist narratives vis-à-vis the ordinary citizenry.[120] While elite mythmakers promote nationalism, or other ideologies, as doctrines benefiting the masses, there is little doubt that the prime material beneficiaries are nationalist elites themselves.[121]

If ethnic entrepreneurs engineer nationalist convictions, how do they assemble these identities? Tönnies described a natural and organic community as a *gemeinschaft*. But a nation is not a *gemeinschaft*, it is a *gesellschaft*—a fabricated or artificial society.[122] How does one transform an artificial construct in such a way that it appear to be natural? Ethnic entrepreneurs face a formidable challenge—they must foment an identity that unites coethnics across class lines while simultaneously excluding outsiders. There is no first-person plural without a corresponding third-person plural.[123] In this process, ethnic entrepreneurs exploit preexisting folk customs, beliefs, and other readily accessible sociocultural elements in order to define group boundaries.[124] What had been, at one point, the habits and practices of rural life—or some remote existence—are incorporated into the common national narrative.[125] Ethnic entrepreneurs forge an artificial sense of kinship by objectifying symbols and a shared set of cultural characteristics.[126] It is imperative that we separate group identities from the cultural traits publicly used to demarcate the features describing *us* versus *them*. As Barth noted, group identities can endure the loss of the characteristics employed to portray them.[127]

Cultural objectification is not a spontaneous event—it is a very deliberate process. The repertoire of distinguishing cultural attributes is vast. Enumerating all of the discerning features, highlighting the differences between *us* and *them*, is a daunting, yet necessary, task.[128] How should the intelligentsia promoting a new national identity proceed? In order to diminish the costs associated with group mobilization, ethnic entrepreneurs will be parsimonious and characterize their community on the basis of a limited set of traits such as language, religion, or phenotypical characteristics.[129] The traits ethnic entrepreneurs ultimately select coincide with the elite's strategic interest of ensuring their privileged role within the group, all the while excluding outsiders.[130] Ethnic entrepreneurs employ tangible cultural features as if they were stones to build a national identity's outer shell, or public face. The first-person plural will be cast in a positive light. *Our* features are displayed as particularly noteworthy, morally sound, or aesthetically desirable. Through stereotyping and demonization they may be working on defining others as much as establishing the parameters for the first-person plural.[131] Therefore, society's privileged upper stratum must effectively mark the boundaries between in- and outgroup members. Simultaneously, nationalist elites must objectify their group's identity in such a way that they maintain their ideological dominance *within* their community.

Early twentieth-century Puerto Rican nationalism provides a good example of just what can occur when a leader, even a highly respected one, tries to articulate a national chronicle that runs counter to the long-term interests of the nationalist elite advancing the cause. A distinctive Puerto Rican identity, vis-à-vis Spaniards, was already entrenched before the Spanish American War of 1898—the conflict that transformed this Caribbean island into an American colony.[132] This change in sovereignty unveiled an opportunity to redefine the parameters of *puertorriqueñidad*—Puerto Rican-ness.[133] Early twentieth-century Puerto Rican nationalism was manifested in two formats. One was radical, confrontational, and militantly separatist; the second, and more widespread of the two, was reformist, cooperative with American authorities.[134] This second variant was autonomist, not separatist. Pedro Albizu Campos, the Harvard-educated leader of the Nationalist Party in the 1930s, represented the most confrontational and uncompromising segment of the nationalist intelligentsia.[135] To this day, he is exalted by independence supporters on both the island and in the diaspora in the United States as a paragon of *puertorriqueñidad*.[136] Under his leadership, the Nationalist Party spearheaded the diffusion of key cultural symbols associated with a gallant and more assertive Puerto Rican identity.[137] Various Latin American nationalists from this period, including Albizu Campos, looked to writers such as Uruguay's José Rodó for intellectual inspiration.[138] While he admired the technological advances of the United States, Rodó encouraged Latin Americans to reject the soulless utilitarianism of the Anglo North.[139] Albizu Campos found his inspiration in Catholic Spain. His studies in the Boston area inspired his perception of nationalism. With the Irish Free State movement as his nationalist paradigm, Albizu Campos attempted to objectify Roman Catholicism as a defining feature of his people's identity.[140]

At the time Pedro Albizu Campos articulated his nationalist message, most Puerto Rican islanders were Roman Catholic and a clear majority of Americans were Protestant. Still, even in the 1930s, there were tens of millions of Catholics in the United States. Their presence certainly undermined a sharp division between a Catholic *us* versus a Protestant *them*. Furthermore, by the 1930s, there were already thousands of Puerto Rican converts to Protestantism. By its nature, religion is a cultural trait that is most effectively dominated by clerics. Hence, as opposed to lifting the status of the secular and nationalist intelligentsia—one comprised of teachers, poets, and lawyers—the objectification of Roman Catholicism would have fortified the standing of priests and bishops. Following the Spanish American War, officials in Rome replaced Bishop Toribio Miguella y Arnedo with Bishop William Ambrose Jones. From this point on until the mid-1960s, the vast majority of the diocesan leaders were American-born Anglophones.[141] Albizu Campos's attempt to politically galvanize Catholicism clashed with the interests of a conservative and American-dominated local church hierarchy.[142] Religion was a less than ideal boundary marker separating Americans from Puerto Ricans, given the considerable size of the Catholic minority in North America. And rather than reinforce the secular ethnic elites promoting nationalism, it inadvertently raise the status of a rival elite.

In contrast to religion, language proved to be a far more effective ethnic group boundary marker. The percentage of Puerto Ricans capable of speaking even rudimentary English in the first few decades of the twentieth century was extremely low.[143] On the other hand, exceedingly few American administrators appointed to staff the territorial government or federal agencies were capable of speaking Spanish. For the few who endeavored to learn the local language, their thick accent served as a constant reminder of their alien origins. Extended to the United States as a whole, the proportion of Spanish speakers during this period was relatively low outside the southwestern states. From the perspective of the local intelligentsia, language was also a more effective preserver of their ingroup status. Even in cases of mass literacy, society's secular intellectuals generally have greater command of the language's standardized version. Additionally, the learned are also more familiar with the language's literary canons and traditions. As opposed to religion, language was a trait that secular intellectuals could dominate, thus assuring their long-term standing in the community as the guardians of the *sacred tongue* rather than the *sacred texts*. Pedro Albizu Campos remained a revered figure among Puerto Rican nationalists, but secular nationalists simply ignored the confessional dimension of his political rhetoric.

Elite motivations in a nationalist project are rather clear. Then again, the "essence" of nationalism is not found in the small coterie of elites who design it but in the rank and file implementing the nationalist vision.[144] If the incentives for elite participation are unambiguous, the impetus behind the involvement of nonelites is uncertain. Although a risky gamble, victorious ethnic entrepreneurs hope to reap tremendous rewards—particularly in the form of patronage—for their participation.[145] Large-scale movements, on the other hand, simply do not have the resources to directly compensate all participants for their individual contribution. Neither do they have the resources to hire enough monitors to scrutinize all community members in order to assess who should be rewarded for their cooperation, or sanctioned for their treachery, and to what degree. Society's highest ranking members stand at the head of the line to reap the material rewards of their movement's successes—choice civilian and military positions within the nationalist government, lucrative contracts, prestigious titles and honors, and other incentives. These coveted rewards are allocated according on one's specific contribution to the nationalist campaign. The other type of reward is nonexcludable.

Following victory, blue-collar jobs in the public and private sector, for example, may be limited to members of the dominant ethnic group. Regime leaders may mandate the printing of all public signs, or the transmission of media broadcasts, in their language. All ingroup members could benefit from such a change. Unless they are bilingual, outsiders could be handicapped by such a move. But rewards such as these are distributed to all group members regardless of their particular participation in the nationalist campaign. They are, by definition, nonexcludable public goods. Since these nonexcludable goods cannot be restricted, they are open to all regardless of the level of participation, or even defection. As Mancur Olson explained, this creates an inherent incongruity between a rational strategy for the collective and its ordinary members.[146]

Group leaders must find ways to "privatize," to somehow make exclusive, collective benefits to assure cooperators' greater benefits than defectors.[147] After all, individual and exclusive benefits represent the fodder that feeds collective action. Samuel Popkin wrote, "Whether a self-interested peasant will or will not contribute to a collective action depends on individual—not group—benefits."[148] When the only rewards on the table are public goods, rational individuals are temped to free ride on the backs of others. Long before Olson published his tome, Jean-Jacques Rousseau commented that the common good could not be derived from an individual's sense of self-interest.[149] From Thomas Hobbes's perspective, collective action is inconceivable without the forceful hand of the state or a well-armed institution.[150] These thinkers shared with Olson a concern for explaining the logical incongruity between individual interests and the collective's best interests.

Movement longevity or triumph is not likely until, and to the degree that, the masses depend on ethnic entrepreneurs rather than other elites.[151] That dependency is often centered on information as much as it is on tangibles.[152] For Michael Hechter, the free-rider paradox can only be countermand through an effective set of institutions monitoring and sanctioning possible defectors.[153] As he put it, "Without control, group solidarity is, at best, a chimera."[154] But we run into yet another dilemma—accounting for the resources necessary to individually reward village- and street-level norm enforcers. This is the *second-order free-rider paradox*, and it is just as problematic as the original free-rider paradox.[155] Beyond the issue of paying norm-enforcing agents, group leaders must still keep an eye out for these monitors.[156] Thus, rational choice analyses have demonstrated significant deficiencies in predicting nonelite participation in large-scale collective endeavors.

Olson's *free-rider paradox* represents one of the most significant challenges to theories within the rational choice framework that seek to explain the logic behind popular participation in collective action.[157] As Jon Elster put it, there is no more difficult or important problem in the social sciences than explaining collective action.[158] Nationalism is difficult to explain in terms of individual rationality precisely because of the collective action problem.[159] Detractors have questioned the heart of the rational choice approach's methodologically congruity—attempting to assess an inherently collective phenomenon with an innately individualistic approach.[160]

CONCLUSION

Nationalism studies conducted within political science have paralleled larger trends in the discipline. Thus, over the past half century, three major research paradigms have each contributed to the larger debate over the essence of this phenomenon. From the perspective of scholars operating with the political culture approach, nationalism was a deep-seated inclination that was both antediluvian and ingrained in our very genes. Subsequently, scholars operating from a structuralist framework viewed nationalism as either the growing pains associated with modernization or the consequence of interregional economic exploitation. Rational choice theorists have explored the invented nature of national identities and the strategic interests of ethnic entrepreneurs. So far, none of the three approaches has adequately addressed the logic behind the ordinary individual's participation in nationalist activities. The following chapter will begin to directly tackle the *free-rider paradox*. Perhaps the challenge is not explaining irrational behavior; instead, our aspiration should be to understand that rational actions are not solely limited to the pursuit of tangibles.

CHAPTER 2

RATIONALITY'S JANUS-LIKE NATURE

THE WRITINGS OF BENTHAM AND MACHIAVELLI DISCUSSED in the previous chapter constitute integral parts of the rational choice cannon. These works strongly influenced the way in which many social scientists understood the nature of rationality. Among these disciplines, economics was the first to feel its influence and it was also the field that felt its impact more than others. Subsequently, economics played a key role in introducing utilitarian principles to the other social sciences. As a result, its biases tinted the lenses through which these disciplines understood rationality. Rational beings were ones who pursued material or other tangible rewards and endeavored to eschew material or tangible sanctions. This trajectory of this intellectual transmission significantly impacted the manner in which nationalism scholars perceived rationality. Such a limited view of rationality was encouraged by a deeply entrenched presumption that our *so-called* emotive and rational thinking processes were totally distinct.

Research findings in the social, behavioral, and natural sciences question that dualist supposition. Some classic thinkers and contemporary research scientists suggest that emotions are an integral part of the way in which people gauge the most efficient paths to reach their goals. The manner in which individuals strategically deliberate their alternatives applies to our material-seeking side as much as it does to our emotive side. Perhaps the problem is not found in the rationalist framework itself but in some of the key assumptions traditionally made by rationalists who studied nationalism in the past. Nationalist rhetoric is saturated with emotional appeals, and rational choice frameworks can be censured for inadequately addressing that emotive dimension. Our analysis must tackle the issue of emotions head-on.

EMOTIONS VERSUS RATIONALITY

Lone among the social sciences, economics had the greatest impact on disseminating rational choice assumptions throughout its sister disciplines.[1] Capitalist economics normally begin with the assumption that individuals are geared toward the accrual of material goods.[2] The means by which we measure prosperity are clearly discernible objects, such as currency. Rational beings, it was presumed, sought items that any objective analyst could examine. Not only is the object of the capitalist's desire tangible, money also has the advantage of providing the analyst with specific units for cross-case comparisons. Over time, these fundamental assumptions swayed the way in which other social scientists set the boundaries of rational behavior.

Wealth-seeking individuals did not simply stumble across prosperity. Affluence was a blueprint they had to carefully draft. Lady luck could always play a part in anyone's successes. Nevertheless, happenstance is never a reliable plan of action. Instead, wealth seekers needed to sketch a mental map of the best way they could achieve their goals given their particular circumstances. Economists learned early on that in order to understand individual decision makers bent on maintaining, if not augmenting, their financial standing, one had to assess the way in which they made their choices. This introduction from economics significantly impacted the way in which most social scientists assessed the question of rational behavior and psychological motivations.

Economists have the luxury of comparing utilities for wealth seekers. A utility is a gauge of individuals' preferred outcomes that takes into account their enthusiasm, or reluctance, for risk taking.[3] We expect rational individuals to pursue the alternative that yields the greatest utility.[4] Those who are oriented toward pecuniary outcomes prefer a job offering a monthly salary of $4,000 versus a comparable contract compensated at only $3,000 per month. The same individual weighing two alternative employment opportunities a few years down the road—say, one offering $6,000 and another at $5,000 per month—not only prefers the higher salary over the lower, but this individual values the loftier wage at $1,000. This sum is the same difference between the earlier set of rival salaries. Here the options at the two different periods are spaced exactly 1,000 currency units apart. We can move beyond a mere ordinal comparison that tells us little more than *greater than* or *less than*. The precise nature of these financial units provides observers the benefit of employing precise measurements. Not only can we compare these particular preferences over time, but we can also assess the relative value of different financial outcomes once we factor in the probability of materialization.

Imagine, for instance, that someone had $100 to invest. To simplify this example, this investor was limited to two choices. This budding venture capitalist could deposit the $100 in a simple savings account. Alternatively, this novice entrepreneur could purchase one hundred dollars worth of lottery tickets. A savings account paying, let us say, 2 percent interest per annum will yield a profit of $2 after twelve months. Contrast this dividend with the lottery. Hitting the jackpot could generate, for our financier, $10 million. Certainly, $10 million is astronomically greater than a paltry $2. Yet, not only can we compare the absolute values of the two different outcomes, we can also evaluate the weight of these two outcomes given their probability of fulfillment.

In a government-assured banking account the probability of earning the $2 in interest is extremely high. Unless we fear the collapse of the state, we could presuppose that the likelihood of receiving that meek interest is a near certainty. On the other hand, the probability of hitting a multimillion-dollar jackpot, even with one hundred $1 tickets, is infinitesimally small. Our investor might have as good of chance of winning the lottery, even with one hundred tickets, as being struck by lightning. When we ponder the probabilities of different outcomes, not just their absolute difference, we can understand why it is financially more prudent to invest the $100 in a savings account than spend it on lottery tickets. It goes without saying that comparisons made by professional economists are far more complex than the comparisons presented here. Nonetheless, the main point is that these outcomes can be compared cardinally. This kind of precision may be a regular feature of most economic analyses but it is atypical in most social science inquiries.

While other social scientists may have to settle with comparing ordinal preferences, economists may indulgence, depending on the precise nature of their study, in comparing cardinal preferences across actors. It is one thing to argue that one actor prefers one set of policy preferences more than another set. For example, assume that a group of nationalist politicians favored declaring their idiom the sole official language. Topping their legislative agenda would be promulgating a new statute, or even a constitutional amendment, declaring theirs as the only legally sanctioned national idiom. Given the realities of negotiating in a legislative body, we would understand that their dreamed option might not be realistic. These nationalists may not have enough parliamentary seats to pass their ideal language law. Such nationalist lawmakers would rather support a statute establishing theirs as the *first* of two languages rather than endorse a bill instituting official bilingualism or language parity. Based on the classic attributes, these are objectively rational, political actors. They could differentiate their alternatives, rank them, categorize them transitively, pick the option that came closest to fulfilling their preferences, and when confronted with the same choices, they would make the same decision.[5] Legislative strategizing in this manner is wholly consistent with the fundamental principles of instrumental rationality but such an assessment lacks the exactitude commonly found in economics.

Over time, noneconomists employing a rational choice framework generally saw a material or pecuniary foundation to individual motivation in purposeful action.[6] Monetary rewards could explain elite motivation in nationalism. Certainly, elites—the ethnic entrepreneurs that played the role of venture capitalists in a nationalist campaign—stood at the head of the line doling out what few individual selective incentives the group could offer. In a confessor-like manner, elites anointed themselves guardians of the nation's essence—the intermediary between the ordinary folk and the nation's unseen purity.[7] This assumption led Albert Breton to assume that the working classes should be less inclined toward nationalism than their white-collar co-ethnics.[8] The typical person in these analyses, to one degree or another, is epitomized by the classic *Homo economicus*, or economic man. Capitalizing on profits and other tangible gains was deemed the axiomatic endgame of every rational actor despite the fact that earlier theorists developed more inclusive notions of rational behavior.

Outside of economics, many thinkers simply took for granted that rational and emotive thought were two utterly disparate phenomena. Emile Durkheim, for example, believed that people were invested with both a body and separate soul.[9] Within the field of nationalism studies, Walker Connor made a similar point when he underscored that nationalist leaders make their appeals through emotions and not reason.[10] If emotions and reason are disparate phenomena, there is no point in employing a strategic actor model outside of the pursuit of tangible rewards or steering clear of material pain or punishment. This is a line of reasoning that René Descartes would have recommended. Descartes conceptually estranged emotions out of the realm of rationality. His "dualist notion" segregated the mind from the brain and body.[11] This assumption did more than just impact philosophy. Over the years, this dualist tradition influenced the way in which Western medicine examines and treats diseases.[12] In *The Discourse*, Descartes postulated that these were two completely distinct mental processes—one emotional, another rational. Rationality, he insisted, represented the superior of the two. Descartes promoted the principle that we should all strive to lead our lives by reason rather than our emotions or senses.[13] In *The Passions of the Soul*, he commented, "And all the struggles that people customarily imagine between the lower part of the soul, which is called sensitive, and the higher, which is rational, or between the natural appetites and the will, consist only in the opposition between the movements which the body by its spirits and the soul by its will tend to excite simultaneously in the gland."[14]

Beyond Descartes, this dualist thesis was reinforced by religious influences. Jewish and Christian theology long associated emotions with transgressions and surrendering to one's passions.[15] In Proverbs, emotions are ridiculed while calm rationality is lauded: "The patient man shows much good sense, but the quick-tempered man displays folly at its height. A tranquil mind gives life to the body, but jealousy rots the bones."[16] One will find similar language in the Christian scriptures. In the Second book of Timothy, St. Paul proposed: "So, turn from your youthful passions and pursue integrity, faith, love, and peace, along with those who call on the Lord in purity of heart."[17] Excerpts from these texts left little doubt that emotions were something we should curb, or at least attempt to repress, for the greater good of society and ourselves. Rational beings suppressed their emotions. To give into them led not just to irrationality but also paved the way for the commission of sins.

EMOTIONS PLUS RATIONALITY

Before we simply accept the thesis that so-called emotive and rational thought processes are completely separate phenomena, we should heed Rose McDermott's advice. She counseled us to take another look at rational choice's foundational texts. She strongly suggested that modern scholarship employing this approach deviated from the path laid out by its intellectual progenitors. Bentham's work was never limited to material wants or financial aspirations: "Notions of pleasure and pain were eliminated from the understanding of utility when utility was changed from a psychological to an economic construct. To the extent that current models of expected utility theory exclude emotion, they betray their intellectual foundations."[18]

A complete view of rational beings must take into account the pursuit of both material and nonmaterial goals. Appraising the rational choice approach, Rodney Barker noted that the real problem was not with the supposed irrationality of those who engaged in collective activities, but with an "inadequate conception of rationality, which takes identities and interests as given, rather than as dynamic, and which fails to take account of identity cultivation, maintenance, and expression, as a major part of public life."[19] Drew Westen said, "Although Western philosophy and culture have a history of viewing reason and emotion as opposing forces, what becomes clear from understanding their evolution is how ultimately they typically work together."[20] If emotions were an integral part of the original utilitarian calculus, then economists were not completely wrong for centering on tangible goals. Rather, they were myopic. As opposed to relying exclusively on an economist's reading of Bentham, it will be useful to return to the original source ourselves.

Individuals aspire to maximize their pleasure and minimize pain, Bentham insisted.[21] He clearly recognized the power of lust over money and power in steering human behavior. His *Principles of Morals and Legislation* acknowledged that some people thirst for material possessions. Yet a single-mined focus on tangible goods is incomplete. He noted that some people pursue something different. Bentham outlined four sources instigating pleasure and pain: the physical, the political, the moral, and the religious.[22] The joys and sorrows of the first three sources must be experienced within one's natural life. Religious pain or pleasure, he gathered, could be experienced in either the hereafter or the present.[23] Physical and political sources of pain and pleasure could be described in tangible terms. On the positive side, they could motivate individuals to pursue food, consumer goods, luxury items, public office, or other material wants. Its negative correlate would have us steer away from the pain associated with poverty, want, homelessness, or expulsion from office. But the other two sources of pain and pleasure he mentioned were moral and religious. In a purely material sense, a devout person could pursue entry into Heaven in a bid to avoid the pains associated with Hell. But when most people contemplate moral and religious motivation, they do not think in terms of tangible goods, but in satisfying spiritual needs that fall outside the realm of material wants.

Subsequently, Bethman went beyond discussing sources of pain and pleasure to enumerating key examples. What brought pleasure? He enumerated fourteen sources of contentment: sense, wealth, skill, amity, good name, power, piety, benevolence, malevolence, memory, imagination, expectation, those who are dependent on association, and relief.[24] Flipping the coin, what induced pain? Bentham cataloged twelve things:

privation, sense, awkwardness, enmity, ill name, piety, benevolence, malevolence, memory, imagination, expectation, and those who were dependent on association.[25] At first, one might be struck by his lists given that half the items on one list also appear on the other. Benevolence can be a joy to the individual who wanted to be generous. That same act could be painful to the miser who complies with benevolence out of some sort of societal or familial obligation. After a few moments, one may take note that elements in each of the two lists are material and nonmaterial. Quite a few of them, in fact, could be interpreted either way. As McDermott commented, the intellectual underpinnings of utilitarian thinking were not limited to the pursuit of material goods.[26]

Bentham was not the only utilitarian thinker who thought that strategic decision makers could pursue nonmaterial goals. According to John Stuart Mill, most individuals have stronger self-centered feelings than social ones. But for those who have strong social sentiments, these feelings are deemed natural.[27] Such deeply internalized sentiments impact an individual's core identity and their willingness to partake in a collective endeavor. John Stuart Mill commented, "The social state is at once so natural, so necessary, and so habitual to man, that, except in some unusual circumstances or by an effort of voluntary abstraction, he never conceives himself otherwise than as a member of the body."[28] While Mill does not swing the door wide open to contemplate a nonmaterial realm, he nonetheless left the gate ajar. Perhaps the breach between emotions and rationality is not as wide as Descartes would have had us believe.

Opposing Descartes' dualist assumptions stood Jean-Jacques Rousseau. In his *Discourse on Inequality*, Rousseau suggested that our emotions are integral to our capacity to reason. Furthermore, he insisted, our passions advance our reasoning faculties: "It is by the activity of the passions that our reason improves itself; we seek to know only because we desire to enjoy; and it is impossible to conceive a man who had neither desires nor fears giving himself the trouble of reason."[29] For this illustrious figure from Geneva, emotive and logical thinking are not the severed mental processes Descartes described. They are parts of a greater whole. If these phenomena were parts of a larger and integrated sum, then the way in which Descartes and his intellectual progeny perceived rationality was excessively limited.

Rousseau's integrationist thesis has found support among a host of scholars outside the social sciences researching rationality and human behavior. Their work should not be interpreted by social scientists as an attempt to depose their theoretical approaches; rather, they should be seen as complementary. These scholars inform us that understanding rationality is not a matter of selecting between nature and nurture, but in appreciating how these two processes work in tandem. Alford and Hibbing explained, "The message is not that nature trumps nurture but rather that nurture is our nature—and that the precise nature of our nurturing tendencies depends upon environmental conditions."[30] Some of these researchers presupposed that the alleged disconnect between so-called emotional and rational thought processes is quite artificial and erroneous. Antonio Damasio is one of these scholars. Self-styled emotive and rational thought processes do not emerge out of differing portions of the brain.[31] These processes "intersect," in a manner of speaking, in the same regions of the brain. He stated, "In short, there appears to be a collection of systems in the human brain consistently dedicated to the goal-oriented thinking process we call reasoning, and to the response selection we call decision making, with a special emphasis on the personal and social domain. This same collection of systems is also involved in emotion and feeling, and is partly dedicated to processing body signals."[32]

Jonathan Turner suggested that emotions were absolutely necessary for human evolution and survival.[33] Early hominids imbued with strong emotional ties were more likely to form interpersonal bonds and thus collaborate with one another in a hostile environment. Cooperation on the prehistoric plains of East Africa was imperative to the survival of small bands of our hominid forerunners that could not effectively protect themselves from predation. The same emotional hardwiring that facilitated self-defense pacts also contributed to successful hunting. Later on, this teamwork would facilitate animal husbandry and sharing food and shelter with one's fellow group members in times of scarcity. Some certainly would contemplate, or even insist, in attributing this development to divine intervention. Yet even in a community of pure egoists, there is the chance of a mutation producing a cooperator. Generally, cooperators are more successful than pure egoists; thus, over time, collaborative beings would be more successful at reproduction and passing on their more collectively oriented genetic predisposition to subsequent generations.[34] But the human brain is not just an enlarged ape brain.[35] The area of the brain that is most important in the development of hominid emotions is larger in humans than in our fellow hominids, both in terms of absolute size and relative to others as a percentage of total brain volume.[36] Our brains, larger than those of previous hominids, were designed not only to be more materially calculating, but also more responsive to emotions.

Without strong emotional ties, early hominids were less likely to survive in a harsh environment. Emotive bonds increased the likelihood of cooperating with others, and this collaboration augmented an individual's chances for surviving. This occurred even in cases where cooperation was less than perfect.[37] Indeed, Robert Frank is one of several scholars emphasizing the material benefits of cooperation: "Trustworthiness, provided it is recognizable, creates valuable opportunities that would not otherwise be available. The fact that trustworthy persons *do* receive a material payoff is of course what sustains the trait within the individual selectionist framework."[38] Given repeated positive interactions, cooperators were more likely to reciprocate in the future leading toward constructive tit-for-tat cycles.[39] Arguably, if not ironically, sympathetic emotions could be classified as an egotistic quality since such a sentiment is likely to generate reciprocity.[40] Of course, cooperation is never absolute—it varies by degrees.[41] Long-term cooperation must also entail a certain degree of forgiving minor infractions. It is also more likely to succeed the more individuals interact with one another.[42] Toward this end, societies foment numerous conventions in an attempt to regulate individual behavior.[43] Rather than serve as guarantees of material rewards, emotions lie at the heart of the national project.

PLEASURE IN PARTICIPATION

It is absolutely imperative to clarify one vital point. Unlike Shaw and Wong's primordialist thesis, this is not an argument favoring biological determinism.[44] Nationalists frequently reference assumed bonds of blood. Their *myth of common ancestry* is laced with allusions to a shared familial past. Despite the lofty stances of nationalists, and even some scholars, natural selection did not create nationalism or nationalists. Ethnic ties were not forged at the core of our DNA. Rather, natural selection "partially shaped" crucial facets of our social behavior.[45] Over time, natural selection favored beings with a reflexive penchant toward cooperation. Over the generations, natural selection benefited individuals who were, in the words of John Alford and John Hibbing, *wary cooperators*: "Humans are cooperative, but not altruistic; competitive, but not exclusively so. We have an innate inclination to cooperate, particularly within defined group boundaries, but we are also highly sensitive to selfish actions on the part of other group members. This sensitively leads us to cease cooperating when that cooperation is not reciprocated, to avoid future interaction with non-cooperators, and even to engage in personally costly punishment of individuals who fail to cooperate."[46]

Those with strong emotive bonds were more likely to cooperate than pure egoists. In a hostile environment, cooperators were more likely to nurture their offspring into adulthood. Thus cooperators, born with a penchant for working together, were more likely to pass on their genes to a subsequent generation. In the end, "all social cooperation ultimately arises as an extension of the natural impulses to sexual coupling and parental care of the young."[47] Over time, natural selection increased the proportion of cooperators in human society. It is worth repeating that natural selection did not create nationalism; evolutionary processes simply augmented the likelihood of being born with *cooperatively oriented* genes.

Early cooperation centered on kin groups or those with whom we work with closely.[48] While evolutionary forces did not produce modern notions of nationalism or ethnicity, they did foment conditions that nationalist leaders subsequently exploited.[49] Nationalist elites later took advantage of this proclivity by weaving a myth of common ancestry, selling national identities as an extension of familial ties. While evolutionary forces did not produce nationalism, they created conditions nationalist leaders took advantage of in due course.[50] Ethnic entrepreneurs attempt to fulfill an important human need—the craving to belong.

Emotional necessities cannot be satisfied in isolation: "Individuals inherently and consistently long to establish identity of their own. They meet this need, or strive to meet it, through identification with significant persons, as well as with social and political entities."[51] In concert with this line of thinking, Etienne Balibar stated that individual identities are indivisible from groups: "*All identity is individual,* but there is no individual identity that is not historical or, in other words, constructed within a field of social values, norms of behaviour and collective symbols."[52] Indeed, identities are always built via comparison. The term female does not hold much meaning without the male designation. Youth has no meaning without a corresponding cohort of elders. Languages are merely means of communication—conduits through which we exchange ideas—until they encounter others. At that point, they are transformed into labels that point out and segregate not only who speaks *A* or *B*—a matter of action—but who is an *A*- or *B*-speaker—a matter of identification and group belonging. Homogeneity is not a fertile terrain for the proliferation of identities.

Our emotional side is an integral part of our nature—how we think and how we evolved over thousands of generations. People prefer to deal with those they trust rather than those they do not, even if the proposed payoff from an individual we do not trust is high.[53] Culture and shared customs are transformed into the "common knowledge" laying the groundwork for cooperation.[54] An outreached hand is, in many societies, a signal that one would like to meet and peacefully interact, even if the gesture is performed by a stranger. It is not usually seen as a prelude to conflict. There was a time when a greeting of *pax vobiscum*—"peace be with you"—was both a common salutation and an outward sign, in many parts of Europe, that one was encountering a fellow Christian. The fact that someone attends the same services in a house of worship is a signal, albeit extremely imperfect, that this individual shares a code of conduct, that this is a trustworthy soul. The rituals and codes of behavior transmitted in a religious setting provide adherents with the vocabulary necessary to effectively communicate even with strangers. Larry Arnhart noted, "Symbolic communication and conceptual abstraction allow human beings to sustain relationships in the absence of face-to-face proximity."[55] These shared cultural characteristics become the fodder used by ethnic elites in a bid to satisfy our emotional needs presented in the form of the nation—the mega extended family.

This may help us to explain one of the fundamental paradoxes of nationalism. As Benedict Anderson said, nations are artificial constructs: "It is *imagined* because the members of even the smallest nation will never know most of their fellow-members, meet them, or even hear of them, yet in the minds of each lives the image of their communion."[56] Russell Hardin concurred; all identities, including national ones, are inventions.[57] Even in Marxian analysis, one must attain class-consciousness before one will see class-oriented action.[58] Despite this artificiality, self-described nationalists buy into the notion that theirs is an organic community an extended family, of sorts.[59] Although nations number in the thousands or millions, ethnic mythmakers employ the discourse of familial intimacy.[60] So their myth of common ancestry, a modern invention, purports to *prove* the existence of ancient familial ties by pointing to old icons nostalgically recalling earlier eras or shared traits such as a common language or creed. Of course, ethnic entrepreneurs can rejoice in the knowledge that there is no one alive from that long gone era who could refute the nationalist entrepreneur's claims.

Individual identities connect to groups by way of shared experiences. Inherently, Anderson's *Imagined Community* is too immense for group members to know one another personally and share direct experiences the way people do in small face-to-face communities. Nationalist identities must be crafted in such a way that the artificiality of large-group attachments—sentiments based on something other than personal contact—is presented as something as natural as the camaraderie shared between neighboring families. Part of the solution to making nationalist identities feel natural is for nationalist elites to build their sense of collective unity atop the shared experiences of existing and widespread symbols and cultural performances. This is what Haunai-Kay Trask, a Hawaiian nationalist, attempted to elucidate in a speech delivered during a Stanford University conference in 1990: "Immigrants to Hawai'i, including both *haole* (white) and Asians, cannot truly understand this cultural value of *mālama 'āina* [care for the land] even when they feel some affection for Hawai'i. Two thousand years of practicing a careful husbandry of the land and regarding it as a mother can never be and should never be claimed by recent arrivals to any Native shores."[61] In this example, the understanding that looking after this particular place, guarding it as if it were one's blood relative, is a sacrosanct duty is an attribute shared by in-group members. More than a shared object of veneration, this nationalist anthropomorphized the earth as a mother. Regarding the land as if it were one's parent is a popular belief shared—we are led to believe—by most *true* Hawaiians. Historically recent newcomers of European and Asian ancestry were automatically excluded. Such shared experiences eliminate outsiders who cannot fully share the meaning of special icons, dances, and other outward manifestations of a cultural identity.

Through political socialization, leaders sensitize group members to a common set of cultural icons and shared subjective historical narratives that address the collective's destiny as one people.[62] Among society's elite, intellectuals play the most direct role in generating a coherent national narrative.[63] This process began with the birth of nationalism during the French Revolution. Festivals during this period borrowed extensively from religious rites—spectacles with which the common folk were already familiar.[64] This was a necessary step given that nationalism walks hand in hand with increased popular participation in the political process. It was not enough to watch. The fellowship of nationalists was summoned to partake in the drama of nation building. George Mosse elucidated, "The direct involvement of masses of people forced politics to become a drama based upon myths and their symbols, a drama that was given coherence by means of a predetermined ideal of beauty."[65] Through rituals and performances that include festivals, parades, public pledges of allegiance, and official commemorations, these symbols are displayed and the abstract identity is made incarnate, at least in the minds of believers:[66] "Acceptance of and participation in ritual, one of the instruments of standardization, is vital, if not indeed obligatory, if the system is to be sustained, but belief in the ritual and the set of explanations attached to the ritual are less important....In this sense, ritual is more a stylized statement of belief than a fully fledged internalization of what the ritual supposedly expresses."[67] Once institutionalized in symbolic and ritualistic form, out-group members can reinforce group identities.[68] In-group members are treated in a privileged manner; outsiders are peripheralized if not persecuted. Not all group members internalize the nationalist myth to the same degree. Some never internalize it all, but they silence their nationalist agnosticism in situations where they fear severe repercussions for publicly confessing their heresy. Ethnic leaders can expect to augment the scope and intensity of their collective identity to the degree they convince or recruit more stanch devotees.[69] True believers represent the gestation pools for an army of norm enforcers.

Elite mythmakers are not the only ones in society with their own worldview. From urban factory workers to campestral laborers, ordinary citizens embrace their own cultural mores, icons, and forms of symbolic representation. Their symbolic cosmology has been the driving force of popular cultural interaction for countless generations. But the material and educational status of the lower classes hampers their ability to eloquently articulate and disseminate their views.[70] Regarding the ordinary peasant, Antonio Gramsci said, "He respects the social position of the intellectuals and in general that of state employees, but sometimes affects contempt for it, which means that his admiration is mingled with instinctive elements of envy and impassioned anger."[71] Robert Michels was much harsher in his description of society's rank-and-file members—he said, "The incompetence of the masses, which is in the last analysis always recognized by the leaders, serves to provide a theoretical justification for the domination of these."[72]

Those at the upper echelons of society have a potent advantage over in-group counterparts—access to information and the capacity to disseminate it. Logically, elites endeavor to transmit information, including a national narrative, which best suits their interests. Some may suspect that elites are holding out but detractors rarely have the hard evidence to back up this supposition. Even if they did, elite opponents are not likely to possess the means to disseminate their critique.[73] This elemental imbalance of scholastic power helps empower intellectuals as the self-appointed disseminators of objective knowledge and rather subjective myths. In cases of large-scale political mobilization, such as revolutions, "the native or traditional ideology of the common people requires to be wedded to and merge with an ideology or a 'theory' (to repeat Marx's term) of a more sophisticated and more 'forward-looking' kind coming from 'without'— that is, from a higher social group."[74] Acting as social mangers, intellectuals are the primary agents that convert "cultural data" into what they hope will become socially accepted "natural truths."[75]

In the absence of alternative information or a credible counternarrative, the elites' subjective interpretation of ethics, socioeconomic relations, and history may become ingrained. Elites have access to the means of distributing their biased viewpoints via disseminating textbooks, disseminating messages in public squares and at the pulpit, erecting monuments, organizing parades, and other official commemorations.[76] Through repetition, intellectuals attempt to entrench their particular version of events.[77] When elites have fashioned a narrative that is so deeply internalized that it is no longer publicly questioned, we have crossed a pivotal threshold from an ideal that is merely dominant to one that is hegemonic.[78] Antonio Gramsci described hegemony as "the 'spontaneous' consent given by the great masses of the population to the general direction imposed on social life by the dominant fundamental group; this consent is 'historically' caused by the prestige (and consequent confidence) which the dominant group enjoys because of its position and function in the world of production."[79] Once instituted, a hegemonic belief functions like a scientific paradigm, dividing what is mainstream from that which is outlandish, extreme, eccentric, or even heretical.[80] Over the years, these narratives were internalized shaping their respective political discourse for generations.[81]

Individuals imbued with a strong commitment to a particular group identity—especially an identity that is hegemonic—live in an attitudinal realm whereby one's pleasure is inextricably connected to complying with the collective's principles. Their pleasure increases by expressing their identification to their chosen collective identity. Moreover, it rises to the degree these solidarity-driven individuals collaborate within one another, thus enjoying the positive rewards from joining in the collective action, plus taking pleasure in the bonds of amity that are forged between fellow activists. Two eminent scholars, William Riker and Peter Ordeshook, commented that collective action rewards went beyond material goods: "From participation, men also get prestige, friendship, the fun of playing the game, the satisfaction of identifying with some cause, and so on."[82] Expressing an identity has meaning *only* when it has been manifested through partaking in the collective endeavor: "Utility maximization should not only take into account the utility of what *we have* (and the activities we carry out) but also the utility we get from what (we think) *we are*….Many of our actions give us symbolic utility in the sense that they increase our welfare by defining what we are in a way that we find desirable."[83] In this light, casting a vote for a nationalist party, for example, is not just a utilitarian means of electing a preferred candidate; it is a method of expressing or personifying one's ideology.[84] Pleasure is derived from *doing* what is right in the eyes of one's peers and community. Group identity motivates individuals out of a sense of duty and rewards its backer with esteem and self-esteem.[85] Improper actions inflict sorrow, shame, or other negative emotions.[86]

SOCIAL REWARDS AND PUNISHMENTS

Just what are the rewards socially oriented people seek? The quest for positive emotions, such as honor, is universal. Jon Elster contended that we can control our thirst for honor or restrain our enjoyment over other people's envy; but we cannot fully suppress it.[87] Honor, according to Jean-Jacques Rousseau, is part of the social contract.[88] And David Hume wrote, "'Tis evident, that pride and humility, tho' directly contrary, have yet the same object. This object is self, or that succession of related ideas and impressions, of which we have an intimate memory and consciousness."[89] The pursuit of honor and dignity, wrote Thomas Hobbes, is one of the key traits distinguishing people from animals.[90] Self-love, Jean-Jacques Rousseau commented, is a natural feeling found in all animals; on the other hand, pride is an emotion found only in human society.[91] As innately social creatures, our sense of belonging to a community and our quest for love are sentiments that can be fulfilled only by other people.[92]

Through performance, the movement's advocate enjoys an intense satisfaction that can only come about by actively contributing to the joint venture. Leaders are aware of this emotive dynamic and they distribute psychological payoffs selectively based on an individual's level of cooperation.[93] For the die-hard believer, participation in the national project increases our self-esteem.[94] Participation in the nationalist struggle provides individuals with the opportunity to socialize with like-minded folk who embrace the belief that the first person plural is comprised of honorable people who perform righteous deeds. "Nationalism provides a way for us to join together with others, to be convinced that we are good, and to live in the service of a just cause."[95] In the case of a highly social individual, being deprival of such a sentiment fuels anger and may contribute to a sense of resentment.[96] In the final analysis, it is up to each individual group member to participate in the collective endeavor.[97]

The hunt for praise during one's lifetime, and fame after it, drives individual action.[98] Social payoffs may come in both selective and non-exclusive varieties. The foundation of collective action is made up of the selective social payoffs that are generated by society's army of norm enforcers. And the craving for these benefits often surpasses the desire for material goods.[99] One can feel great satisfaction in performing a task on the group's behalf. But honor and praise cannot transpire in isolation. There is no praise without witnesses who can attest to the individual's participation.[100] These witnesses present their evidence before a very special court—one that operates outside the parameters of the state, adheres to its own rules of evidence, and quickly passes judgment on those it deems worthy of praise or guilty of dishonor. "Public opinion forms therefore a tribunal before which the claims to honour are brought, 'the court of reputation' as it has been called, and against its judgements there is no redress."[101] The only individuals receiving praise will be those who directly took part in the collective action.[102] Of course, what is lauded or condemned is action or the lack thereof. Desire for acclaim or fear of being ostracized cannot be divorced from one's sense of self-esteem or an individual's subjective perception of their place in their society.[103] No society can candidly assess an individual's true motivation. This opens the door for hypocritical cooperators likely a critical component to the early development of collective action.[104]

Social activist testimonies furnish us with a window into their motivations and how they perceive participation. Lynn Stephen transcribed and translated the testimony of María Teresa Tula, a run-of-the-mill working-class Salvadoran who became an extraordinary peace activist and human rights organizer. María's group sought the whereabouts of their relatives who disappeared under the country's brutal military rule. Many husbands reprimanded their wives for their work in CO-MADRES—the grassroots human rights organization to which María belonged. Some men even beat their partners for their activism. María was arrested and tortured by the country's military authorities on suspicion of being affiliated with El Salvador's leftist insurgency. She and her companions paid a substantial, and very personal, price for their involvement. CO-MADRES was comprised of working-class women; elite Salvadoran women had their own organizations. María commented on some of the differences between these bourgeois feminists and her colleagues from the popular classes: "Sometimes we meet with these feminists, but all they do is talk, roaring like lions, but not doing anything. They go on marches, but they don't really do anything, just march around in the name of feminism."[105]

Working-class women may not have called themselves feminists but they were far more subjugated than any of their bourgeois counterparts.[106]

María's companions insisted on politically organizing women and demanding that the Salvadoran government disclose their loved ones' location, even if the location was an unmarked grave. She and her fellow activists insisted on direct action through constant public pressure on government authorities. Ultimately, they aspired to topple the regime that kidnapped, and, in some cases, killed, their family members. María proudly explained, "These humble women have demonstrated that they have the political, ideological, and military capacity to make changes in El Salvador. Being united for women's rights won't do us any good unless we change our government."[107] Within CO-MADRES, only direct action was praised, a rhetorical commitment to the cause was insufficient. From their perspective, speechifying was the only action generated by their upper-class counterpart. Personal involvement also demarcated insider from outsider. Nonparticipating upper-class women may have labeled themselves feminists, but they were a sham in eyes of María and other grassroots Salvadoran activists. These women paid a high price for their participation. Their precious reward never belonged to the material realm—it was social and emotional.

A commitment to one's group is rarely unconditional. Solidarity is a variety of "conditional altruism."[108] This *conditional* element applies to a tiny minority of group members in any society. Generally speaking, we label the unconditional cooperators *fanatics*. Leaving aside that minuscule segment in society, the vast majority of our *conditional altruists* are kept in line not only by the potential social rewards conferred for active participation, but also by the potential social penalties imposed on nonconformists. Breton and Dalmazzone contended that ostracism and rejection are more likely to influence behavior rather than beliefs.[109] Michael Hechter noted that groups have several *symbolic* or *social* sanctions at their disposal, including honor and prestige on the positive end and shame on the punitive side.[110] Due to their highly subjective nature, the efficacy of these measures relies on the dissemination of shared values within a particular community.[111]

Intragroup control is managed through a number of mechanisms.[112] In the case of social movements—and nationalism is no exception—punishment frequently comes in the form of gossip, rumors, and other negative forms of social commentary slandering one's reputation. In his study of popular culture and religion in Nicaragua, Roger Lancaster illustrated the potency of hearsay in enforcing group norms. Within their community, individuals are expected to sponsor a gathering, a celebration the Immaculate Conception of the Virgin Mary, the *Purísima*—literally, the "most pure." Expectations notwithstanding, some do not comply with this obligation. In response to the failure to live up to one's social obligations ordinary citizens dispense social sanctions in the court of public opinion. The sentence in this case came in the form of verbal an assault on the guilty party's reputation. Roger Lancaster noted, "One may refuse to throw a Purísima that lies within one's means, but at some risk: consistent refusal will label oneself *pinche*, a particularly dreaded derogative, signifying 'stingy.' A 'stingy' person in a popular barrio is first subjected to gentle and friendly prodding by his immediate neighbors. If this proves futile, he will become the subject of increasingly hostile gossip. If this, too, proves ineffective, the gossip continues but takes on an increasingly *public* and often confrontational character."[113]

Intuitively, the very act of dispensing such social penalties generates both a positive and a negative social payoff. The nonparticipant receives, in the extreme, a series of public reprimands. Such a punishment is meaningful only to the degree that the individual in question has a social connection to the group meting out the retribution. At the same time, public attacks on the honor or dignity of the uncooperative generate a kind of social insurance policy for the accusers. In his 37th maxim, François La Rochefoucauld said, "Pride plays a greater part than kindness in the reprimands we address to wrongdoers; we reprove them not so much to reform them as to make them believe that we are free from their faults."[114] Circuitously, these judges and juries dispense their brand of social justice, all the while washing their hands of any possible complicity in that transgression.

Nationalist movement leaders cannot enforce group norms at all places and all times. Enforcing norms is much easier within small groups. Even the most centralized of large political parties, for example, cannot operate effectively without party chapters at the grassroots. Large-scale campaigns, such as the American civil rights movement of the 1960s and 1970s, were built atop local church organizations.[115] The key to social sanctions is our emotional dependency on the group in question—the community within which we interact and the community within which we share a common set of expectations.[116] Such reliance on the group makes us vulnerable to humiliation and shame: "To think of oneself as a bad person is bad enough; the additional through that others view one in the same light is nearly intolerable."[117] Shame, an extremely public penalty, is a powerful force within tight-knit communities, and it is stronger sensation than guilt, a private indignity.

The fact that we gossip is itself a reliable indicator that we are concerned about the subject or topic in question.[118] Gossip is a weapon that enhances the status of the norm's self-appointed spokesperson,[119] but condemnation from a group with which we feel no loyalty is irrelevant. As James Scott noted in his study of rural Malaysia, wealthy individuals were immune from the sway of material incentives to engage in collective action.[120] The social sanctions sent their way—penalties in the form of gossip, slander, etc.—meant little where there was no dependency on the group in question. The same would not be true were the slander emanating from these economic elites' peers. Still, given that gossip is usually intracommunal, there is the chance, if not a strong probability, that nongroup members will be impervious to disparaging comments against them.

LONGING TO BE A CHAMPION

The foregoing discussion does not imply that the masses are helpless lambs lined up for a slaughter. Common folk have many choices. Among those alternatives is the option to ignore their leadership's pleas. Perhaps the ordinary citizenry may remain seated while the privileged few call their citizens to action. Then again, they might align themselves with rival elites in open insurrection. Over a century ago, Ernest Renan said that a nation's existence is a "daily plebiscite."[121] In this perennial campaign, elites eagerly exploit state-controlled public education systems in a bid to inculcate national norms. They must never assume, however, that their social, economic, and political status entitles them to automatic popular submission.[122] As Sam Kaplan noted, "Politically dominant groups working in conjunction with state agencies have the clout to linguistically determine the parameters of collective identity for the entire citizenry, that is, to implement authoritative meanings of language and thereby mold men and women in the images of canonized politics. At the same time, no political concept can deliver complete order because both the language of politics and the politics of language are deeply entrenched in contingent power relations at *all* levels of society."[123] A people already committed to a national ideal do not readily jettison the icons denoting that identity.

It will be useful to examine two cases of deeply entrenched national ideals—the first is from Mexico, the second, from Iraq. Arguably the most sacrosanct icon in contemporary Mexico is the icon of Our Lady of Guadalupe. According to legend, in 1531, the Virgin Mary appeared on Tepeyac Hill in Mexico City to a local peasant, Juan Diego, in the form of an indigenous woman. During the Aztec era, this same mount was the locus of a sanctuary to the Aztec mother goddess, Tonantzin.[124] The faithful believe that her image was miraculously impressed on Juan Diego's poncho, and it is this article of clothing that is preserved in a basilica built in her honor on Tepeyac. Catholic pilgrims travel considerable distances to pray at this shrine. Symbolically, this brown-skinned Madonna syncretically fuses a religion that developed in Europe with the indigenous societies in the Americas. Beyond the parameters of popular Roman Catholic belief, the iconic image of the Virgin of Guadalupe has been intimately associated with Mexican national identity.

In 1988, one Mexican artist savored a taste of the public's wrath over his interpretation of the Lady of Guadalupe. The state-owned Museum of Modern Art in Mexico City decided to exhibit some of the works by an avant-garde artist named Rolando de la Rosa. Several of his works asked viewers to challenge their preconceived notions of about Mexican culture and society through controversial, if not provocative, imagery. But the most contentious work featured the Guadalupe. In one of his montages, de la Rosa overlaid the face and exposed breasts of Marilyn Monroe atop an image of Our Lady of Guadalupe.[125] Incensed protestors stormed this museum, threatened to set fire to the building, and threatened to lynch the artist for his "satanic blasphemy."[126] Responding to the public's outcry, the Mexican government withdrew de la Rosa's work.

To diehard Catholics and Mexican nationalists, this representation was a direct affront to their faith and national pride. Néstor García Cancilini was correct when he pointed out that religious imagery is historically inaccurate and comparatively arbitrary.[127] Nonetheless, one takes a substantial risk when asking people to contemplate, if not tackle head-on, what they perceive to be their most sacrosanct beliefs, particularly in museums. It is a mistake to treat the museum-going general public as if it were a group of conference-attending academics. Adults, unlike children, cannot be obliged to enter, let alone learn from, a museum. No, the general public must be "intrigued and cajoled."[128] Timothy Luke went even further when he argued, "Entertainment values have so saturated museums that one cannot assume that the theme parks provide only amusement while museums generate only enlightenment."[129] A museum is rarely a place where one enters for critical analysis. Its collections display the narrative that its organizers want the public to see. When curators attempt to go beyond entertainment and foster deep thought and discussion, they often succeed in merely provoke the public's wrath.[130]

Another example illustrating the pitfalls of attempting to overhaul a well-established national identity comes from Iraq. In the first months of

2004, the U.S. government learned that lesson. Iraq's American-appointed government resolved to symbolically wipe the slate clean and herald the dawn of the post-Saddam Hussein era with a new emblem. Fundamental changes in political leadership are often underscored with transformations to the emblematic representations of state, especially a new flag and coat of arms. The old standard featured a red-white-black horizontal tricolor. There were three green five-pointed stars in the central white stripe and the *Takbir* the phrase *Allah-hu-akbar*, or "God is Almighty" was embroidered between the green stars. This modular tricolor remains a common characteristic in many Arab flags.[131] Seeking to dissociate itself from the Hussein regime, the Iraqi Governing Council proposed adopting a new national standard featuring a blue crescent moon centered on a white background suspended over three thin horizontal stripes in the pattern blue-yellow-blue. These stripes were supposed to evoke the Tigris and Euphrates rivers. The crescent moon was a common feature in the flags of many Muslim states.[132] Flag designers hoped that the public would celebrate a new era with this innovative pennant.

Immediately, the proposed flag met with public scorn and widespread rejection from Iraqi society. Nationalist myths are strongest when they are based on narratives centered on the preexisting state and when associated with the society's *staatsvolk*, or dominant group.[133] This banner was neither. An occupying power, an illegitimate ruler, was imposing a new symbol. The country's overseers both domestic and foreign—did not appreciate that the majority viewed their authority to oversee Iraq as illegitimate. Concurrently, the administrative authorities did not appreciate the profound and pervasive esteem felt for the old standard. The old banner prominently paraded a Pan-Arab identity embraced by the majority of the population—minus, of course, its sizeable Kurdish minority. Alternatively, the design and color scheme of the proposed national emblem appeared extraordinarily similar to only one other flag in the region the emblem of Israel.[134] In the end, Iraq restored the previous flag minus the stars. The popular indignation expressed during this episode illustrated that elite attempts to objectify a new identity contradicting popular and ingrained notions of nationhood can fail. Mass participation cannot be taken for granted.

It has been suggested that emotional rewards, and fear of emotional sanctions, lie at the bedrock of nationalist collective action. The scarceness of selective tangible rewards severely limits the capacity of national elites to copiously distribute these kinds of incentives. Comparatively speaking, social rewards cost much less to generate. As beings with both social and material wants, individuals covet the benefits that come from positive emotive recompense and try to avoid negative emotional punishment. Nationalism, a modern ideology built around a myth of common ancestry, allows individuals to reap an exceptionally precious emotive reward—one that is commensurate with the lofty status of the macro-extended family of nationhood. The communal accolades bestowed on those who safeguard their families are significant, but the praise jealously reserved for those who defend the mega-extended family—the nation—is even greater. Identities, including national ones, start as internal feelings. Ultimately, however, believers feel a need to express that emotion through exploits. Herbert Blumer commented, "Without action, any structure of relations between people is meaningless. To be understood, a society must be seen and grasped in terms of the action that comprises it."[135] Through actions, ordinary mortals are transformed into heroes.

Thomas Hansen's analysis of Hindu nationalism in India gives us a glimpse into the delight derived from performing one's identity. One of the pivotal episodes in contemporary Indian politics transpired at the Babri Masjid in Ayodhya. Located in the northern state of Uttar Pradesh, this mosque was constructed in the sixteenth century under the reign of Babur, the first Mughal emperor. Yet for Hindus, that same location was revered as the birthplace of their deity, Ram. On December 6, 1992, a throng descended on this locale and demolished the mosque. Volunteers from the militant Hindu nationalist Rashtriya Swayamsevak Sangh (RSS), who had just returned from Ayodhya, commented on what they witnessed, what they did, and how they felt: "In Ayodhya the excitement was tremendous. *Everybody felt this is the foundation of the Hindu nation....*So many of our leaders had been insulted and so much wrong has been done to us. Whatever had been done [in Ayodhya] was to bring together the Hindus and show them how outsiders are violating them and their country. Once the Hindu power is established...the Muslims will be shown their place."[136]

From the perspective of the congratulatory witnesses, in addition to those who actually took part in the mosque's destruction, the events of that December day represented a national vindication for perceived historic wrongs against the Hindu majority. Indeed, the interviewee boasted that this act represented the "foundation of the Hindu nation." There was no question that they felt immense gratification at the mosque's demolition. Given their exuberance, one is left wondering whether the interviewees were not just mere spectators. From their perspective, the destruction of this mosque was a response to past insults and previous wrongs. Additionally, the militants who made these comments were adamant that their agenda was not limited to reinstating one of their holiest shrines. Their plan was to subdue the influence of outsiders by putting Muslims in "their place." It was not enough to express fury in words—it had to be performed. This expression of national identity involved the destruction of one community's holy shrine. Furthermore, it inaugurated a period of intense social unrest. But this was not a dress rehearsal. The participants in this drama claimed they were performing an act of national exaltation and their performance was judged as such by friend and foe. For Hindu nationalists, those who participated in the Ayodhya campaign were national champions. Of course, one community's heroes are another's delinquents, or even terrorists.

Our lust for honor and pride prompt our collective actions, and yet our potential deeds are limited in accordance with our station in life. Acknowledging the confines of our actions is important in this discussion. José Ortega y Gasset said, "I am myself plus my circumstance."[137] François Rochefoucauld commented, "All men have an equal share of pride; the only difference is in their ways and means of showing it."[138] With their vast resources, elites have the luxury of greater mobility. Flexibility, in terms of varieties of performance, is inherent to those with greater resources. A highly literate person has the option of seeking fame through writing poetry or historic treatises—something outside the scope of the illiterate or the person with scant access to popular or classic literature. Wealthy individuals can aspire to reach a kind of immortality through their generosity. To this day, many associate the Medici family with the Italian Renaissance, the name Carnegie with libraries, and many institutions of higher education bear the names of their founding patrons. That kind of prominence is restricted to those with financial means.

All individuals seek self-respect and the appreciation of others: "Our wish to deserve the praise of others fortifies our virtue, and praise accorded to intellect, valour, and beauty encourages these things to grow."[139] Honors are bestowed on those who demonstrate courage under fire—those who pursue a challenge when there is no certainly of victory.[140] The highest of honors, full-blown glory, is reserved for those who aspire to be viewed as *"better than (all) others."*[141] Exploits performed in the name of the nation do not merely benefit the lone activist—they benefit the entire nation. Through great deeds carried out in the name of the collective, ordinary group members elevate their standing as protectors of the macro-extended family—the nation.

Where does this discussion regarding the tactical pursuit of nontangibles leave altruism? Emile Durkheim said, "Wherever there are societies, there is altruism, because there is solidarity."[142] Although their collectively oriented behavior parallels one another—individuals trying to maximize social benefits and their altruistic counterparts—their motivations are quite distinct. Our strategic collective activist does indeed expect compensation, notwithstanding in the form of social goods rather than material benefits. Such comportment is "determined by sentiments and representations which are exclusively personal," and Durkheim said that altruism could not have emerged from egoism.[143] A true altruist gives without expecting anything in return, and this runs counter to a fundamental assumption of strategic behavior models.[144] John Stuart Mill said, "The utilitarian morality does recognise in human beings the power of sacrificing their own greatest good for the good of others. It only refuses to admit that the sacrifice is itself a good. A sacrifice which does not increase, or tend to increase, the sum total of happiness, it considers as wasted."[145]

One possible trajectory is to follow François La Rochefoucauld's lead. This seventeenth-century French moralist implied that all human behavior was motivated by *amour-propre*, or self-love.[146] La Rochefoucauld said, "We are held to our duty by laziness and timidity, but often our virtue gets all the credit."[147] Self-interest, he insisted, explains why we censure transgressions or laud virtue.[148] So, for this thinker, there is no altruism, only self-interested motivation. His answer would certainly take care of explaining a significant anomaly. Still, what it adds in terms of parsimony it detracts in terms of accurately reflecting the complexities of the human mind.

While it is an intriguing topic, ascertaining the origins of altruism remains outside the scope of this project. One does not have to go as far as La Rochefoucauld to insinuate that altruism does not exist. We do say, nevertheless, that individuals can be as strategic about social rewards and sanctions as they can logically pursue material benefits and try to avoid tangible pain. The decision to participation in collective action—participating in a parade, joining a demonstration, voting for a favorite political party, or taking up arms against one's adversary—is not a spontaneous act. Individuals *choose* to participate, or, conversely, to opt out. Either way, theirs is a conscious choice and it corresponds to the same underlying logic as the archetypal wealth maximizer or vote-maximizing politician.

CONCLUSION

After examining some of the foundational works of utilitarian thought, we see that these intellectual precursors to the rational choice approach conceived instrumental rationality in broad terms. Their assumptions should have allowed modern-day scholars to realize that the fulfillment of emotive or social benefits was just as logical as the satisfaction of tangible goods. Economists were not wrong for assuming that wealth maximization was rational. The source of the difficulty has less to do with economics than with the other social sciences. After all, they not only borrowed the concept of rationality from economics, but they also, unnecessarily, took this concept along with its fixation on material rewards and sanctions. What tips the scales for the average individual—whether to pursue material or social rewards—is the degree to which that person feels an emotional bond with the group in question. Obviously, that emotive connection varies from group to group. Individuals are more likely to feel this commitment with intimate groups such as families. This may help to explain why nationalist leaders articulate their mission in the name of the *nation*, the presumed mega-extended family. In the following chapter, we shall examine a way in which to model this material-social dynamic.

CHAPTER 3

MODELING SOCIAL AND MATERIAL RECOMPENSE

IN THE FIRST CHAPTER, WE CONTENDED THAT nationalism is an inherently political phenomenon. Like ethnicity, nationalism adheres to the belief that community members are linked by presumed ancestral bonds. Nationalism takes this belief in a shared ancestry one step further by insisting upon a correspondence between cultural and administrative boundaries. A nationalist movement may limit its aspirations to the creation of an autonomous region within an existing state. Or it may demand a complete rupture with the existing state either in the form of establishing an independent country or breaking their region from the current sovereign and joining another state. Over time, nationalist movements may oscillate between soft-core autonomism and hard-core separatism. Nationalism, as a political concept, hinges itself to that of the sovereign state.

Subsequently, we discussed the nature of rationality. Its introduction to the social sciences via economics significantly affected the way in which these disciplines perceived rational thinking and behavior. Rather than limit ourselves to the overly narrow confines of maximizing material gains, a more complete portrait of instrumental rationality must encompass the aspirations of many to maximize social or emotional goods. The classic *Homo economicus* seeks financial wealth. Its social counterpart craves not tangible goods but honor, praise, and satisfaction. In this chapter, we shall take the first steps toward presenting these dimensions of our strategic thinking as integral parts of a unified whole. As a political phenomenon, let us begin by examining a well-cited work employed to describe the strategic behavior of political parties and their leaders—Anthony Downs's *Economic Theory of Democracy*.

FROM DOWNS TO TSEBELIS

Although it was written more than half a century ago, Downs's tome remains one of the most prominent works in the field of electoral politics. His model changed the way many perceived political parties, their leaders, and their professed ideological orientations.[1] Traditional assessments of political parties emphasized their platforms and underlying ideological leanings. Bucking the prevailing trend, Anthony Downs and Robert Michels asserted that, despite appearances, political parties were not fixated on these matters. At the dawn of the twentieth century, Michels wrote, "The modern party is a fighting organization in the political sense of the term, and must as such conform to the laws of tactics."[2] Decades later, Downs wrote that "parties formulate policies in order to win elections, rather than win elections in order to formulate policies."[3] Thus, ideological pronouncements and grand policy statements were simply means to win public support. From economics, we understand that private firms are profit-maximizing institutions. Their products are merely the means to generate revenue. Analogously, prospective parties were, at their core, vote-maximizing institutions.

In the same way that new customers alter the realm of commerce, the introduction of new voters change the political environment. Commercial firms modify their advertising, and even their product lines, in response to changes in public preferences. Likewise, political parties modify their platforms in the hopes of seizing a larger portion of the electoral pie. Altering party positions on key issues, as is the case with transforming one's merchandise, is easier to understand conceptually than it is to execute. Modest shifts in party platforms are more believable than sudden radical swings. Manufacturers known for producing low-cost and poor-quality commodities will have a hard time shifting their status to makers of high-end and superior goods. Reputations, good or bad, have a remarkably long shelf life. Similarly, a political party known for its association with the Left, with peace movements, or with the clerical establishment may discover that the voting public has a hard time swallowing its sudden adaptation into a centrist or conservative party, a party of hawks, or a newly anointed secular party. Both the buying and voting publics insist on consistency and some level of predictability.

Parties attempt to garner as many votes as possible in much the same way that rival commercial enterprises vie for a larger market share.[4] Candidates for office in autocratic one-party regimes take their reelection for granted.[5] Their counterparts in democratic polities must earn, or cajole, public support for their tenure in office. Downs's rational political parties and politicians neatly fall in line with classic economic assumptions of rationality. The objects they are accruing—votes, in this case—are unmistakably tangible goods. A vote for party A is a loss for its rival, B.[6] Downs's vote-maximizing assumption is quite conservative. Individual politicians focus on one tangible target—vote accumulation. This is political science's counterpart to the *Homo economicus* conjecture—the financial hunter engaged in the pursuit of greater profit. Chasing after anything else is supposed to be an irrational act.

Vote maximization lies at the core of the standard analyses of democratic interparty competition. Parties championing left- or right-leaning manifestos follow this strategy. Nationalist parties are not an exception. The key difference here is that they do not struggle along a Left to Right continuum.[7] Where the national question dominates the political scene, parties compete along a center-periphery axis.[8] The *center* end of this spectrum endorses greater concentration of power in the metropolitan capital. Pro-*center* parties vehemently oppose devolution of power to cultural minorities and rapaciously contest nondominant ethnic groups' assertions to the right to self-determination. At the other end of this ideological continuum—the *pro-periphery* endpoint—parties demand a complete rupture with that metropolitan state. Here is where we find separatist movements and political organizations. Either extreme can represent a nationalist party. Dominant ethnic communities can be represented by a nationalist party as well as by minority communities. Prevailing ethnic communities often flex their demographic muscle by trying to centralize power vis-à-vis the country's minorities.[9] Minorities or colonial subjects, on the other hand, will want to break with the central state.

If the political battle lines are drawn in terms of center versus periphery, these parties have the luxury of associating themselves with either the Right or Left. Such leanings are historically accidental and expedient. Thus, over time, nationalist parties may appear to oscillate along the Left-Right axis in order to appeal to larger segments of the public. Conversely, nationalist party critics may try to stigmatize their autonomist or separatist rivals in terms of negative labels associated with the Left or Right. For example, Puerto Rican independence supporters were labeled Fascists in the 1930s and early 1940s; during the cold war they were deemed Socialists and Marxists. Québécois and Catalan nationalists were frequently deemed radicals in the 1960s and then business-friendly in the 1980s. Their commitment to Left-Right principles and rhetoric changed over the decades. But their commitment to advancing their autonomist and separatist claims against the central state remained stable.

Vote maximizing assumptions do a fine job explaining party leader behavior under most instances. Yet there are instances when political parties appear to behave irrationally. Such aberrations point out that occasionally, and quite intentionally, party leaders advocate unpopular stances. Alterations to a party's platform are not, per se, irrational. Parties do this quite frequently. But when they do so, the change is usually explained in terms of appealing to shifting voter preferences. As is possible in another realm of life, party leaders may err. They may have erroneous information or incomplete information regarding amendments in the public's policy preferences. Nonetheless, the supposed illogical misstep we are discussing was not the result of faulty information about the public will. To the contrary, they marched forward knowing that electoral devastation awaited them. Let us briefly examine vacillating policies in a polity where the nation question dominates electoral politics.

In the words of José Trías Monge, a former chief justice of Puerto Rico's Supreme Court, a half millennium of history has left this island as the *oldest colony in the world*.[10] From the late fifteenth until the late nineteenth century, this island was a possession of the Spanish Crown. Since the Spanish-American War of 1898, it has been an U.S. overseas territory. Throughout those centuries, this colonial ward has seen the emergence of a myriad of political parties, each championing a host of different issues. The only ones with any staying power were those that committed themselves to resolving the seemingly interminable debate over Puerto Rico's status. Since World War II, the party system has solidified around one party representing each of the major status alternatives. In terms of center-periphery relations, they are: statehood, the *status quo* as an American "Commonwealth," and independence.[11] Debates over the status question are not just arguments over the constitutional mechanics of center-periphery relations. They are inextricably tied to the larger dispute over the compatibility, or lack thereof, between Puerto Rican identity and various notions of American national identity. As part of that dispute, politicians have argued over the status of adopting an official language versus a commitment to bilingualism.[12]

In the early 1990s, the leadership of the *Partido Popular Democrático* (PPD, or Popular Democratic Party) took up the issue of whether to replace the old official languages law. Starting in the 1970s, the issue popped up every now and then, but the PPD elites left it alone, fearing the electoral consequences. To the surprise of many islanders—and representatives of the U.S. government—PPD Governor Rafael Hernández Colón signed the bill into law, replacing official bilingualism with official unilingualism.[13] This party was, and remains, the stalwart defender of the Puerto Rican autonomist movement and the champion of the current *Commonwealth* status with the United States. As a U.S. territory, the Puerto Rican government had the legal authority to modify its local statutes, including its language laws.[14] In 1991, the ruling PPD dropped English as one of the two co-official languages in favor of a new statute declaring Spanish the sole official language of the Puerto Rican people and its territorial government. For the bill's proponents, the new language law simply reflected an important Puerto Rican reality. Spanish is the primary language of over 90 percent of the island's inhabitants.[15] Furthermore, most islanders are moderate nationalists.[16]

To the casual outside observer, any reluctance to amend the old bilingual law might seem odd given the island's unilingual reality. Advocates of Puerto Rican statehood fervently condemned this shift in the language law as a symbolic attempt to distance Puerto Rico from the United States. Official unilingualism opponents were worried less about the island's electorate than how the federal government would respond. Many Puerto Rican islanders were nervous that Washington, D.C., might economically retaliate against this overseas territory for dropping English as a co-official language. Islanders assumed that the American public, and certainly U.S. lawmakers, felt an intractable bond between the English language and American identity.[17] Shelving English as a co-official language could be perceived in Washington as a slap in the face.[18] Still, despite the publication of public opinion surveys indicating disapproval of such a statutory change, the PPD pushed ahead with its linguistic agenda and the party was punished in the subsequent elections with a resounding defeat.

How do we account for such an anomaly to the customary conjecture that parties are always trying to maximize votes? Party leaders, Downs taught us, are not fixated on promoting policies or fulfilling ideological preferences; they only want to taste the fruits of holding office. Non-nationalist parties aspire to savor the privileges of governing the polity. These assumptions need to be moderately adjusted with regard to leaders of nationalist parties. Publicly nationalist parties proclaim that their ultimate agenda is to modify the character of existing center-periphery relations. Autonomy or independence sits atop the platforms of nationalist parties championing the plight of minority groups. For their counterparts representing dominant ethnic communities, it may be a matter of championing forced cultural assimilation of their heterogeneous population. Does this mean that there are rational vote-maximizing parties and *less than* rational nationalist parties? Perhaps, as one scholar has suggested, party leaders may simply promote a policy for personal reasons.[19] Or, conceivably, some are driven to win elections—so called "ambitious" parties—while others are more concerned with policy—so called "ideological" parties.[20] Perchance there may be a distinction between rational and irrational parties. All of these speculations implicitly question the universality of Downs's core premise.

It is not necessary to overthrow the fundamental thesis of power-maximizing institutions or their leaders. Perhaps we are assuming that parties are fixated on winning elections when these political institutions are strategically focusing on other gains. Such speculation suggests that party leaders perceive the art of politics, or the political game, as something more than election-day victories. Nationalist party leaders can be described as power-maximizing elites. However, they feel that in order to accomplish this, they must do so within a different political system. Standard rational choice analyses start by asking how actors strategically proceed in order to achieve their goals, taking into account the constraints of the existing structure. An actor's actions, in other words, are rational given their structural environment. But here we are talking about a group of political actors who not only operate within existing conditions but also are dedicated to altering the political system's core structure. Nationalist leaders are not satisfied with reaping the benefits of dwelling in the stately rooms of the existing political edifice. Instead, they want to relish in the possibilities of residing in the grand accommodations of another political manor. These elites believe that the nature of the existing constitutional order disadvantages them. For minority nationalist parties, greater regional autonomy, or outright independence, satisfies that desire. Nationalist parties representing dominant groups may attempt to reshape the existing political order in a centralizing direction.

In the previous example, the PPD was the champion of Puerto Rico's current status as a U.S. "Commonwealth." As the champion of moderate autonomism, this party competed with the hard-core separatism of the *Partido Independentista Puertorriqueño* (PIP, or Puerto Rican Independence Party). But its primary partisan rival was the *Partido Nuevo Progresista* (PNP, or New Progressive Party). The PNP advocated converting this territory into the fifty-first state of the United States. By promulgating the 1991 Official Language Act, the PPD elevated Spanish as the one and only official idiom. In so doing, the PPD knowingly laid the groundwork for a major setback in the November 1992 elections. Polls consistently revealed the electorate's unhappiness with this statute—a bill signed into law only months before the November 1992 elections.[21] Through this symbolic piece of legislation, the PPD flaunted Puerto Rican nationalism. Puerto Rican islanders were not the primary audience. The PPD's true intent was to display this identity to U.S. mainlanders. The party's leadership was aware that Congress is the only body that is constitutionally authorized to admit states into the union. Outside the public limelight, PPD strategists calculated that such an audacious gesture could diminish support for the status alternative they dreaded the most—Puerto Rican statehood—in Washington. This party lost an important election. In the process, it fortified its cherished status as an American Commonwealth.[22]

The uniqueness of Puerto Rican politics is not the culprit. Nationalism is not the source of our problem. Our principal encumbrance is not the presumed irrationality of political parties. Rather, our challenge is ascertaining the true—and, at times, concealed—focal point of the politicians' fixation. While our attention was focused on the discernible electoral game, some prominent political actors were concentrating on another battlefield.[23] Political analysts who set their eyes exclusively on the realm of electoral politics overlook other critical political arenas. These alternative settings may be the true focal point of the politician's obsession. Susan Batty and Vesna Danilović noted, "The observer fails to see that the formulation of preferences in the arena of interest is conditioned by simultaneous political interaction in other arenas."[24] Rationality does not impose an electoral agenda on political parties. Rather, it supposes that their leaders pursue their objectives deliberately and strategically.[25] George Tsebelis opted to tackle this paradox head-on.

Belgium, the focus of Tsebelis's study, represents an example of a consociational political system. Profound chasms segregate society members along confessional and ideological lines.[26] These interboundary antagonisms are reflected in the electoral sphere. Different parties purport to represent particular blocs. Leading political figures fashion "cartels of elites" in order to promote political stability—ones loyal to their bloc, not just the standard parliamentary coalition.[27] Elected officials face popular displeasure when they cooperate across partisan lines.[28] Vote-maximizing politicians in consociational democracies would not extend a hand to their counterparts across the parliamentary aisle were they seeking to reflect the popular will. Appeasing constituents, however, can be a costly decision. Legislative deadlock is a common feature of these political systems unless one social bloc comprises an electoral majority. To avoid such a scenario in multiparty consociational systems, lawmakers occasionally bypass the popular will and cooperate across party lines. As one should expect, these parliamentarians treat lightly in this political minefield in order to avoid the public's wrath for their cooperation. Thus, these political strategists play a political game in two realms—one is centered in the parliament itself, the other pertains to the electoral contest.[29]

George Tsebelis wrote that in order to study consociational democracies, one had to take into account the existence of two political battlefields—one is electoral and the other is parliamentary. He modeled consociational politics as a *nested game*. Politics here shares something in common with a *matryoshka* dolls. The outermost figurine conceals another one inside.[30] In this case, the electoral arena is visible and exceedingly public. Downsian assumptions dominate here. The parliamentary realm is just as contentious as its electorate counterpart. Political intrigues here, on the other hand, take place behind closed doors. While improving legislative cooperation may be irrational in electoral terms in these democracies, the politicians trying to foment it are not behaving illogically. They are as just as strategic as their standard vote-maximizing counterparts. What differs is their ultimate goal.

Politicians fulfill their ultimate pleasure if, and only if, they hold office. Unless they aspire to take power through the barrel of a gun, even nationalist parties cannot hope to fulfill their agenda unless they are elected into office. Investing time and energy in a campaign, the business of securing the voters' support, was the means to achieve that end. Pain is what followed after defeat at the polls. Downs informed us that politicians seek a dividend in only one form—the electoral kind. That dividend is the office holder's or office seeker's reward or *payoff*. Symbolically, we can represent a payoff as "PO." We can characterize a generic individual with the subscript "*i*" and we can signify the electoral realm with a subscript "*e*." Downs's classic vote maximization model assumes that an individual politician's payoff equals their electoral payoff. We can write that core assumption as follows:

$$PO_i = PO_{ei} \tag{3.1}$$

Still, thanks to Tsebelis's assertion, we understand that politicians can, and sometimes do, aim for nonelectoral goals. In the Belgian case, the alternative realm was legislative. In nationalist politics, the national question is the alternative arena.[31] To accommodate this sphere of political action, Tsebelis added a parliamentary arena to his model. We can represent this battlefield with the subscript "*p*." The public is not conscientious of every aspect of parliamentary politics. When they are not very attentive to legislative deliberations, office holders feel they have a freer hand to govern and they can chance swerving from vote maximization.[32] A model of political decision-making in consociational democracies needs to assess the relative weights of these two domains. Most of the time lawmakers will value their reelection above all else. Exceptions to this rule favor a smoother parliamentary process. Tsebelis employed the letter "k" to stand for the weight of popular impact on the legislative issue at hand. At times, k is worth one; occasionally, it is worth zero. Under his model our individual lawmaker is forced to choose between these two political realms. After Tsebelis assembled all of these elements—the individual's electoral payoff (POei), the individual's parliamentary payoff (POpi), and popular input or the relative weight of the two battlefields (k)—Tsebelis devised the following model:

$$PO i = k PO ei + (1-k) PO pi \qquad\qquad (3.2)$$

In this model, k casts the deciding vote whether the individual parliamentarian pursues electoral advantage or promotes a smoother operation of the legislature. If the k is worth one, our individual lawmaker pursues electoral advantage. Alternatively, in cases when it is worth zero, this political actor sides with maximizing a parliamentary payoff.[33]

MODELING RATIONALITY

Certainly there are instances when nationalist politicians opt to pursue their aims through the ballot box. The battle between Puerto Rico's PPD and PNP parties over an official language law as a means of attracting Washington's attention is symptomatic of polities where the national question dominates the partisan sphere. Similarly, the Liberal Party and the Parti Québécois have, for decades, locked horns over the breadth of language legislation in Quebec. But electoral outcomes are not the prime reason why it was necessary to assess the relationship between core assumptions in Downs and Tsebelis. The advantage of Tsebelis's model is its ability to account for balancing two sets of distinct payoffs. A nested games model is quite useful for examining the interplay between the material and social rewards individuals seek.[34]

Our individual nationalist, as is the case with individual legislators in consociational democracies, contends with satisfying two realms. One sphere is strategically focused on tangible goods. This is where we find our classic *Homo economicus*—the hunter in pursuit of material benefits—and our Downsian counterpart. A second is centered on social rewards. Here we find the domain of the *Homo sociologicus*. The classic *Homo economicus* is driven by the lust for wealth and tangible goods and his trepidations are also material such as financial decline, risking physical injury, or imprisonment. Likewise, the *Homo sociologicus* searches out the pleasures derived from bonding with others, receiving their praises, and dreaming of glory.[35] A socially driven person seeks to avoid social pitfalls such as a deterioration in one's social standing, the onset of shame, or public humiliation.[36] Social connections fundamentally alter the way an individual weighs preferences. Florence Passy wrote, "Social relations create and sustain a structure of meaning that contributes to the definition of individual perception or preferences.[37] All individuals, nationalists or not, must deal with these two sets of needs.

Rather than view these orientations as diametrically opposed to one another, it is important to understand that all individuals possess both social and material desires. Any model of collective action must contend with the reality that activists weigh these two sets of interests. Not surprisingly, these interests may collide with one another. The intensity of our emotional attachment to the group in question determines which of the two realms is valued more highly than the other. Jon Elster contended, "On the one hand, people have a strong desire to promote their material interests. On the other hand, people have a strong desire to maintain a positive self-image. For most people, the self-image includes a belief that they are not motivated only or even mainly by material interest."[38] Not every nationalist group member feels the same level of group commitment. The emotive bonds that individuals feel vary from group to group. That variance has a major impact on our willingness to engage in collective action. For some collectives—say, for a social club—we are willing to sacrifice a few hours a week. It is possible that we are also disposed to make a modest donation or subscript to one of their publications. At the other end of the continuum—say, our families or perhaps our nations—we might be willing to lay down our lives and those of our progeny. Simply because others associate someone with a particular ethnic group does not guarantee that this person identifies with that label. We may feel no attachment to a particular group whatsoever. Where we feel no emotive connection, we might be induced to cooperate if we are materially compensated for our efforts or if we are afraid of some form of reprisal for our noncompliance. Our cooperation with this grouping will not take place until the collective musters enough tangible rewards to entice our participation. Conversely, this group may inflict sufficient material penalties to beguile our collaboration.

Tsebelis's model assessed two arenas—one electoral, another parliamentary. Likewise, our rational nationalist must balance two sets of possible rewards or sanctions—a material and a social payoff. We can represent a material realm with the subscript m and our social side with the subscript s. An individual's material payoff is $POmi$, while an individual's social payoff is represented as $POsi$. Weighing disparately on each of these realms is "j," which, in this model, symbolizes the individual's emotive or psychological attachment to the group. One could perceive this as an individual's sense of solidarity or emotional attachment with the group. Solidarity or identification with a group significantly alters an individual's calculus whether or not to engage in collective action.[39] Using Tsebelis's model of consociational politics as our cornerstone, we develop the following:

$$PObi = (1\text{-}j)POmi + jPOsi \qquad (3.3)$$

Any sense of solidarity with the collective will vary from one person to another. We should not assume that any two group members have internalized the same level of emotional attachment to the group. Indeed, it is important to emphasize that someone might not identify with their ethnic community at all. But a person's emotional attachment to the collective, or perhaps their psychological dependency on the group, is the most significant determinant of their willingness to partake in collective action.[40] Furthermore, since we belong to various groups, we have dissimilar emotional attachments to different collectivities.[41] We all assign diverse groupings differing values of j. With regard to an individual's sense of solidarity with their nation, the j could be very high, say, equal to 0.75, or perhaps it is minuscule, say, equal to 0.25. A j equal to zero indicates an individual with no emotional connection to the collective. At the other end of the spectrum, a j equal to one would be typical of an absolutist or zealot.[42]

This model leaves room for change over time. A j is not a variable set in stone. Emotional attachments to a group identity are likely to be stable during most periods. We are socialized into our families. Likewise, national identities are usually inculcated from a very early age. National ideologies are taught and reinforced through state and nonstate actors and institutions. Positive feedback, negative stereotyping, and discrimination all contribute to the fortification of our national sentiments. Leaders hope that, over time, these notions are ingrained and internalized to the point they are taken for granted—in Gramscian terms, a hegemonic belief. Still, some groups articulate a collective narrative in such a way that out-group members can be absorbed. Assimilation for them is possible.[43] Furthermore, our faith in our national identities might be reinforced by our confidence in our leaders. Leadership failures provide opportunities for sowing the seeds of doubt about a host of beliefs. While this might lower our j levels over time, the opposite is also true—repeated successes attributed to group leaders can augment individuals' j levels.

Implicitly, this model underscores the importance of cultivating those with a high level of j. Ethnic entrepreneurs concerned with fomenting collective action are aware that not everyone has the same level of emotional commitment or identification with their group. Hard core activists represent but a small portion of all any group's total membership. Yet their role in maintaining and promoting the organization's interests is imperative.[44] Without the impassioned devotees and unquestioning followers, most nationalist movements would fail. Those cases where individuals have a j valued at one represents nationalists with an extremely intense sense of group solidarity; they value social payoffs in absolute terms. Such individuals will risk life and limb for the collective good. These individuals are rewarded with personal esteem, a private feeling, and public recognition leading to a more pronounced social status.[45] Centuries ago, Machiavelli warned us about the dangers inherent in those who regarded honor highly compared to those who merely pursued monetary compensation: "In a word, the greatest danger with mercenaries lies in their cowardice and reluctance to fight, but with auxiliaries the danger lies in their courage."[46] In more recent times, Mia Bloom noted, "Individual esteem is bound to group status, physically and symbolically. Sacrifice and risk employed on behalf of the group become valuable virtues, rewarded by social status."[47] Those with a j at or near one constitute the core of our *true believers*. In time, they may become martyrs.[48] Through their performance, militants generate both tangible and social payoffs. The social reward goes to the activist; the material beneficiary of their collective action is the group itself. José Ortega y Gasset reflected on the narcissistic side of heroism: "...to be a hero means to be one out of many, to be oneself. If we refuse to have our actions determined by heredity or environment it is because we seek to base the origin of our actions on ourselves and only on ourselves. The hero's will is not that of his ancestors nor of his society, but his own."[49]

Ethnic entrepreneurs endeavor to disseminate myths that inspire nonelites in a transclass endeavor to generate group solidarity. Elites diffuse their myth of common ancestry through educational institutions, the pulpit, and various forms of media. Their goal is not to convey objective historical treatises but to instill highly subjective interpretations of past events. The sagas purporting that *we* were good and *they* were not are relayed in the form of romanticized narratives. Anthony Smith explained, "Since the aims of nationalist educator-intellectuals are not academic, but social, i.e., the moral purification and political mobilization of the people, communal history must be taught as a series of foundation and liberation myths and as a cult of heroes."[50] Heroes are glorified; traitors are scorned. The nonactive members, the ones who were neutral when the call to collective action was rung, are treated with piqued indifference or disdain.

Nationalist myths purport to convince the ordinary citizenry that collaborating with the nation is akin to cooperating with their relations. So, nationalist elites start by seeking out individuals who hunger for group inclusion. A good place to search for such individuals is among the socially mobile, yet vulnerable, intelligentsia.[51] Their contribution is pivotal, particularly during the early stages of building their movement and mobilizing their community. They constitute the group's base or activist core. Subsequently, ethnic entrepreneurs will then have the daunting task of recruiting, or even *converting*, those with reduced emotive attachments to their group. As elites enlist the support of people with lower levels of group solidarity—j less than one—they will count on the *true believers* to act as eyes and ears, monitoring potential deviations from the group norm and even executing sanctions for uncooperative behavior. At the opposite end of the spectrum lie individuals with a j at zero. These people have no emotional bond to the group identity ethnic elites are fomenting. In all likelihood, they channel their emotional sensibilities in a different direction—perhaps toward another collectivity. These are not unfeeling citizens but individuals who are indifferent toward *our* community. Other identities captivate their passions.[52]

It is critical not to hastily exclude persons with a low j from our study of nationalism. They still might participate in the movement. Indeed, their cooperation may be invaluable. Without a sense of psychological affection toward the collective, the activities of individuals lacking in-group solidarity depends on the supply of private or excludable tangible payoffs.[53] Their participation in a collective endeavor is contingent upon providing enough positive selective incentives to encourage cooperation or, inversely, a sufficient level of negative selective incentives to threaten retribution for insubordination. Societies with a high percentage of solidarity-driven individuals are inherently flush with a plentiful supply of norm enforcers who can assess participation levels and disseminate sanctions. Like some disingenuous elites—perhaps more than just a few—they participate in order to reap the financial rewards associated with a successful struggle or to avoid being the next victim in a purge of defectors.[54]

Between the two endpoints—a j at one and j at zero—we find the vast majority of our citizens. At the early stages of a nationalist movement, it is safe to assume a j survey would reveal not a normal curve but a skewed distribution—extremely few with a j of one and the vast majority clumped toward the opposite end of the spectrum. Perhaps a distribution of our followers and their j levels would reveal a deeply institutionalized or even a hegemonic identity represented as a skewed curve but, this time, flowing in the opposite direction. The polar opposites—extremely ardent enthusiasts and individuals with no commitment to the group—are easier to assess.

This model differs from classic Downsian assumptions in another important way. A hypothetical distribution of j levels across any society would reveal a solidarity curve. Assuming the ability to plot j levels in a community observers would appreciate that the higher the height of the j-curve, the greater would be the number of societal members who feel the same intensity of group solidarity. We assume that ethnic entrepreneurs persistently fight to change the shape of that curve. Their greatest preference is to induce higher levels of group solidarity. In other words, they would like to foment a skewed curve—one favoring a higher percentage with a j at or near one. The greater the number of individuals with intense feelings of group solidarity, the easier it is to mobilize collective action in general and more militant collective activities in particular. Classic Downsian electoral strategies propose that political leaders need to appeal to the median voter to amass the largest number of possible votes. We do not assume that ethnic leaders need to cater to the median level of j.

Ethnic entrepreneurs assign tasks commensurate with varying levels of group solidarity. This is not a game of *one size fits all*. Ethnic elites may ask all group members to vote for a nationalist party. In many democratic polities this is a low risk venture and is not considered an onerous burden even for those with modest levels of group solidarity—a j around, say, around 0.5. Participating in a demonstration or a strike, however, is riskier. Group leaders might ask all sympathizers to collaborate with these activities. But they are more likely to recruit activists with more than modest levels of group solidarity for these assignments. Ultimately, nationalist leaders may ask for volunteers to serve in a military capacity. While ordinary citizens may provide rations or lodging, only those with the highest levels of group solidarity are likely to report for duty. The group's capacity to extract collective action and impose greater obligations increases when the collective in question is in command of a state. With a bureaucratic apparatus at their service, ethnic leaders are in a better position to coerce greater levels of collective action. In the end, whether they command state or not, group leaders do not have to demand the same collective activities from everyone. They can and do assign different tasks proportionate to varying levels of group solidarity.

All individuals, scholars propose, have heterogeneous priorities.[55] At times, we prefer one set over another. Different preferences are often based on the divergent roles we perform. Our responsibilities as a blood relative differ substantially from our obligations as members of a social club.[56] We are also in a better position to fulfill social commitments after we have satisfied fundamental material needs. For Maslow, assorted preferences are a result of the fulfillment or deficiency of ranked needs.[57] Thus, the desire for tangible goods, such as food, takes priority over the quest for love. Once that critical material want is satisfied we can then pursue others. While we have a hierarchy of needs, there is no doubt that we seek emotional nourishment from our immediate environment.[58] Our social needs compel us to take into account the caprices of our peers, neighbors, and larger community.[59] After all, they are the ones who provide social rewards. Simultaneously, they deliver castigating verdicts on our failings. Thus, social and material needs should be perceived as two sides of the same coin as opposed to completely disconnected phenomena. In order to understand individual motivation, we must attempt to comprehend a person's subjective perspective.[60] That assessment must take into account that people mull over *both* economic and social payoffs.[61]

Primary groups, starting with families, elicit the highest levels of psychological attachment. Common life experiences serve as constant reminders that individuals make tremendous personal sacrifices for their children, siblings, or clan members. In contrast, most of us would be surprised to hear about an individual making the same kinds of sacrifices for, say, a neighborhood association or a professional organization. Given the passion that some feel for sports teams or political parties, perhaps they could be situated somewhere between familial loyalty and devotion to one's social club. The degree to which nationalist elites succeed in generating collective action—whether in the form of voting, encouraging participants to join in a demonstration, or recruiting the rank and file to join an armed struggle—will depend on their ability to evoke a potent poignant response. Unlike standard political party leaders, in Downs's approach, ethnic elites do not merely respond to the nationalist public; they are always trying to mold it. Among the most forceful human sentiments are those associated with familial bonds. Hence, ethnic entrepreneurs must define the nation as more than just another ordinary social group. In order to generate large-scale collective action, the ethnic group and the nation must be effectively characterized as a colossal extended family.

THE SECOND-ORDER PARADOX

State agencies, civil society, and even ordinary individuals all are capable of generating social benefits and sanctions. Government officials accomplish this in the form of official recognition such as awarding metals or determining who marches in a parade. The praiseworthy are often selected to perform important public rituals such as raising a flag or laying a wreath in a celebration. The government can also immortalize those whose labors brought glory to the nation by putting their names on monuments or naming streets after them.[62] Nonstate actors ranging from ordinary citizens to organized religious groups can also engage in generating selective social payoffs, both negative and positive. They can take the form of a parade, an honorable mention by the community's cleric, or other such public ceremonies. In poems, songs, and novels, their exploits are related to future generations. More than just praising the past, these gestures intend to foment future collective action. Yael Zerubavel observed, "Each act of commemoration reproduces a *commemorative narrative*, a story about a particular past that accounts for this ritualized remembrance and provides a moral message for the group members."[63] Within each society, these series of commemorative narratives are sewn together into a much larger *master commemorative*—a romanticized celebration of a society's past that leaders trust will inspire future collective action.[64] Socially ambitious individuals seek out this commendation.

Self-esteem is an intimately personal emotion. While one can show outward signs of a positive or negative self-image, frequently individuals mask their self-esteem from others. Although it is a private emotion, it is fomented or diminished by others.[65] This emotion is comparative.[66] Patrick Hogan said, "To a great extent, people's self-esteem appears to rely on their feeling that they are in a dominant position over someone else, or that some group to which they belong and with which they identify is in a dominant position over another such group."[67] Generic praise is far from the ultimate goal. A watered-down social payoff is worth little to the diehard believer. The true prize is to receive adulation from particular people—those with privileged position in society. As Aristotle said, "Honour seems to depend more upon the people who pay it than upon the person to whom it is paid…It seems too that the reason why men seek honour is that they may be confident of their own goodness."[68] The value of a social reward or sanction is positively associated with the rank of the person distributing that payoff. The higher the social rank of the person distributing the praise, the greater the value and impact of the tribute. Praise from a teacher, the classroom head, is good. But praise from the mayor, the town leader, is much better. Congratulations from both of these pales in comparison to accolades from a national leader. Those tributes are delivered in the name of the entire ethnic community.[69]

Grassroot notables are more than capable of generating social benefits and sanctions. Still, the impact of admiration from one's neighbor cannot compare to the public commendation imparted by a larger organization or even the state seizing for itself the mantle of the nation incarnate. That same appreciation from a neighbor in a uniform—the vestment adorning someone as a representative of the state—or a grand title is worth considerably more. Aristotle said, "But they who aspire to gain honour from persons of high character and wide information are eager to confirm their own opinion of themselves; they delight therefore in a sense of their own goodness."[70] A strong sense of honor, an emotion generated by the praise of others, helps to boost one's self-esteem. Still, one's self-image is not a social benefit. Augmenting that self-image in the eyes of one's chosen community determines what constitutes a benefit.[71] Pride and honor are comparative feelings and we feel at our greatest while in the company of those with lesser amounts.[72] Envy is particularly strong in terms of those closest to us in rank and social standing but not those who exceed our station.[73] Exaltations from our superiors send a clear message that our actions on behalf of the many afforded us the opportunity to surpass our station, even if for a brief moment.

The previous discussion brings us to the next question: why should individuals bother to shower another with praise? A more perplexing issue is why individuals inconvenience themselves by volunteering to perform as norm enforcers? Lauding someone for their good works, thus generating a positive social payoff for the recipient, or chastising a social deviant, inflicting a negative social payoff on our subject, may take little effort. Regardless, performing a guardian function imposes a cost that a norm enforcer must bear. In a word, we have ended up, one more time, at the doorstep of Olson's *free-rider paradox*. Instead of asking why the believer should cooperate with the group, we now inquiry why a norm enforcer should find it in their self-interest to stand vigil over group member behavior and safeguard the collective's interest. We would have an easier time understanding the motivation behind norm sentinels were they paid. Extremely few, if any, are hired to fulfill that function. If states cannot afford to situate a police officer on every corner, nonstate actors are in an even more precarious financial circumstance. This challenge, as aggravating as the original *free-rider paradox*, has been termed the *second order free-rider paradox*.

Following Rose McDermott's advice again, it would be prudent to start by examining some of the classic thinkers who helped us to reevaluate our exceedingly narrow perception of rationality. David Hume and François La Rochefoucauld suggested that there are, in actuality, selfish motivations for performing a norm-enforcing role. We can look at this in either a positive or negative light. Starting from a vantage point of sincerity, individuals would not want to acclaim a virtue they did not share. Such a view suggests that the cooperative group member has been judged to be *one like us*. A skeptic might rephrase that last sentence and insinuate that individuals are not interested in extolling righteousness unless they wanted others to believe in their rectitude.[74] Taken in a less-than-flattering light, this alternative interpretation suggests that the cooperator is being judged based not on how we behave but on how we want others to *believe* we act on the group's behalf. As Hume put it, "We may observe, that no person is ever prais'd by another for any quality, which wou'd not, if real, produce, of itself, a pride in the person possest of it."[75] La Rochefoucauld said, "To praise noble deeds unreservedly is in a sense to have a share in them."[76] He is more explicit in his 143rd maxim, where he claimed, that "we overpraise the qualities of others more out of satisfaction with our own opinion than respect for their merit, seeking to draw praise upon ourselves while appearing to praise them."[77] This does not imply that we love to engage in the act of lauding itself. La Rochefoucauld understood that from an entrepreneur's perspective, it was simply the cost of doing business. He noted, "We dislike praising, and never praise anybody except out of self-interest. Praise is a subtle, concealed, and delicate form of flattery which gratifies giver and receiver in different ways: the latter accepts it as the due reward of his merit, the former bestows it so as to draw attention to his own fairness and discrimination."[78]

In the dominion of social payoffs, activists are publicly commended for their efforts; their deeds are openly heralded. Norm deviants, in kind, are reprimanded for their failure to live up to societal expectations. The payoff to the performer can come in either the positive or negative varieties. Whether they are extolling virtues or condemning transgressions, norm regulators simultaneously generate another reward—one for themselves. The very act of refereeing social conduct is an overt signal that eulogizing jurors regard themselves worthy to make a pronouncement over someone else's actions or failings. Presumably, one does not have the right to sit in judgment over another unless such a person already lives up to—or *claims to live up to*—the code of conduct in question. Generally speaking, most individuals in a society do not dare challenge norm enforcers for fear that they might turn their juridical gaze on their challenger unless one had clear and convincing evidence of their hypocrisy.[79] Playing the role of arbitrator represents a societal promotion, in a manner of speaking. It elevates someone's unofficial in-group status from the ranks of the mundane citizenry to a protector of sanctified code of conduct by which all group members were supposed to live. That norm defender may be respected or dreaded. In any case, their perpetually vigilant eyes and sharp tongues have an amazingly effective way of keeping many in line. At the neighborhood level, they may be scornfully classified as the local *busybody* or gossip. As an envoy from the state or nation, these grassroots adjudicators may be designated informants. Lacking a paycheck for their work, in most cases, these individuals are still amply rewarded by their societies for their dutiful service.

Thus, a full portrait of norm arbitration must take into account the production of two distinct products. First, norm referees manufacture social payoffs for a third party. Participants enjoy a social reward; noncooperators are compensated with a social reprimand. Second, they pat themselves on the back for defending their community's social order. Self-congratulation for norm arbitration is a public affair thus lifting up the norm judge's in-group stature. Through public commentary, circulating rumors, and spreading gossip, norm enforcers remind their neighbors and peers of their praiseworthy function as societal protectors. The intensity of the reward, or reprimand, is contingent upon the level or intensity of the collective activity or the outrageousness of the defection. Outside the state, deep in the crevices of civil society, ordinary citizens operate as norm enforcers. Without priestly robes, they flaunt their judicial role, thus augmenting the value of their autogenerated reward, through innuendo, gossip, and ridicule. Norm enforcers are compensated and this payment is selective. As is the case with informants in a police state, grassroots norm enforcers are paid, but only to the degree that they are active in the profession.

Individuals will be willing to engage in collective action for praise, assuming they have an emotional or social connection to the group in question. When weighed against one's material interests, the potential gain by voting, engaging in a parade or demonstration, or other nonviolent act may be great indeed. Naturally, as the potential material cost of engaging in collective action increases—such as cases of ethnic warfare—the total individual payoff may deter collective action in all but the most committed group members, such as martyrs. National communities have a host of tasks that must be fulfilled, and these missions of varying risk levels are carried out by group members with differing levels of group solidarity.

Conclusion

The model presented here seeks to highlight the utilities individuals must weigh when calculating their decision whether to participate in collective action. The proclivity to lend a hand increases to the degree individuals depend on the group in question. Emotional dependency on the group may be supplemented with a material dependency, particularly when the nation has command of a state and is in a position to disseminate salaries as well as social payoffs. For the rational pleasure-seeking *Homo sociologicus*, we seek praise, pride, and honor and attempt to avoid admonish, shame, and disgrace. Even if the benefits and sanctions of social interaction are nonmaterial, this still leaves us with the question of why grassroots enforcers would bother to generate the social rewards or sanctions at all. Part of the solution to this quandary is to understand the benefits accrued by norm enforcers. Indirectly, those handing out praise present themselves as exemplar community members. After all, only a member in good standing has the right to sit in judgment of others. Thus, those who praise the deeds of others simultaneously generate positive social rewards for themselves. This is no less true for the generation and dissemination of social sanctions for noncooperation or betrayal. Unlike the limited material rewards distributed to elite cooperators, such as patronage posts, social rewards and punishments can be easily generated and disseminated by society's rank and file. Producing them is very inexpensive. And despite the low cost, they are very effective against noncooperative individuals, particularly if the defectors have an elevated level of emotional commitment to the group. Social rewards or sanctions are not effective on out-group members. In the following chapter, we shall examine some cases of moderate or nonviolent forms of collective action and the kinds of social rewards that motivated cooperators, including the varieties of social sanction that influenced their strategic behavior.

CHAPTER 4

ODE TO A HERO

NOVELS, POEMS, SONGS, BOOKS, AND A PLETHORA of public monuments are emblazoned with the chronicles of brave souls who made valiant personal sacrifices for the greater community. Government-sanctioned textbooks lavishly praise the courageous prince and the valiant general. Official and unofficial chronicles glorify the deeds of the common citizen who also exerted tremendous effort on behalf of the many. Social rank does not determine one's status as a hero—that is established by deed. Leaders at the apex and at the grassroots present the champion's gallantry as an example we should all follow. Legends also echo the tragic misdeeds of the group's adversaries. But even harsher words are reserved for traitors. Avoiding shame's stigma and fear of shunning for deviating from social norms can be powerful motivators.

Students of the classic Hellenic era may recall that heroes were not godly beings; they were the offspring of the Olympians and ordinary mortals. They were imbued with superhuman abilities but they were not divine. Within their communities, national leaders promote the hero's cult. They laud the one who stood above the ordinary masses but not high enough to be one with the supernatural. We acclaim the pursuit of that *in-between* status. Thus, the label of "hero" in this chapter is rather fitting. Here the focus is not on the most zealous nationalists—the ones willing to take up arms and those who volunteer for martyrdom. Rather, these are the ordinary individuals who comprise a nationalist movement's rank and file. Their actions are deliberate and unambiguous but they are also cautious and somewhat conservative. Unquestionably, these souls feel a profoundly strong bond with *their people* and they joyfully await the positive social rewards associated with cooperating with their cause. Still, this link is not absolute. Their activities represent the unassuming stuff of which most nationalist exploits are made. This chapter focuses on ordinary activists—those with a j greater than zero but less than one. These are souls who willingly forego material benefits in the name of a loftier ideal. Given their emotional or psychological attachment to the group, they weigh their social utility above the material.

FIGHTING WORDS

Depending on the particular circumstances, nationalist leaders lobby their community members to collaborate with or fight against the *status quo*. When it comes to defying the established authority politically significant social action comes in a wide array of forms and levels of intensity ranging from gossip's mellow whispers to the furious blast of armed insurrection. Virile warriors brandishing a sword in hand serve as the prototypical representation of the national resistance fighter. As with many social phenomena, more fervent manifestations habitually grab the public's attention, overshadowing other forms of defiance or collaboration. Only a small percentage of crises will ever rise to the level of political confrontation designed to overthrow existing relationships of subordination and oppression.[1] Recurrently, we find more subtle expressions of resistance that can be categorized under the larger rubric of "weapons of the weak."[2] Like so many other phenomena, acts of resistance against the adversary are deeds that display cooperative behavior toward *our* collective and these can be situated along a continuum. Regardless of its specific manifestation, all manner of defiance share an unfettering determination to incessantly contest some aspect of the *status quo*. Recurrently, agents of defiance regularly justify their future goals by appealing to the *status quo ante* or some romanticized version of the past.

The primary focus of this tome is on nonelite participation in the nationalist enterprise. Presumably, elites can count on selective tangible traits to compensate their compensation. Still, that does not prevent elites from feeling emotions or even engaging in activities, in whole or in part, to satisfy their emotions. Like all other members of society, they, too, must weigh their social and material payoffs. Indeed, Rodney Barker suggested that many of the rituals regimes engage in to foster greater legitimacy are actually geared toward themselves and not the masses.[3]

Let us begin with an example of cooperation in a nationalist struggle carried out by an elite. This individual's actions were not being scrutinized because of his rank or prominence. Rather, he was singled out because of his choice of armaments. Out of the vast repertoire of weaponry, our volunteer elected to use speech as his rapier. In this exchange, the choice of employing one language over another was more important than the literal concepts uttered. No blood was shed, no blows were delivered, and no one was incarcerated. The only things tossed back and forth were the sounds of human voices. In the grand scheme of things, particularly in the volatile environs of the Middle East, many would consider this a trifling skirmish. What makes this gesture part and parcel of the larger struggle is its replication. At that moment, this member of the intelligentsia was aware that his most effective blade was not clenched in the palm of his hand. Rather, it rested on the tip of his tongue.

National identities are not dependent on the objectification of any one cultural feature. That being the case, numerous nationalist movements differentiate themselves primarily, or in part, on their vernacular.[4] Part scholar and part language romantic, Jean Laponce stated, "A language is not a mere tool of communication; it is also a community definer."[5] The insurgents in the French Revolution insisted that a common language, the dialect of Paris, would unite their people in contrast to a multitude of regional languages and dialects that were deemed feudal and hinted of pro-monarchy leanings.[6] For over two centuries, nationalists have extolled languages as the features uniting a national community.[7] Its popularity can be attributed to the influence of late eighteenth- and early nineteenth-century German Romantics, particularly Johann Gottfried Herder and Johann Gottlieb Fichte.[8] In 1808, Johann Gottlieb Fichte uttered the following words during his thirteenth *Address to the German Nation*: "Those who speak the same language are joined to each other by a multitude of invisible bonds by nature herself, long before any human art begins; they understand each other and have the power of continuing to make themselves understood more and more clearly; they belong together and are by nature one and an inseparable whole."[9] In the early nineteenth century Alexis de Tocqueville claimed, "Language is perhaps the strongest and more enduring link which unites men."[10] Ronald Schmidt contended that at the heart of the *politics of language* lies a kind of "identity politics," where enthusiasts and militants contest one another in a bid to mold public perceptions of *us-versus-them* and incorporate that ideology into state policy.[11] Both scholars and activists understand the powerful role languages can play in the objectification and display of national identities. From pauper to prince, we can all understand sounds enunciated in *our* national tongue. Those expressed by outsiders, even if they are fluent in our language, will always carry the stain of a peculiar accent and thus bear the mark of an outsider.

Academics are frequently engaged in describing and evaluating the actions of others. Depending on the field of study, the deeds being analyzed may have transpired eons ago. In this case, interestingly enough, the defiance was carried out by the author himself. Yasir Suleiman, a Palestinian linguist residing in the United Kingdom, shared with his readers a fine example of temperate resistance. Arabic was, for him, more than just a *lingua franca*; it was a sacred tongue and a tangible sign of national and cultural solidarity with his fellow Palestinians and Arabs. Different rules of grammar, verb conjugation, and lexical nuances do not make war with one another. Suleiman pointed out that "linguistic conflict is not conflict between languages or language varieties per se, but between speakers of a language, or those of different languages, who compete over resources and values in their physical and cultural milieu or inter- and intra-group situations."[12] As a proud Palestinian and a linguist, he understood the powerful connection between vernacular speech and national identities.

In his book *A War of Words, Yasir* Suleiman discussed his encounters with Israeli soldiers and police. Most Israelis, and likely most Western travelers to the Holy Land, would look upon these armed officers as simply state agents. Chances are that few Arabs, particularly Palestinians, would see them as anything other than the embodiment of the enemy regime. Conflicting national aspirations combined with seriously disparate levels of economic development help to produce a volatile mixture—one ripe for near-spontaneous outbursts. When he was addressed by these law enforcement agents in his native Arabic, Suleiman refused to respond in kind. Replying in Arabic would have been a signal that he was playing the game by their rules. He thought about his choice and he decided to reply in English. Suleiman proclaimed, "My refusal to use Arabic with Israeli soldiers, Jewish or Druze, is impregnated with symbolic meaning. It signaled an attitude of defiance on my part. It also represented an act of cultural resistance to the occupier; a token one perhaps, but one which nevertheless held a lot of political meaning for me."[13] From the start, Suleiman's comments draw a sharp line between *us* and *them*, and that line is emphatically demarcated with his use of the pejorative term "occupier." With this term he attempted to debase the legitimacy of the Israeli presence in the homeland of his forefathers. Fascinatingly, he clumped together two sets of Israeli citizens—Jews and Druze—despite their disparate linguistic, cultural, and religious backgrounds.[14] Suleiman almost casually dismissed the Druze from the greater Arab family despite the fact that Arabic is also their mother tongue and their faith's shared history with Sunni and Shiite Islam.

Beneath the surface there is also a romantic element to his confrontational description of the Israeli military. Manifest in Suleiman's use of the term "occupier" is a desire to return to a pre-1948 world, or even a time before the first significant waves of Zionist-era Jewish immigrants—or *Olim Hadashim*—began arriving at the twilight of the nineteenth century.[15] As is the case in many protracted conflicts, the same event is referenced in completely different ways. What Israelis call their independence from the British, Suleiman and his fellow Palestinians and Arabs classify as the *Nakba*—the catastrophe. The author's idyllic *status quo ante*, at least in demographic terms, is temporally located toward the end of the Ottoman period. The political dimension is far more problematic.[16] At the intersection of Ottoman and British rule, Arabs were a clear majority in the land between the Mediterranean Sea and the Jordan River. Administratively, these inhabitants' legal status was changed from Ottoman citizens to subjects or colonial wards of the British Empire. Then again, glorifying the past is always a selective process. His idealized setting would exclude both Jewish immigration and Istanbul's administrative authority.

Having distinguished the first- from the third-person plural, Suleiman was prepared to engage in battle. First, he needed to select his preferred armament, and he chose the medium of communication itself. He spoke in English rather than Arabic in a tense, if not provoking, setting with a soldier. Employing a language he mastered against a soldier who, in all likelihood, had yet to attend a university gave him an upper hand in exchanges with ordinary Israelis. While one can assume that he spoke Arabic far better than the majority of Israeli soldiers—Jewish or Druze—this professor was aware that Arabic held a low status for Israelis *vis-à-vis* English. A stellar command of his native tongue and *lingua sacra* did not empower him over an Israeli Defense Forces (IDF) soldier. But a robust command of English—the language of Israel's chief ally, the United States, Western popular culture, and the dominant language of a great deal of international commercial and scientific exchange—was another matter. Using English in a heated discussion with members of his adversary's armed forces gave him, even if momentarily, the tactical high ground.

The manner in which Suleiman carried out his act of defiance was impregnated with an inherent and paradoxical duality. On the one hand, he acted as an average Palestinian, a community member with a strong sense of group solidarity, standing up to an adversary. His action made no sense outside the context of claiming to represent his collective. It was performed in the name of his people. On the other hand, even if only a "token" gesture, he executed a feat that was at least one notch above what the average Palestinian would do or could do. After all, how many ordinary Israelis or Palestinians could surpass the English language skills of a university professor who taught in the United Kingdom? Thus, he set himself above his rivals and his fellow compatriots. His actions consisted of a less-than-amicable exchange of words rather than a physical confrontation. Any escalation beyond an unpleasant exchange of words would likely have resulted in physical violence, confinement, or worse. Suleiman's exploit reminds us that the resolve to partake in a collective action is not a spontaneous response. It is a premeditated act that is rather modest in scope most of the time.[17]

Another interesting aspect about this small act of defiance is the reward structure. Who is present to compensate resistors for their actions? One could argue that as an academic, Suleiman is a privileged person. Intellectuals already enjoy the privileged position within their society's elite. In this case, his exploits were chronicled by none other than himself and disseminated by his publisher. Anyone who reads this book, or his students who listen to his lectures, will be familiar with what he did. His compensation was selective since only he would benefit from this reticent act of resistance. In his dual role as an elite and an activist, we cannot determine for certain whether his payoff was tangible, social, or a combination of the two. In any case, he was not compensated for any action beyond his *War of Words*. Higher levels of return would be reserved for those who engaged in more intense forms of nationalist opposition. The actions undertaken by elites do not challenge the classic free-rider paradox. Members of the upper crust will be selectively rewarded by other elites for their individual feats and sanctioned for particular faults. The free-rider paradox is a conceptual problem faced by those attempting to explain the exploits of ordinary citizens. Now we face the challenge of trying to understand the logic behind the heroic act carried out by the many.

TONGUE-TIED IN KYIV

As an elite member of his community, Suleiman could be selectively and materially rewarded for his individual actions. His nationalist defiance was the tactical choice to employ a language that would strategically advantage him over an adversary with relatively fewer linguistic skills. Examples of nationalist resistance abound regardless of social rank and prestige. There are numerous cases where language selection performs an important task in the nationalist's toolbox. Let us shift our attention from the eastern Mediterranean to the northern Black Sea. Laada Bilaniuk's study of language usage in the modern Ukraine represents a case in point. Language preservation and diffusion are closely associated with an idiom's overall prestige.[18] In diglossic situations, an idiom's stature is also directly related to the number of roles it performs such as the primary language employed at home, on the streets, in business establishments, in government offices, and in houses of worship. Until the demise of the USSR, the Russian language was associated with high social standing and educational achievement throughout the Soviet Union's fifteen constituent republics. Furthermore, Russian speakers could relish in the cachet that theirs was one of the official languages used at the United Nations. Adding to the idiom's prestige was the Soviet Union's ideological and military grip on most of Eastern Europe during the cold war. Since the downfall of the Gorbachev regime, the Russian language's status has significantly eroded.

In the Suleiman example, the rapier of choice was one standard language in opposition to another. Had he responded to the Israeli soldier in Arabic, the professor could have answered back in a number of variants of modern colloquial Arabic or Classic Arabic. Today most people in the Ukraine speak standardized Russian, standardized Ukrainian, or a varying patois of the two called *surzhyk*.[19] Standardized and popular variants of these related forms of speech fall are constituents of the same family of Slavic languages.[20] Depending on the context, these variable forms of speech may merely be forms of communications or arms in a nonsanguinous nationalist exchange. Although Ukrainian and Russian nationalist mythmakers trace their emergence to a common juncture— the ninth-century Kyvian Rus'—that shared past has not quelled disparate claims over the appropriate role for each language.[21] Linguistic differences can be transformed into effective nationalist armaments even if the dissimilarities are relatively minor.[22] Laada Bilaniuk observed, "The close genetic relationship of Ukrainian and Russian underscored how even small differences in linguistic variants could accrue great symbolic weight."[23] Elites' ability to exploit linguistic differences as national identity boundary markers springs from the popular presumption that these cultural attributes are durable notwithstanding the reality that living languages are constantly adapting to new circumstances.[24] Indeed, the only *pure* languages are those that do not change, and we commonly refer to these as *dead* languages.

Long before the birth of the Soviet Union, the Russian rulers imposed restrictions on the Ukrainian language. As far back as Czar Peter I, the imperial court limited the publication of books in the Ukraine.[25] Persecution of the Ukrainian language, in forms subtle and gross, continued throughout the Soviet era. Communist Party leaders in Moscow envisioned forging a new socialist society wherein non-Russian ethnic identities, and the languages associated with them, would eventually dissolve into the forgotten pages of history.[26] Under Lenin, Russian was ideologically rehabilitated from a symbol of the newly defunct imperial order to the language of the impending workers' revolutionary struggle.[27] It is true that the federal structure of the USSR preserved a certain degree of cultural autonomy for the titular ethnic groups in the fifteen constituent republics. But the domination of a highly centralized Communist Party assured the ascendancy of Russian above all other Soviet languages.[28] Out of the many varieties and dialects of Russian, Soviet rulers displayed a marked partiality toward a very traditional and conservative Russian—a dialect unmistakably associated with Moscow "high culture."[29] Throughout the Soviet era, speaking Ukrainian in public was deemed evidence of backwardness and suggested that one sympathized with Ukrainian nationalism or even separatism. As a consequence, during most of the twentieth century, the Russian language dominated the most prominent facets of the Ukrainian public sphere, particularly in the larger urban centers.[30]

This linguistic juggernaut began to show signs of vulnerability during the heyday of Gorbachev's *perestroika* reforms. Little could he have imagined at the time that by attempting to restructure the political system, he unwittingly opened the Pandora's box. Some leaders in the republics interpreted Gorbachev's statements as a green light to experiment with change. In the spirit of greater openness, and justified as a bid to reform the Communist system to promote its long-term prognosis, the government in Kyiv declared Ukrainian the Republic's official state language.[31] In keeping with Newtonian principles of motion, for every action there is an equal and opposite reaction. Moscow's anger turned into a counter-reaction. The Supreme Soviet of the USSR responded to this gesture by promulgating its own statute—one declaring Russian the official language of the Soviet Union. As events unfolded, this Moscow-centered initiative became inconsequential as the Union's constituent republics seceded one by one.[32] In the wake of the Union's partition, Ukrainian stood as the official language of a new sovereign polity. Changes in language policy typified altering ethnic relations. Shifting language policies within the USSR's old constituent units boosted the social standing of the republics' titular ethnic communities by attempting to elevate them to the level of the new republic's *staatvolk*.[33]

Changes in government policy have yet to keep pace with the heterogeneous linguistic state of affairs in the contemporary Ukraine. Upon its independence from the Soviet Union, Ukrainian became the official language of a new sovereign country. Government repression of this language ended. Relatively quick changes in government policy could not alter an array of attitudes and deeply entrenched linguistic practices overnight. In a society where many are dominant or exclusive Russian speakers, *surzhyk* has become more prevalent. While nationalist leaders exalt cultural homogeneity, cultural hybridity is the global norm.[34] But it is frequently chastised by ethnic mythmakers and entrepreneurs for failing to live up to their image of cleanliness from outside—read, *corrupt*—influences. Although very artificial, so-called pure cultural features are continuously contrasted with the *other*.[35] Ukrainian nationalists and linguistic traditionalists reproach this colloquial speech as a bastardization of their pristine tongue.[36] Rather than meld the two, some simply select one language; at times, that choice is made regardless of the other speaker's preferred language.[37] To many, this might appear like a return to the Tower of Babel, even though employing two distinct languages in the same conversation, or even code switching between the two, is quite the norm where linguistic frontiers meet and sometimes collide. Nonreciprocal bilingualism in the Ukraine is on the rise.

In the course of her research, Laada Bilaniuk interviewed a Ukrainian nationalist in his late thirties who was identified by the pseudonym Taras. The further Taras pursued his formal education—from boarding school to college—the greater was his contact with the Russian language.[38] Given the power and prestige of this language during the Soviet era, many of the Russian speakers he encountered were upwardly mobile ethnic Ukrainians. During the Soviet era this was not unexpected. While attending university, Taras developed a deep and lasting friendship with a Ukrainian nationalist. In time, he expressed his nationalist feelings more publicly and Taras was eventually expelled from the school for his vocal opposition to Russification.[39] While he unambiguously opposed Russification during the Soviet era, he did so within socialist parameters. He expressed scorn for Russian cultural chauvinism and not revulsion for Marxist principles. Taras said, "We felt that the regime had fouled up communist ideals and enslaved Ukraine, and that Ukraine needed to be free so that an unblemished communism could be created."[40]

Openly challenging Russification at that time, even if done under a Marxist guise, was tantamount to ideological heresy in a regime that displayed little tolerance for ideological heterodoxy. The KGB, the Soviet secret police, interrogated him and his college roommate. Taras pronounced, "All those discussions with the KGB, even though they were demoralizing and broke me to some extent, at the same time they also reified my nationalism."[41] Rather than repress his Ukrainian nationalism, this harassment only intensified his nationalist feelings. For someone who identified passionately with his national community, maltreatment by his foes was certainly unpleasant but it came with its own reward. As someone with a high level of solidarity with his Ukraine, his persecution by the state was a clear sign of his dedication to his nation. That kind of social standing cannot come from free riding.

Ukrainian—to be more precise, *standard* Ukrainian—was Taras's *national* language. He insisted that this would be the sole language in his household. Indeed, nation-building projects are incomplete until they make their way into the home—the locus of the "inner domain"—the Edenic core of the national soul.[42] But life is rarely experienced in black-and-white terms. Sharply separating these inner and outer domains is easier said than done. Despite his wishes, Taras was never far from Russian speakers, even in his own abode. Occasionally, he found it necessary to temper his nationalist passions in his wife's presence since Russian was her mother tongue.[43] For a male nationalist adhering to traditional gender norms, having an outsider wife poses a problem when the mother is expected to transmit cultural intimacy, including the nation's language, to the next generation. Regarding the development of Indian nationalism under British rule, Partha Chatterjee said, "The home was the principal site for expressing the spiritual quality of the national culture, and women must take the main responsibility for protecting and nurturing this quality."[44] Nationalist movements have a paradoxical quality when it comes to gender roles. On the one hand, they ask women to become active participants in the political struggle to liberate the entire community. Deniz Kandiyoti noted, "On the other hand, they reaffirm the boundaries of culturally acceptable feminine conduct and exert pressure on women to articulate their gender interests within the terms of reference set by nationalist discourse."[45] Nationalist movements have a socially conservative, if not chauvinistic, bent, and the epicenter of that traditionalism is the home.[46]

Taras' first major conflict with his wife over his nationalism arose when she referred to him as *papa* rather than *tato* when speaking to their daughter.[47] *Papa* was the Russian term for father as opposed to the Ukrainian *tato*. Besides his irritation with his wife, Taras was also annoyed with his own mother. After retiring she moved to Kyiv. As one might expect, relocating to a major metropolitan area exposes newcomers to a host of new ideas, mores, and customs. Among the new trends his mother picked up was word borrowings from Russian. Although she was a retired teacher, a well-educated person, her speech was becoming increasingly *surzhykified*. For her son, this linguistic modification was an abomination. As he put it,

"They are taking away my mother tongue, the language my mother once spoke to me."[48] It is interesting how Taras classified *her* language shift as a deprivation of *his* heritage. Complying with nationalist norms was not only an obligation he imposed on himself, he also *volunteered* his family members whether they were willing or not.

Even before the Ukraine's independence from the Soviet Union, Taras insisted on performing his national identity in a public, though limited, manner. Such displays often incur tangible and very personal costs. Taras reported that he had a group of Russian-speaking friends. By custom, he spoke with them in their language. For a true nationalist, appeasing friends can cost in terms of one's self-esteem—the sense that one is betraying one's principles. With no warning he decided that in order to be true to himself he would speak to them, henceforth, only in Ukrainian.[49] Stunned by this revelation, not all accepted his new personal language policy. One Russian-born friend was manifestly offended and insisted that she did not want to see Taras anymore. Another, a friend of mixed Russian and Ukrainian heritage, accepted this change. This more accepting friend later became his wife.

Like Suleiman, Taras passionately felt that his identity was a core facet of his life and this dimension needed to be publicly performed, even if in a circumscribed manner. As we learned, his Ukrainian identity was displayed at home, in his "inner domain." Although it was preserved, it was executed in a less-than-perfect manner. His Ukrainian identity was also exhibited in the "outer domain." His opposition to Russification under Soviet rule sidetracked his college career and brought him the undesirable attention of the USSR's old secret service. Taras paid a substantial price, materially speaking, for practicing his beliefs. He clearly felt that the upside of his gestures, the pride from showcasing his Ukrainianness, was worth the sacrifice. In social terms, Taras's insistence on speaking only Ukrainian with his inner circle of friends cost him a friend. These costs were not shared by all Ukrainians; he bore those costs selectively. The ultimate material beneficiary of his deeds was the larger Ukrainian nation. One by one, Ukrainians decided to recapture their public spaces by using their language in open forums. Marc Levine referred to the *Reconquest of Montreal*.[50] Taras joined likeminded Ukrainians in attempting the *Reconquest of Kyiv*. Was he compensated for his sacrifices? Yes, he was. In his own words, while his interrogation by the KGB was "demoralizing," it also "reified" his nationalist feelings.[51] It allowed him to be "true" to himself.[52] Pride could only befall the performer. The same would be true of shame for noncompliance or inadequate compliance. These emotions were selective and could not be shared with the collective.

FLAUNTING MODERNITY

Ethnic and national identities are supposed to be objictified in terms of characteristics that clearly differentiate *us* from *them*. In this boundary-defining process, one would expect ethnic entrepreneurs to select traits that are rather unique. To do otherwise would risk the possibility of having two groups describe themselves in a similar manner. In that vein, we could imagine that universal attributes would make poor intergroup dividing lines. Although it may seem ironic, supposedly universal principles have been exploited as national boundaries drawing lines uniting *us* and fending off *them*. Socialism a popular philosophy within segments of the European Jewish intelligentsia was employed by the embryonic Israeli state to promote Jewish immigration during the British mandate.[53] Ideologies have been used to differentiate communities sharing common cultural legacies, such as the United States and Canada. At times, universalist ideologies serve to build a coherent national image within heterogeneous societies absorbing new peoples, such as net immigrant recipients.[54] For instance, Seymour M. Lipset claimed that American identity was founded on the bedrock of egalitarianism, anti-statisim, populism, and universalism.[55] Likewise, the incorporation of immigrants has also been woven in the fabric of official multicultural Australian national discourse.[56] When students and observers alike think about the cases where modernity is presented as a core element of national identity, they frequently set their sights on Turkey.

Mustafa Kemal Atatürk, the founder of the modern, secular, and republican Turkish state, engineered and promoted a notion of Turkishness that endeavored to make a clean break with past. His country's old older was headed by the imperial House of Osman—a regime that held temporal power over the Ottoman Empire and spiritual authority as the Caliphs of the Islamic faith. Geography became synonymous with orientations toward technology, religiosity, and social reforms. Despite misgivings about imitating the West, sultans began emulating some aspects of Western modernization as part of a strategy toward building a stronger state as far back as the late eighteenth century.[57] Still, this *ancien régime* exemplified a deeply conservative tradition that represented variance with European notions of modernity. In the aftermath of World War I, Atatürk embraced what the old Ottoman order cast aside. His was a nation-building project—or perhaps we should classify it as a nation-*recreating* enterprise—obsessed with emulating many European aspects. The West allegedly represented social, technological, and pedagogical progress. Perhaps more important to a new republican regime picking up the pieces of a defunct empire was the view that Europe stood for economic and military prowess. Whereas the previous government was intertwined with religious legitimacy, Atatürk's republic sought to cut those ties. His constitutional order meant to establish a separation of mosque and state.

The changes Atatürk envisioned were designed to revolutionize Turkish society down to its very core. His regime also broke with the past by promoting fundamental changes, for example, in language policy. These modifications included altering the language itself—*dil devrimi*, or language reform—and replacing the Arabic script with the Latin alphabet—*harf devrimi*, or letter reform.[58] The imperial language of the Ottoman court was Osmanlıca—a stately variant of Turkish that shared many common elements with popular Turkish but had many loan words from classic Arabic and Persian.[59] Starting in the nineteenth century, Turkish nationalists began advocating a deep-seated change in the way Turks spoke and wrote. But this movement did not take off until the dawn of the republican era. Republican Turks endeavored to drive out Persian and Arabic loan words in favor of a *purer* Turkish language. Furthermore, they embraced a new Latin alphabet replacing the Arabic script.[60] Adopting Latin, the most popular script in western and central Europe, was perceived as a fundamental step toward promoting Turkish modernization.[61]

Constructing an official nationalist narrative is based not on the free-flowing undulation of everyday customs but on a national paradigm that has been artificially locked in the *authentic* past. Of course, in the realm of nationalist and ethnic objectification, to bring up an authentic past implies its bogus converse. Public ceremonies play a major role in the articulation and institutionalization of the authentic past. These large-scale public rituals romanticize a pivotal moment in the past. They remind observers, in an ecclesiastical-like manner, that is the faithful past in contrast to inauthentic or even heretical alternative historic interpretations. As Eric Hobsbawm outlined, the invention of traditions is based on "a process of formalization and ritualization, characterized by reference to the past, if only by imposing repetition."[62] For secular Turkish nationalists, the glorious past they celebrate is the 1930s, the pinnacle of Atatürk's tenure.[63] School children are taught that Atatürk saved the country from foreign exploitation. His virility contrasts with pleasure-seeking, egotistical, weak, backward, and oppressive sultans of an earlier epoch.[64] Reminiscence of that era generates a kind of "nostalgic modernity."[65] Esra Özyürek's study of contemporary Turkish identity explored the privatization of that nostalgic modernity—the ways individuals took it upon themselves to glorify national identity associated with Atatürk's tenure.

In the course of her research, Özyürek interviewed an elderly woman, a retired teacher named Meliha. This author took advantage of Meliha's recollections in an effort to connect with the glorious early years of the republic. With exuberant pride Meliha remembered what it was like to grow up in that era. Her contemporaries fondly looked back on a time when it appeared that the entire nation was reciting, in unison, one uniform nationalist sonnet. Atatürk's enemies, domestic and foreign, had just been beaten and there was no visible dissention from Kemalist principles.[66] One of her recollections reveals a great deal about the role of the individual, even the youngest of citizens, in the articulation of national identity and its public performance. In three short sentences, Meliha revealed quite a bit about the interplay between citizen, nation, and the local community. She commented, "The songs, games, marches they taught us in school in those years were made to remind us of war, stir our feelings against the enemies. We would sing marches against the Greeks and the Italians as if they were still invading our land. I remember we would go out with flags in our hands singing these marches, and all store owners would walk outside and applaud us."[67]

First, we see the state fervently at work inculcating nationalist principles and ideas by way of its leading didactic arm—the public school system. Healthy doses of patriotic lessons and exercises are a regular feature of most state-run curricula. Such messages are designed to foment national pride, loyalty to the regime, and to generate collective action in the future. Sam Kaplan said, "The habitual routines, rituals, and discourses to which children are exposed during their years of schooling are all designed to inscribe them with a prereflective background to civic action."[68] Second, the state's nationalist curriculum defined "us" (the Turks) in contrast to "them" (foreigners, or Greeks and Italians). Such a sharp divide could not be bridged by a mere handshake or other expression of amiability. After all, that *us-them* partition was forged in the deathbed of a dilapidated empire and the cradle of spirited budding republic. Enunciating ethnic divisions can cause considerable hardships when cultural boundaries fail to coincide with jurisdictional perimeters. While Italians were foreigners, the same was not true of all Greeks. Articulating group boundaries can inflict severe repercussions on interethnic domestic relations. Such a separation of the first-person plural from its third-person counterpart invariably disenfranchised the country's longstanding ethnic Greek community from the Turkish national family.[69]

A third and extremely important feature of Meliha's statement was her description of the performative aspects of the children's procession. Identities and group boundaries may be acknowledged as an internal emotion, but, particularly in times of conflict, they must be consummated. Through singing, marching, and waving flags, these children imagined themselves—if not symbolically transformed themselves—from common citizens to aspiring soldiers engaged in defending their homes "as if they were still invading our land."[70] To merely feel this effervescent republican Turkish identity was inadequate. No, the children had to manifestly express it and do so, preferably, in a venue where all could witness. Fourth, their juvenile pageant piquantly admonished adult observers to never forget what would be accepted as a legitimate interpretation of Turkishness. Fifth, symbolic presentation has a discrete payoff to the performer. Partaking in feats intentionally designed to exhibit national identity heightened the children's self-confidence.[71] Sixth, the children were praised not only by the state but also by the community. Teachers, a neighborhood-level representative of the Kemalist state, lauded the children for their street-side production. Concurrently, their performance was commended by community members as they harmoniously paraded through town. Seventh, this nationalist display—as is the case with the vast majority of nationalist collective action—came at relatively little risk to the performers. There is no question that this gesture lionized the nation's defenders who were stationed out on the front lines combating the republic's foreign opponents. Likewise, there was no question that the risks for partaking in this particular act were virtually nonexistent. The same would not apply, of course, were a group of Armenians, Greeks, or Kurds to flaunt their ethnic and national pride down the streets of Istanbul. In the realm of political opera, nationalist performance is a carefully planned event.

Rather than dwell just on the early republican period—the era of Meliha's youth—Özyürek's study also examined a new trend toward privatizing Kemalist nationalism.[72] This identity is not just orchestrated by the state but is increasingly being flaunted by individuals exhibiting rival notions of Turkishness, particularly theologically centered notions of Turkish identity. In the *War of Words*, the author described his own moderate act of nationalist performance. In Özyürek's book, the author's mother provides an example of Turkish identity on display. The author's mother lives in Istanbul's Erenköy neighborhood—a largely secular and upscale community. Following the electoral triumph of local Islamists in the mid-1990s, her mother began wearing a pin with Atatürk's image. She ardently and proudly exclaimed, "I want to show that there are people who are dedicated to Atatürk's principles....I have my Atatürk against their veils."[73] We are not provided with detailed descriptions of the mother's perceptions of this article of clothing. The veil could symbolize the bygone days of Ottoman rule in contrast to Atatürk's modern and republican Turkey. From this perspective, it represents the past. The same piece of clothing could also be associated with more conservative and rural parts of the country. In this light, the veil represents for urban secular Turks agrarian backwardness. Then again, the manner in which some fundamentalist Turkish women cover themselves in public could reflect a penchant for what they perceived as more "authentic" forms of Islamic attire. Were this the case, the author's mother could also be combating unwanted foreign influences. Her simple gesture of displaying the founder's image flaunted her social and political principles in a most public, yet personal, manner. And it solidified her credentials, in case anyone had doubts, that her ideological orientations were unmistakably *modern* and secular.

While the previous example represented a secular gesture that pitted religiosity against modern Turkishness, there are examples of hybrid displays that present Atatürk and Islam as compatible representation of a greater and common national identity. The flavor of nationalism on parade veers from the official secular variety. Nonetheless, for fervent nationalists, the need to perform it is just as palpable as crucial as it is for their secularist compatriots. Such synchronous beliefs became more common following the country's 1980 military coup. During the fleeting years of the cold war, the ruling junta began to suggest that Kemalist and Islamic principles were congruent.[74] Özyürek's mother demonstrated her national identity by wearing a pin adorned with Atatürk's image. A shop owner proudly exhibited his national identity by posting a sign. A merchant in the Beyoğlu district of Istanbul displayed a poster of Atatürk near a *Bismillahirahmanirrahim* sign—a sign proclaiming, "*In the name of God, the merciful and the compassionate.*"[75] This entrepreneur lashed out at the Islamists for failing to recognize that without Atatürk, their country would have been overrun by its adversarial neighbors. He insisted, "These pictures show them [Islamists] that the people of this country love Atatürk. They always did and these always will."[76]

Ingrates must be taught a lesson. Interestingly, this shop owner took it upon himself to perform a tutor's role. Governments do not always produce and disseminate the most sufficient lesson plans for instilling national pride. He took it upon himself to fill the slack. The sign-poster combination acted as his chalkboard in a bid to set Islamists straight that they should readjust their view of the past and the present. Simultaneously, it was an outward gesture to Kemalists that he was in solidarity with them and their interpretation of Turkishness. Perhaps this gesture was also an attempt to convey his interpretation of Kemalism—one that did not need to erect such a high wall partitioning mosque and state. In any event, it was not enough to feel passionately about Kemalist principles; he felt the urge to inaudibly display them in a public setting. In so doing, this shop owner tried to elevate himself to the privileged ranks of the honored custodians of the glorious national ideal.

RESISTANCE THROUGH RESIDENCY

Nationalist goals vary across a wide spectrum. At one end, nationalists may desire increased autonomy within their ethnic enclave. At the other end of the nationalist continuum, they aspire to shatter existing center-periphery relations through separatism or irredentism. In any nationalist movement, it is quite common to find a wide diversity of opinion regarding how far the community should go. Nationalists in the U.S. territory of Puerto Rico plainly exhibit this feature all the while adhering to a strong sense of ethnic and national pride. In the words of José Trías Monge, a former Chief Justice of the Commonwealth's Supreme Court, "Puerto Ricans of all persuasions are primarily cultural nationalists."[77] The vast majority of Puerto Ricans express their nationalist aspirations in its autonomist form.[78] This applies to *puertorriqueños* on the Caribbean home island as much as relates to their ethnic brethren residing in various enclaves throughout the U.S. mainland. For a determined minority, the ultimate goal is the island's independence from the United States. Both in the island Commonwealth of Puerto Rico and in Puerto Rican communities throughout North America, this pro-independence sentiment is strongly associated with the intelligentsia—a typical phenomenon in nationalist movements throughout the globe.

Most studies of Puerto Rican nationalism center their attention on the island itself and the perennial debate over the status question—statehood versus the *status quo* versus independence. A handful assess nationalism in New York City—the largest Puerto Rican enclave in the country. Bucking this trend, Ana Yolanda Ramos-Zayas explored Puerto Rican nationalism in inner-city Chicago. She observed, as have others who have studied Puerto Rican nationalism outside the island, a perplexing dilemma. Namely, there is greater support for Puerto Rican independence in the

United States than on the island of Puerto Rico. Rather than oppose this trend, Chicago only reinforces it. Unlike most Puerto Ricans back on the island, the majority of activists within the Chicago community are staunch separatists. Racism and socioeconomic marginalization abound in many inner-city American communities. In turn, these prevalent conditions have fueled a more militant and pro-independence variant of nationalism. Traditionally Puerto Rican nationalism was perceived as a movement challenging the island's colonial status. Outside the boundaries of its Caribbean homeland Puerto Rican nationalism serves another purpose. It has been appropriated as a vehicle by which *barrio* residents can express their fury over their indignation as members of a socially and economically marginalized community in the "*Land of Opportunity.*"[79]

The nationalist project was not limited to something that would transpire *over there*—on the island of Puerto Rico itself—but would also become institutionalized within their inner-city ethnic enclave. Reserving a special status for the local enclave is not novel. Ethnic communities have a history of conceptualizing both an *internal* and *external* homeland.[80] Advocates of the island's independence have a long history in the United States. Although their numbers were few activists in the nascent Puerto Rican community in New York City began organizing pro-independence activities while the island was still a Spanish colony.[81] The hard-core Chicago activists were distinguished from other social campaigners in the vicinity for their commitment to freeing several inmates who had tied to the revolutionary *Fuerzas Armadas de Liberación Nacional* (FALN), or Armed Forced of National Liberation.[82] They lionized Lolita Lebrón, the leader of the 1954 attack on the U.S. House of Representatives, as the personification of the new revolutionary woman.[83] Her assault on Congress came in the wake of the 1950 nationalist uprising and the establishment of Puerto Rico's Commonwealth government in 1952. Both the Puerto Rican and U.S. federal governments used these violent episodes to justify a multidecade campaign of intimidation and persecution of independence supporters regardless of their espousal of violent or nonviolent actions.[84] Government intimidation and persecution of nationalists included independence supporters on the island of Puerto Rico and their sympathizers throughout the United States.

The epicenter of the nationalist mission in Chicago is the Puerto Rican Cultural Center on Division Street. The center is adorned with nationalist slogans, flags, and signs exclaiming *Viva Puerto Rico Libre*—Long Live Free Puerto Rico.[85] Affectionately referred to by locals as the *escuelita*— literally, the "little school"—the second floor of the center houses the

Pedro Albizu Campos High School. There was no more unambiguous statement of their political leanings than to name a school after Albizu Campos, the uncompromising separatist leader from the second quarter of the twentieth century. This school was founded in the 1970s by a group of Puerto Rican teachers and students expelled from the Chicago public school system for advocating bilingual education programs, calling for courses on Puerto Rican history, and refusing to salute the American flag.[86] While they represented a small portion of all Puerto Ricans in the greater Chicago metropolitan area, the center's teachers and nationalist activists represented an important segment of the local intelligentsia.[87] Although considered politically extreme by many, their unquestionable commitment to preserving and promoting Puerto Rican cultural identity anointed these activists with the mantle of guardians of an authentic *puertorriqueñidad*, or Puerto Ricanness.

Whether or not one agrees with Puerto Rico's independence from the United States, one can at least appreciate the tangible connection between espousing this policy and residing on this particular Caribbean island. If a nationalist wanted to cast off from the harbors of the metropolitan state, it is logical to presume this activist would want to be, at a minimum, a passenger aboard ship. Does it make sense for Puerto Ricans to champion sovereignty living hundreds or even thousands of kilometers from the proposed independent homeland? Even among these most fervent of nationalists, it remains unclear how many would return to the island even if the U.S. Congress conceded its independence. Puerto Rican migration to the United States predates the Spanish-American War of 1898, although the great migratory flood took place in the 1940s and 1950s.[88] Today just over half of all ethnic Puerto Ricans reside outside their island homeland. It is true that physical distance has not evaporated the symbolic role performed by the traditional ethnic homeland.[89] Still, diasporic branches of an ethnic community often employ the political rhetoric of the conditions back in the *homeland* even while negotiating their place in a new setting. Puerto Rican nationalism in a U.S. mainland setting becomes a key conduit through which community members convey their political aspirations regarding Puerto Rico's status vis-à-vis the United States.[90] Venerating the iconic image of Pedro Albizu Campos on the streets of Chicago and proclaiming Puerto Rico's right to self-determination and secession may have less to do with colonial politics on this Caribbean territory than the state of affairs in inner-city Chicago.

Within the confines of the *barrio*, these community residents perceive these nationalist activists as local notables and grassroots intellectuals.

Elite motivation is primarily assessed in terms of selective and excludible incentives. Still, we cannot ignore the fact that these nationalists reside far from the ethnic homeland located at the juncture of the Greater and Lesser Antilles. Geography is one factor that determines the degree to which the highest echelons of the nationalist movement will be able to distribute excludable material rewards compensating activists for their participation. Even if, one day, Puerto Rico broke its existing political bonds with the U.S. federal government and established a sovereign government, there will be little opportunity for that independent government to compensate its many activists scattered throughout the United States.[91] In an environment meager in excludable materials incentives, the impulse to support the nationalist cause cannot be studied in terms of tangible benefits. Logically, it must be examined in terms of social motivations. For these nationalists, their activities represent an important way in which to exhibit their identity. And they manifested that identity in the most *bona fide* way they knew—through the rhetoric of separatism.

While Division Street serves as a prime focal point for member of this ethnic community, not all Chicago-area Puerto Ricans live in this district. As is the case with other ethnic communities in the United States, there is a propensity for those who are financially better off to relocate to middle-class suburbs. Suburbanites will tout the relative safety of living outside urban confines. Crime rates are usually lower and many middle-class suburban communities offer a greater array of educational and social services. For those individuals without a strong emotive commitment to their ethnic community, relocating to the suburbs sounds like a winning proposition. And yet, such a move comes at a price. There are cultural costs associated with living in a predominantly white and Anglophone area. In time, their children socialize not into Puerto Rican culture but into a middle-class white suburban culture. *Puertorriqueñidad* is relegated to the deepest recesses of the inner sanctum—the home. For those who strongly identified with their inner-city community, there was a clear social payoff associated with residing in the one area where they are surrounded by shops and other businesses catering to their culinary needs and streets where their language can be seen and heard. Simply living within the boundaries of the enclaves was viewed by many as a sign of nationalist defiance and a commitment to cultural authenticity. It is important to note that this benefit was available only to those who partook in the activity—here residing within this nationalist district— and its meaning was deemed positive only by those who adhered to the nationalist creed.[92]

According to Rafael Otero, Division Street district residency was an important way in which Puerto Ricans maintained their ties to their culture and people. Although he opposed Puerto Rican independence, Rafael, a local businessman, insisted on staying put in this locale. He affirmed, "If I live in this community and I am part of it, why do I have to go to the suburbs? No! I want to be part of these Puerto Ricans."[93] Not only was Rafael proud to live in this neighborhood but he also felt indignation toward those who fled to the suburbs. Referring to his fellow Puerto Ricans who left the Division Street area Otero said, "If they disperse out there, out of the environment, then they can't be a part of this. There's a lack of loyalty to the Puerto Rican cause....The Puerto Rican who was able to grow, he should contribute something to this community. He owes it to this community."[94] If one lived in the Chicago area, according to this resident and entrepreneur, one had to reside in this zone. Those who did were praised. Rafael made his selective score quite clear for those suburbanites who shirked their nationalist duty to build a true Puerto Rican community.

Rafael Otero was not the only community resident to draw links between residential setting and cultural authenticity. Mike Morales also expressed a deep sense of satisfaction for taking a stance and opting to dwell in the *barrio* despite the costs. Mike was not stuck; he is a lawyer for an investment firm. He boasted, "I still live in Logan Square....I will never move to the suburbs, though. I won't do that to my kids. Because I know what happens to the kids of parents who do that. They grow up around white kids, never knowing about being Puerto Rican, feeling insecure."[95] Unlike some of his neighbors who were yoked to this location because of poverty, Mike had the opportunity and the means to move out. To do so, however, would exact too high a cost.

What may be viewed as a mere real estate decision, selecting a home and a neighborhood became a sign of political action for nationalists in this one community. Living here means, possibly, forgoing some of the material benefits frequently found in the suburbs. Urban living is frequently associated with severe social problems and criminal activity. Such a relationship may be factual, but we should not close the door to the possibility that it is a suburban myth. Still, regardless of their ethnic ancestry or national identification, educated professionals are constantly encouraged to leave working-class inner-city neighborhoods. Only those who embrace a robust pride in their Puerto Rican identity insist on staying even when their incomes allow them a larger range of residential options. They attempt to prove their *puertorriqueñidad* through their actions, and, in this case, the exploit is an insolent determination to remain in an urban ethnic enclave associated with a people and with the most ardent manifestation of their nationalist politics. The positive sociopsychological benefits associated with this action are felt only by those who are active.

HOMECOMING IN ZION

The decision to stay or leave Division Street's Puerto Rican enclave entailed a host of economic, social, and cultural sacrifices for its residents. Nonetheless, they made it clear that this was a place—perhaps *the* only locale for hundreds of kilometers—where Puerto Rican nationalists could openly and satisfactorily perform their identity. We can find some interesting parallels in another group of current, and perhaps former, U.S. citizens. From the hustle and bustle of the urban sprawl at the southern edge of Lake Michigan, we now set our gaze on the tranquility of the southern Negev Desert. William Miles's analysis of contemporary Zionism focused on two Israeli collective farms near the port of Eilat—Yahel and Lotan. These particular agricultural communities are quite unique. First of all, most kibbutzim are secular.[96] Additionally, few American Jews immigrate to Israel.[97] Among the few American Jews who do immigrate to Israel, most are religious. When they do immigrate, most of these American immigrants settle in major urban centers.[98] In a twist of multiple ironies, Yahel and Lotan were founded as religious, but nonorthodox, kibbutzim. They were settled primarily by American Jews who tended to come from affluent homes. These remote and arid settings were selected as the environments where a hardy bunch of North American expatriates could carry out their wish to live out Jewish lives in the Jewish state.

Historically, the thought of Reform Jewish immigration to Israel, let alone establishing a Reform kibbutz, would seem, to many, an astonishing development. After all, in the late nineteenth century, this movement discarded the possibility of establishing a Jewish homeland in Ottoman-ruled Palestine.[99] In so doing, they dismissed the notion of mass Jewish immigration to the Holy Land and ignored the warnings of Herzl and Pinsker that their people urgently needed to establish a refuge, a country of their own. Bemoaning the state of Jewish life in the Diaspora, Theodor Herzl proclaimed, "We have honestly endeavored everywhere to merge ourselves in the social life of surrounding communities and to preserve the faith of our fathers. We are not permitted to do so."[100] Assimilation and full acceptance into other societies was not possible for Jews, he insisted, unless they were willing to sacrifice their faith. Indeed, even after Jews converted, the clerical leadership of their new faiths maintained a leery vigil over their new flock. Leon Pinsker hypothesized that anti-Semitism, like his people's wandering, would simply never end.[101] As an alternative, the Reform movement's 1885 *Pittsburgh Platform* jettisoned a Jewish *national* identity in favor of a strictly Jewish *religious* identity. This document proclaimed, "We consider ourselves no longer a nation, but a religious community, and therefore expect neither a return to Palestine, nor a sacrificial worship under the sons of Aaron, nor the restoration of any of the laws concerning the Jewish state."[102] Such skepticism toward Zionism among Reformists dissipated with the advent of World War II and news about the Nazi regime's "*Final Solution.*"[103] Although few American Reform Jews left North America, henceforth the majority accepted immigration Israel's place as a Jewish refuge. This being the case, why did this handful of mostly North American Jews give up their materially comfortable lives in order to move to Israel? Additionally, if they felt the need to relocate to Israel, why not simply move to Tel Aviv, Jerusalem, or other urban centers?

Moving to a kibbutz represented a considerable commitment to an ideal. One does not simply "join" a kibbutz; one is "absorbed" into this collective community.[104] Only a handful of Israelis live on kibbutzim. Still, kibbutz living has been romanticized for decades by Israelis and non-Israelis alike.[105] If the decision to settle in the land of Israel was expounded as a sign of masculinity, the subsequent choice to move to a kibbutz only accentuated that manly image. Physically demanding agricultural work coupled with reclaiming the land of their forefathers defied nineteenth- and twentieth-century negative stereotypes of the frail Eastern European Jew. Early Zionist planners challenged these representations and romanticized the settler in Eretz Israel as the virile antithesis to the anti-Semitic portrayals of Jews as feeble people.[106] This masculine image was propagated in the late-nineteenth and early twentieth-century Zionist promotional art. It accentuated, in particular, the Jewish settler outside the city environs, at home in nature and engaged in agricultural pursuits.[107] Interestingly, Palestinians adopted this thesis of Zionist masculinity as the narrative around which they would subsequently built a nationalist counternarrative.[108]

Constructing a new Jewish society through agricultural labor and self-sufficiency was central to Aaron Gordon's vision of a future Zionist home.[109] Born in Russia in the middle of the nineteenth century, Gordon died on a kibbutz in the Galilee less than two years into the British Mandate. He lamented the state of the Jewish ancestral land—a realm that had been "abandoned, and wasted, and delivered into the hands of strangers."[110] Returning to the place promised to Abraham's and Isaac's descendants was not only part and parcel of national deliverance but also intimately linked with an internal or personal emancipation. Gordon exhorted, "We must return to nature, to creative work, to a sense of order, and to a spiritual life, in short, to family-nationhood."[111] Romanticizing the land and the glories of conquering a frontier was a lure to entice newcomers with idealistic images of conquering a virgin land. What is more, this kind of "naturalistic nationalism" was also a means tying a people to a land and thus symbolically indigenizing them to their new setting.[112]

American immigrants to Israel were an anomaly. Nonetheless, a few immigrated and opted to bypass the country's major urban centers in a bid to create new lives in their *promised land*. In so doing, they also circumvented more comfortable American-styled lifestyles. In this remote location they could fulfill their dreams and Gordon's vision. For some of these American émigrés, part of their mission was to reconstruct a *shtetl*—an East European Jewish community that some of their grandparents and great-grandparents would have known as home. Over the centuries, this bygone world was bounded by oppression. In the *shtetl*, that repression came in the form of anti-Semitism from their Christian sovereigns and neighbors. In Yahel and Lotan, the sweltering severity of the desert heat provided the primary source of suffering.[113]

No one motive adequately explains the decision by these middle class and outwardly secular American Jews to make such a journey. Still, many were attracted as a result of their dissatisfaction with their North American lives coupled with "youthful idealism."[114] Regarding the kibbutz's origins, Michael, one of Yahel's founders, commented, "Perhaps it was the brashness of youth and the lingering madness which had led us from the comforts of 'normal' existence to this stark and lifeless desert. But we laughed at the challenge and called our laughter idealism."[115] Another kibbutz member admitted that the decision to relocate from the United States to an Israeli collective farm constituted a significant material sacrifice. Nonetheless, she claimed that kibbutz members received, in return, something far more significant—satisfaction.[116]

Presented in theatrical guise, a kibbutz resident quoted his rabbi, who said, "Israel is the Broadway of Jewish life. Not everyone can play on Broadway—but if you can, that's the place to be."[117] Presenting Israel as the Jewish "Broadway" connotes the highest level of achievement. If one is Jewish and strongly identifies as such, living in the Holy Land represents the ultimate fulfillment of Jewishness. Some of the immigrants

Miles interviewed felt a stronger national identity with Israel than the land of their birth, the United States. One kibbutznik compared daily living and contentment in Israel with life in the United States: "Here, I have a twenty-four hour Jewish community."[118] Through their deeds, returning to the land of their ancestors, these new Israeli immigrants played a critical role, in their minds, in helping to build and improve the Zionist dream. Miles noted, "Yet virtually all [of the new immigrants] accept the material trade-offs that they have made to build, in however small a measure, and in however compromised a form, a progressive Jewish community and, by extension, a better Jewish State."[119] These tradeoffs included a marked decline in their material standard of living and the realization that they were relocating to a volatile part of the world. Making material sacrifices does not make sense except in those circumstances where the undertaking generates an alternative reward structure. Such a structure applies only to those who already strongly identify with their group. Despite their comfortable upbringing in the United States, these immigrants' Jewishness surpassed their Americanness. Among friends and family members, they are honored as community defenders, as heroes. These accolades did not apply to everyone; they were selectively handed out to those who uprooted their lives and decided to make *Aliyah*.

CONCLUSION

When we discuss reward structures and collective action, we must immediately differentiate in- from out-group members. In the eyes of their community members, the actions undertaken by these moderate nationalists qualify as heroic deeds. Their exploits would be praised by acquaintances and relatives alike. But it is important to underscore that these were not soldiers engaged in mortal combat. Then again, they chose to perform their identities in a way that many would not for fear of the repercussions. Nationalist ideologies bind elite and mass. The actions of these activists will be held up by nationalist leaders as models of exemplary citizenship that others should follow. Whether the deed was a matter of uttering the right words, parading ones' identity through marches, posting a sign, wearing a button, or choosing where to live, the activities in question were not undertaken without risk or cost. Performing their national identities entailed tangible variable risks and costs, and each individual must assess how far they are willing to go at any particular moment. Still, these nationalists anticipated the appropriate action, given their specific situation, and opted to act firmly yet modestly. These and other examples are representative of the kinds of nonheadline-grabbing reticent deeds that constitute the overwhelming majority of nationalist collective action. These are the kinds of activities that generate personal satisfaction and regularly win the praise of community members. The following chapter will assess more intense forms of nationalist performance. Here individual nationalists up the ante, imperiling their lives in the name of the great cause. While they are not representative of the median nationalist activity, their exploits do become the stuff of legends.

CHAPTER 5

DUTY, HONOR, AND THE SUPREME SACRIFICE

GENERAL DOUGLAS MACARTHUR DELIVERED A SPEECH AT the United States Military Academy at West Point entitled "Duty, Honor, Country" on May 12, 1962. In the hands of a skillful orator, the words shared with this finite group of students could have just as easily been imparted on true believers anywhere. It is reasonable to assume that these young cadets were faithful adherents to the national creed. After all, in a stable democratic polity, joining the ranks of the armed forces is rarely associated with economic advancement. The words MacArthur uttered are most fitting in their original setting—in the presence of a group of warriors in the making. In that speech, the former Supreme Commander of the Allied Powers addressed the significance of personal sacrifice in the course of national struggle. He said, "However horrible the incidents of war may be, the soldier who is called upon to offer and to give his life for his country is the noblest development of mankind."[1] Combatants are judged based on their actions and the risks they undertake; they are not appraised on their appearance in a uniform. Only those who participate in the national cause are praised. Glory's most magnificent summit is breached only by those who make or risk the ultimate sacrifice. They join the hallowed crypt of the nation's greatest heroic figures and martyrs.

Through taxation, regimes extract from their citizenry the pecuniary resources to operate the apparatus of state. In times of war, that extraction accelerates and moves beyond withdrawing financial assets to siphoning human assets. For many young people, the price they are expected to pay for their national membership comes in the form of military conscription. Those who are conscripted often comply with their leaders' orders out of fear of imprisonment. In contrast, the classic volunteer is eager to heed their nation's call to arms and flaunt their national pride. Some draftees will become casualties, just like their neighbors who volunteered into service. While the end result will be the same regardless of how they entered the armed forces, their motivations are not. This chapter focuses less on those who were drafted but more on those who willingly or even eagerly volunteered. In the course of mobilizing a nationalist campaign, ethnic elites may not possess the state-like resources to efficiently recruit soldiers or the financial means to pay them a salary. Solidarity-driven individuals—those with a j at or approaching one—freely and contentedly sign up because they passionately believe in the righteousness of their cause, the inherent goodness of their people, and the steadfastness of their convictions.

Reporting for Duty

Returning momentarily to an example from the previous chapter, there are concrete costs associated with forgoing a comfortable life in the Chicago suburbs. Socially mobile middle-class Puerto Ricans had to decide whether to stay in the heart of the inner-city ethnic niche, if they grew up there, or move to this community if they were new to the Chicago metropolitan area. In that case, action was evaluated simply by physical residence. While residents paid a price for living in the inner city as opposed to the suburbs, the potentially negative consequences associated with these nationalists' decisions does not come close to those associated with partaking in an armed struggle. Some may have sympathized with the FALN revolutionaries but few enrolled in their militia. During South Africa's apartheid era, the burdens shouldered by activists were much higher. Performing identities through residency was not an option in a segregationist regime where racial and ethnic classifications determined where one was allowed to live. For some, demonstrating nationalism was a matter of partaking in demonstrations or strikes where violence could, and often times did, erupt. Others took matters one step further and enlisted in the armed struggle against the white minority regime. This was Letlapa Mphahlele's path. As opposed to playing a part in the more moderate African National Congress (ANC), he volunteered his services for the more militant Pan Africanist Congress (PAC).[2]

From his childhood in the 1960s, Letlapa recalled hearing a song that had a momentous impact on his political resolve: *Afrika lefase la bo ntat'arona le tserwe ke makgowa* (Africa, our fathers' land, has been taken away by whites).[3] Land was not the only thing unjustly appropriated by the white minority regime. In sync with the ruling elites' dominant ideology, the public school system needs to impart one dominant and subjective nationalist narrative. State-sanctioned South African mythmakers in the pre-Mandela era constantly reinforced their thesis of racial separation and white superiority. As a black child growing up in South Africa, a young Letlapa discovered that even history was commandeered. In his autobiography, Letlapa commended on the absurdity of learning about important figures in European history while officially sanctioned textbooks omitted any mention of his ancestral origins or of notable Africans.[4]

Regimes in charge of educational bureaucracies make sure that the historic figures they present are either benign to the dominant order or extol the virtues of the ruling community whether it is numerically, economically, or militarily dominant. George Fredrickson remarked, "White American children can casually divide up to play 'cowboys and Indians,' but it is hard to imagine Afrikaner youngsters playing 'Voortrekkers and Zulus.' Traditional enemies who remain dangerous are not romanticized and made into heroes with whom children can identify."[5] In the South Africa of that era, virtually any black figure fell into that hazardous category. Denied a place in school texts, marginalized communities will anoint their own heroes and redeemers. Role models must prove their worthiness through their deeds, not just words. As a teenager, Letlapa's political consciousness soared with the Soweto Uprising and the murder of the legendary Steve Biko.[6] The 1976 Soweto Uprising began when a group of black students protested the government's policy forcing them to learn Afrikaans rather than English.[7] Letlapa channeled that exuberance into organizing a student union. After his high school's principal proscribed this student organization, he decided to leave the country and head to Botswana.[8] While living in exile, Letlapa became an active member of Apla—the PAC's military wing.[9]

Letlapa moved to Lagos, Nigeria, where he read some of the fundamental writings of the South African liberation movement, including the ANC's Freedom Charter and the speeches of Mangaliso Sobukwe, the Pan Africanist Congress' founder. He was attracted to Sobukwe's assertion that "the oppressed had to be liberated mentally first."[10] Indeed, a fighter without an emotive connection to the cause will wage war; but such cooperation with the collective is contingent upon on the constancy and adequacy of material compensation or the anxiety over being punished for dissenting. First and foremost, a participant in any large-scale collective endeavor must feel solidarity with the group. Such sentiments are vital for the generation of selective social benefits. Still, Letlapa's fervent commitment to South Africa's liberation did not vaccinate him from holding prejudicial attitudes of his own. While playing soccer with his comrades in Botswana, Letlapa admitted that he and his friends looked down on the local Basarwa community. In comparison with his friends and family, Letlapa saw the Basarwa as a primitive and backward people. But by looking down on the Basarwa, he realized that he was putting into practice some of the same prejudicial attitudes prevalent in the regime he was fighting to overthrow. He confessed, "We did not see the irony in our attitude: we, the victims of racism, had false notions of racial superiority over fellow Africans."[11] The struggle against the white minority regime and the racialized South African socioeconomic configuration did not ensure the internalization of a sense of equality crossing racial or ethnic boundaries. Apartheid's brutality provided, nonetheless, the prime conditions for black youth to fervently identify as native Africans, which later facilitated their collective activities in opposition to the racially segregated social, political, and economic order.

In his memoir, Letlapa informed his readers, in no uncertain terms, that he took great pride in his role in the South African struggle.[12] He also made clear that he viewed positive thinking and a commitment to direct action as critical qualities for any revolutionary. That longing occasionally diverged with the PAC's orders. Walter Toboti, the PAC leader in Zimbabwe, informed Letlapa that he was going to be promoted and appointed PAC's new representative in Uganda. Many individuals in his position would have looked favorably upon such an advancement, but not Letlapa: "Toboti was happy and he congratulated me. He saw this as a step forward for me, but I viewed it as a step backward: my dreams of going to fight in Azania [South Africa] were shattered."[13] Such a decision would have pulled Letlapa away from the front lines, from the locus of action. As an enthusiastic soldier, one who derived a tremendous sense of pride over his involvement in the struggle, direct action was the primary way in which he could generate a positive social reward. Group representatives do hold prestige within both their home communities and those where they are sent. Still, regardless of official rank and designation, diplomatic officers rarely see fighting on the front lines. Letlapa's honor, his sense of self-accomplishment, could be fulfilled only through personal involvement on the battlefield—by directly contesting his adversary.

Letlapa's viewpoint on the importance of direct action was also shaped by his experiences in a Botswana jail. He was arrested by the Botswana authorities for smuggling weapons into South Africa. As a landlocked state sharing a long border with South Africa and South African-ruled Namibia, one can understand why the regime in Gaborone was reluctant to antagonize its militarily powerful neighbor. During his incarceration

Letlapa heard news about an engagement between antiapartheid combatants and the white South African army. While in the Gaborne Central Prison, he reported, "Our spirits soared when we heard of clashes between Azanian guerrillas and the South African forces."[14] His delight was twofold. One can feel delight in the exploits of *one's own* people by mere identification. While this is the classic victory of *us versus them*, it is also a nonexcludable good. The only way he could have reached the zenith of emotional joy would have been to partake in the same campaign. His sense of elation was somewhere between these two benchmarks. Letlapa, as a soldier, was an active part of the struggle but he was not involved in this specific battle.

One episode in particular revealed that while Letlapa's sense of group solidarity was strong, it was not at one ($j = 1$). While in prison, he led a hunger strike over the distribution of food. European and Indian prisoners were supplied certain kinds of food. The penitentiary's authorities gave Africans a poorer menu, assuming that Africans could stomach certain foodstuffs better than Asians or Europeans.[15] This unequal treatment provided a major source of irritation. Yet another frustration was the prison authority's refusal to consent to his request to see a private doctor when he fell ill.[16] Fed up with this situation, Letlapa resorted to a hunger strike—one of the ultimate forms of material deprivation. Although he was encouraged to break the strike, he stood firm for a considerable period. Letlapa lamented, "Nothing would torment me as much as the memory of such weakness: immediate gratification at the expense of well understood principles."[17] Eventually he and his brothers in arms shelved their hunger strike after the prison began force-feeding them.[18] Employing the language of our model, Letlapa's j was quite high; otherwise, he would not have joined the armed struggle. Yet it was not equal to one. Under that scenario, combatants yearn for nothing but pride, honor, and glory, even if they have to pay for these social payoffs with their lives.

Revolutionaries, Letlapa insisted, had a responsibility to rigorously adhere to a high code of conduct. In the early 1990s, De Klerk's administration began lifting restrictions on previously banned movements.[19] This period marked the beginning of the end for the apartheid era. As the end of this segregationist regime approached, many rank-and-file PAC members ceased materially supporting their starving cadres. Under these circumstances, some former revolutionaries turned to crime, including the sale and distribution of narcotics. Letlapa vehemently condemned their transgressions. Part of his reasoning was straightforward practicality. An arrested militant is vulnerable to bribery by government authorities who can compel the fighter to spy on his fellow combatants in return for exoneration.[20] Another facet of his reasoning was ethical: "a revolutionary should be the embodiment of healthy social behaviour that anticipates life after the triumph of the revolution."[21] Furthermore, Letlapa added that "revolution is sacrosanct and should be executed by sober men and women."[22] His life as a soldier in the liberation struggle ended with the advent of democratic rule. Still, he and his fellow combatants continued to feel an intense pride that can come only from their direct involvement in the antiapartheid struggle.

BATTLEGROUND SARAJEVO

Sarajevo, a city that was extolled as the site of the 1984 Winter Olympic Games, was brutally disfigured from a shining example of tolerance and interethnic harmony into a frontline in a vicious conflict shattering the lives of millions throughout the Balkans in the 1990s. Rather than focus on the countless refugees and casualties in this strife, we shall focus on one individual and examine how his less-than-absolute commitment to his national identity motivated him to engage in militant collective action. Elvir Kulin's memoirs recounted his three-year engagement in the nascent Bosnian army. His professional goal was to attend college and become an English teacher.[23] Like many of his peers, his personal goals and ambitions were put on hold until a cease-fire between the warring parties could be arranged. His family, typical of most Bosnian Muslims, was fairly secular and his circle of friends crossed confessional boundaries.[24] Before the partition of Josip Broz Tito's Yugoslavia, Elvir lived in an ethnically mixed building where the majority was Muslim. Still, not all residents of Bosnia embraced a philosophy of interfaith brotherhood or tolerance. While urbanites, especially in Sarajevo, may have disregarded religious identities in their daily interactions, the same was not true for those who lived in the countryside.[25] Rural communities constituted the backbone of the nationalist parties that plunged Bosnia into years of warfare. In a March 2, 1992, referendum, the vast majority of the republic's Muslims and Croats voted to secede from the Yugoslav Federation. Bosnia's considerable Serb minority boycotted that vote. Shortly after that special election, the bullets started flying. By the time the belligerency was over, Sarajevo and the newly independent country of Bosnia would be violently segregated along predominantly religious lines.

This aspiring teacher remembered some of the pivotal events leading up to Yugoslavia's obliteration. No one should expect a participant in a conflict to maintain or even aspire to objectivity. For Elvir, the blame for all the bloodshed rested on the shoulders of Slobodan Milošević, Serbia's leader. In the summer of 1989, Milošević delivered a now legendary speech at the site of the Battle of Kosovo Polje. Milošević's oration commemorated a six-hundred-year-old encounter and bewailed its outcome for Serbs. In this confrontation, Prince Lazar, Serbia's monarch, was killed, and the Ottoman Empire continued to expand its military and administrative influence deeper into the Balkan Peninsula. The death of Lazar also spelled the demise of an independent Serbian state until the nineteenth century. Since the late fourteenth century, Milošević claimed, Serbs had consistently suffered at the hands of neighboring groups. He called on his fellow Serbs to unite and defend themselves.[26] Milošević said, "If we lost the battle, then this was not only the result of social superiority and the armed advantage of the Ottoman Empire but also of the tragic disunity in the leadership of the Serbian state at that time.... The lack of unity and betrayal in Kosovo will continue to follow the Serbian people like an evil fate throughout the whole of its history."[27] Such a nationalistic oration impassioned many Serbs, Elvir claimed, including those who lived outside of Serbia.[28] Six centuries later, there were no Turkish troops on Yugoslav soil. Ottomans were no longer the *other*. Instead, many interpreted Milošević's words as an attack on Yugoslavia's non-Serb peoples: Catholic Slovenes, Catholic Croats, Muslim Bosnians, and Muslim Kosovars.

While Elvir condemned Milošević, he had considerably kinder words for Alija Izetbegović, the man who replaced Radovan Karadžić as Bosnia's president in 1990. Izetbegović penned a document in 1970, the *Islamic Declaration*, for which he was incarcerated in the 1980s as a "counterrevolutionary." The Serbian press claimed that this publication demonstrated Izetbegović's determination to transform Bosnia into an Islamic fundamentalist regime.[29] While many in North America and Western Europe might have associated politicized Islam with Iran in the 1980s, many Serbs instead conjured historic images of Ottoman rule. In an atmosphere of political instability following Tito's death and profound distrust, it was easy to for ethnic leaders to incite suspicions about outsiders by attempting to draw parallels between contemporary quarrels and battles fought centuries earlier.

Despite their differing religious traditions, Elvir recalled that many of his friends used to identify with the Yugoslav Republic of Bosnia and describe themselves as *Bosnians*. As ethnic tensions mounted, those who adhered to the traditions of Eastern Orthodox Christianity increasingly began describing themselves as Serbs. In a subtle sign of nationalist performance, Elvir recounts how many of his Serb friends used to correspond using the Latin script. This was the norm in prewar Bosnia. Exhibiting their newly energized identities as Serbs, they switched to writing in Cyrillic letters. These quasi-proselytizing acquaintances encouraged him to do likewise since they insisted that Cyrillic was a "superior alphabet" vis-à-vis Latin.[30] Although the costs associated with this substitution certainly are not earth-shattering, Elvir's description of this mild form of chauvinism illustrates that people frequently engage in nationalist displays even when they entail definite costs. In this case we are referring to the price of changing one's writing.[31] While altering one's writing can entail a great deal of effort, it pales in comparison, say, to the price paid by the new kibbutz settlers in Yael and Lotan. They had to transform a *lingua sacra* into a vernacular—a change in both alphabets and spoken language.

With the outbreak of violence, we see Elvir's ideological panorama painting two distinct realities of *us versus them*. He said, "I tried to understand the actions of the Serbs. It seemed like weapons, and the authority to use them, turned ordinary people with jobs and families into murdering monsters."[32] Part of the demonization of any people involves affixing stereotypical or historical labels. In the Yugoslav wars of the 1990s, Bosnian Muslims were often referred to, by their Serb and Croat adversaries, as "Turks" despite the fact that they are Slavs without any documented ancestral ties to Anatolia. Calculatedly, their adversaries tried to link Bosnia's Muslims to the Ottoman past despite their Slavic origins. On the other side, Muslims and Croats referred to Serbian soldiers as "Chetniks"—a reference to the World War II-era Serbian nationalists who fought against Tito's Partisans, the Ottomans, and the Austro-Hungarians. Elvir said of the Serbs: "Many Chetniks in our war dressed like Chetniks did in the past, with uniforms, white armbands, and beards."[33] Once more, we revisit an interesting temporal dimension to nationalism. While nationalism is quite contemporary, nationalist rhetoric articulates a saga whereby the past is presented as if it should feel l*ike yester*day rather than eons ago. Milošević's famous 1989 speech tried to symbolically bridge a six-century gap. In a similar manner, Serbs and Croats who used the label "Turks" on Bosnian Muslim were attempting to link these local non-Christians to the era of the Sultans. On the other side of the fence, the reference to Chetniks was mean to emblematically turn back the clock half a century. Although Eugeen Roosens's case studies did not focus on the Balkans, his assessment of the resourcefulness and exceedingly imaginative powers of nationalist mythmakers is as illuminating in this case as they are to any other case. He said, "In the ethnic arsenal you can partially forget what you know if others do not notice or do not mind. You can add things if exact knowledge is not available. You can choose a suitable variant if different theories exist. You can combine and transplant....Almost everything is possible, as long as no falsehoods are told that are too obviously refuted by common knowledge and as long as the adversary is not too strong."[34]

By February 1993, Elvir and his twin brother Amir, both eighteen, were conscripted into the Bosnian army.[35] Although their mother was upset with the news of his enlistment, Elvir claimed that he "felt happy."[36] He served in this militia without an official rank and without pay.[37] As is the case with any fighter, there is always the risk of injury, if not death. If Bosnia had been completely defeated, there would have been no government to care for its injured soldiers. Through his service to his new nation, Elvir exposed himself to great physical peril without the guarantee of material compensation for those potential losses. Army service in a political entity that had just declared its independence would have to depend on a high level of emotional commitment to foment collective action. Elvir said, "I answered a question I had asked myself before I came to the front line: Would I be able to shoot another person? The answer was yes....They would have shot at Amir and me if we hadn't shot at them. It was two less Chetniks to terrorize Muslims, at least for the time they were in the hospital."[38] In this excerpt, Elvir reveals a concern with his *duality*—Elvir was both an individual and a member of the Bosnian Muslim nation. Here he displayed concern both for his personal wellbeing and fidelity to his people and their cause. Of course, as an active participant in the war, he could also take pride in his service to his nation. This was an emotional benefit that nonparticipants could not savor.

Interestingly, like Letlapa, Elvir's dedication to his people was not absolute. An individual with an absolutist fixation on their commitment to the collective assigns the ultimate significance to communitarian identification and group action. Elvir's commitment was strong but it was not unqualified. One day, he was assigned to watch over a group of Serb captives who were compelled to dig trenches for the Muslim armed forces. His orders were to shoot if they attempted to escape over to the Serbian lines. Among the Serbs he recognized was a former elementary school shop teacher, Krsto. Elvir's response was rather interesting for a soldier: "As Krsto looked at me now, I felt embarrassed and ashamed."[39] While Elvir was a nationalist and committed to the cause of Bosnia's separation from the Yugoslav Federation as an undivided country, he was not a blind follower. His identification as a Bosnian Muslim, as a combatant fighting for their cause, conflicted with the emotional ties he built up years earlier with his classmates and his teachers. To avoid such potential hesitancy, many groups expend a considerable effort to demonize their foes and portray them as somehow less than human.

One of the most interesting stories Elvir narrated—an account that gives us wonderful insights into the ways in which individuals with strong bonds of solidarity generate positive social payoffs—did not describe himself, but an eighty-year old man. The man's family name was Botula, and he lived in the village of Stojčevac. This senior citizen decided to remain in his house after his family members fled the vicinity when it became a volatile position on the front lines. The local Muslim commander instructed civilians in this combat zone to hang curtains in their windows to prevent Serb forces from seeing any lights inside the dwelling.[40] In a bold display of defiance, Mr. Botula refused the order and, contrary to the army's instructions, put candles by his curtainless windows.[41] Through them, Serb soldiers could see and hear him pray five times a day. Botula's insubordinate statement reveals a sense of nationalism mixed with a generous serving of geriatric resignation. He said, "If I'm to be killed or wounded by a shell, it is God's will…. My life will soon be over. I can afford to tempt fate. At least I'll die being faithful to my religion and my country….This is my act of defiance against what they are doing to the Muslims in Bosnia."[42] Although he was but one individual, this senior citizen's strong sense of solidarity with his national identity, with his religious identification, altered his assessment of rewards and sanctions. His act of defiance—many would say foolhardiness—was from his perspective vital for the nation. As an individual, his sense of dignity could only be maintained by his particular actions, which meant defending his home against his foes. It may be somewhat speculative but perhaps he just also derived a bit of pleasure from taunting his enemies. In any case, the social reward for engaging in this act of nationalist resistance was selective and aimed specifically at the participant. The material benefits befell the Bosnian collective.

ONE ISLAND, ONE NATION

With the signing of the 1921 Anglo-Irish Treaty, the southern twenty-six counties of Ireland broke away from the United Kingdom, leaving six northeastern counties as a new political entity with a Protestant majority—Northern Ireland. Having established an Irish Free State for the island's Catholic majority, most members of the revolutionary Irish

Republican Army (IRA) laid down their arms against the British state.[43] By the mid-1960s, the Irish Republican Army was an irrelevant force militarily, devoid of any significant political organization either in Northern Ireland or the Irish Republic.[44] But deeply embedded structural conditions in Ulster encouraged the growth of sectarian violence. Following the island's post-World War I partition, Catholics in the North were relegated to the plight of an economically impoverished and discriminated minority.[45] No respite was available in a British public that was largely uninformed about the situation in Northern Ireland and essentially apathetic to the plight of Ulster Catholics.[46] The more severe the form of social, economic, and political marginalization, the less likely it is an individual group member can escape their inferior group status. Cultural divisions of labor reinforce existing *us-them* cleavages. Under these circumstances, collective action finds fertile terrain. Responding to their conditions, Catholics began marching in the summer of 1968 to protest bigotry in housing.[47] The late 1960s marked the beginning of what has been referred to as "the *Troubles*."

In times of despair, one looks for heroes capable of galvanizing the timid and the demoralized. As is common in many nationalist movements, activists in the Irish Republican Army found such champions in a romanticized past. Recounting such a motivation, Gerry McGeough was inspired by a television program commemorating the fiftieth anniversary of the 1916 Easter Rising. A child of eight at the time the program was aired, McGeough recalled feeling a surge of positive emotions watching a group of Irish nationalists defying the British Empire by taking over Dublin's General Post Office.[48] Others were inspired by fiery speeches such as the one delivered by Jimmy Steele revering two IRA combatants. In 1940, British authorities executed Peter Barnes and James McCormick for a fatal bomb attack; the UK government allowing their reburial in Ireland in 1969.[49] At this funeral, Jimmy Steele pronounced the following call to arms in the presence of thousands of sympathizers: "May we hope that from these graves of Barnes and McCormick will emanate a combination of the old and new spirit...a spirit that will ensure the final completion of the task that our martyrs were compelled to leave unfinished."[50]

While many were enthused by such nationalistic imagery, the range of involvement varied considerably from person to person. Participation in a demonstration exacted one set of costs and benefits. Partaking in military operations against the British amplified and added to one's material costs and augmented the social benefits from serving as a combatant. A few, those with an extremely high sense of group solidarity, opted to go all the way. Brendan Hughes, an adult activist in the IRA, recalled how he felt as an adolescent contributor to an armed attack. In August 1969, there were Protestant riots in Catholic areas and some of these rioters came into the vicinity with gasoline bombs.[51] Given his familiarity with a nearby school, a young Brendan Hughes aided an armed IRA fighter by guiding him through this building. Recalling those events from the late 1960s, Hughes said, "It gave me a sense of pride and a feeling that we had something to protect ourselves with. I wanted to be involved in that too because our whole community felt that we were under attack. I wanted to be part of that defense. From then on in, I got involved with the Movement."[52]

As an individual, Brendan Hughes felt pride through his participation. Gratification was echoed by his neighbors and fellow supporters who honored his status as an active soldier in *their* cause. Merely observing or sympathizing was insufficient. Only direct action could generate a positive payoff, whether the activity involved transporting guns or using them. Tommy Gorman noted that in the 1970s, guns were being smuggled into nationalist communities and some people were producing homemade explosives.[53] These munitions producers were not formally trained, and some died in this extremely hazardous endeavor. Rank-and-file nationalists were aware of the dangers but they proceeded regardless of the perils. They assigned their personal security to a secondary concern. They felt it would have been "wrong" to simply sit back while others paid the costs of their struggle.

Severe discrimination, marginalization, and recurring clashes facilitated the formation and solidification of communal bonds. Under such circumstances, participation in the communal struggle is viewed as a normal activity despite the state's classification of nationalist action as subversive and unlawful. Subjectivity in any nationalist tussle is usually one of the first things tossed out the window. Those who perceive themselves as victims or sympathize with their plight classify the group's armed militants as *freedom fighters*.[54] Opposite them are those who claim that these combatants are terrorists. Regardless of which side observers favor, the actions of these fighters are thought out well in advance. John Horgan noted that "the reality of terrorism in today's world is that political movements that use terrorism skilfully manipulate events, and their media coverage, to create for their existing or potential audiences deliberate and often sophisticated impressions and interpretations serving their own particular purposes."[55]

Tommy McKearney joined the Irish Republican Army in his late teens. Representatives of the British government viewed IRA involvement as criminal. That is not the way Tommy saw it. He and others believed that their struggle was thrust upon them. Regarding IRA membership, he said, "I didn't see it any different from any other man joining an army to take part in a defensive war would.…We believed that war had been foisted on us and we were willing to take part in it."[56] Within a community, nationalist action may be recognized as a legitimate activity, but in its most militant manifestations, it is not a pursuit undertaken by all. The Irish Republican Army saw itself as a volunteer militia.[57] Reluctant insurgents posed a threat; they were susceptible to being recruited as informants.[58] Of course, selective enlistment does not protect nonparticipants from being threatened. Punishments are usually dispensed for actions that run contrary to the community's interests. Utmost among the list of possible crimes against the national interests would be treason.

For those with the highest levels of solidarity, no material sacrifice was too high a price to pay for the cause. In Ulster's sectarian divide, that code of honor was put to the ultimate test when several incarcerated members of the Irish Republican Army protested their status within the Maze Prison. Whereas the British government considered them common criminals, these convicted IRA militants saw themselves, and wanted to be treated, as prisoners of war. In response, these men opted to voice their deepest disapproval with a hunger strike. The most famous of these campaigners was Bobby Sands, who was elected the British House of Commons while he was on his hunger strike. Only a few weeks after his election to Parliament, Sands died of starvation. For his followers, Bobby Sand's slow and excruciating death constituted a nationalist redramatization of Christ's death and passion—the summit of nationalist sacrifice for the collective.[59] Another hunger striker was Gerald Hodgkins. Whereas Bobby fasted for sixty-six days, Gerald abstained from food for twenty days. Sands persevered until the bitter end; Gerald Hodgkins lived. He talked about what he felt while ending his hunger strike: "You felt guilty: that you'd actually ended the hunger strike and you hadn't achieved what you set out to achieve. Although you were going to live, you had to live in the knowledge that there were ten men dead who had set out on the same journey. You wonder, 'Have I betrayed them? Have I betrayed their families?'"[60]

Bobby Sands's absolutist commitment to his cause is quite rare. The manner of his premeditated death was evidence of an individual whose j is equal to one or hovers very close to that mark. For such a person, the social realm is all that matters and the material arena becomes irrelevant. Most activists want to live in the hopes of tasting the fruits of their great efforts. In comparison with Bobby, Gerald's reactions correspond more with an above-average militant or fighter than a full-blown martyr. Both men were motivated by a sense of pride and determination for their group—an emotional state that could only be engendered through collective action. These two soldiers in an irregular army also sought to avoid the humiliation that would come with defeat. The key difference was the degree to which they were willing to make material sacrifices for their cause, paying for it slowly and agonizingly with their lives. While Gerald may live with a certain degree of ignominy, Bobby no longer lives—period. Before he passed away, Bobby Sands was aware that his actions would earn him a revered spot in the pantheon of Irish nationalists—those spots reserved for those who fell while engaged in battle. Such a rousing status is bestowed on certain soldiers who pay the ultimate price—those who sacrifice themselves for the national cause.

MARTYRDOM

Utmost among all categories of solidarity-driven collective action are martyrs. These are the individuals that knowingly sacrifice the ultimate material benefit for their cause—their very existence. Traditionally, martyrdom was more frequently associated with religious causes than with nationalism. However, the two categories need not be mutually exclusive. After all, many ethnic entrepreneurs objectify religious characteristics as primary group boundary markers distinguishing *us*, the faithful, from *them*, the heathens. There is no such thing as *religious* nationalism versus *linguistic* nationalism or any other particular characteristic. What differentiates distinct nationalist movements are the cultural features ethnic elites have selected as group boundary markers and manipulated in order to distinguish us from them and attempt. While ethnic elites must separate *us* from *them*, they must also try to maintain their within-group elite privileges.

Elites promise their volunteers short-term benefits in this life and immeasurable long-term rewards in the afterlife. Those seeking praise kowtow before a very public trial. Martyrs, the apogee of socially oriented combatants, prostrate themselves even more so than other volunteers. Those who willingly lay down their lives for their community present themselves to the zenith of elite and communal judgment.[61] As Robert Pape said, "Martyrdom—death for the sake of one's community—is a social construct. An individual may wish to become a martyr and may voluntarily sacrifice his or her life to achieve this aim. However, it is the community that designates the qualifications for martyrdom and judges whether the self-sacrifice of specific individuals meets the requirements for this special status….An individual can die. Only a community can make a martyr."[62]

Complex theological principles are rarely the focus of ethnic entrepreneurs. Rather, nationalist leaders focus their attention on traits that are readily discernible—for example, particular clothing, rituals, dietary habits, or sacred languages (even if the participants are not fluent in that idiom). Remember that the nationalist enterprise must link the erudite in society with the illiterate in a common saga of shared ancestry. Therefore, the story of who *we* are must be simple enough for everyone to understand. One's foes are not just different; they are also evil. The vilification of their adversaries heartens the most extreme responses: "Demonization encourages the two main features of suicide terrorism—the willingness to die and the willingness to kill innocents."[63] When it comes to martyrs, such individuals have internalized norms of honor, pride, and shame to such a degree that material rewards cannot adequately compensate them. In their quest to fulfill the mission, their continued existence takes a back seat to the needs of their collectivity. By so doing, martyrs know they will have earned the maximum positive social rewards that can be bestowed upon any individual. Save for their immediate friends and family, ordinary folk are soon forgotten. But martyrs live on in legend, song, and sometimes monuments. Indeed, Anderson described the tombs of the unknown soldiers as the most "arresting emblems of the modern culture of nationalism."[64] Military cemeteries are nearly universally classified, at least by the dominant ethnic group, as hallowed ground. Subordinate ethnic groups can engage in the same practices, although it may not be as safe to honor their fallen dead in an overly public manner. Deprived of their specific families, friends, and home addresses, martyrs embody the purest form of sacrifice and devotion to their people. Devoid of personal or family names, these martyrs are imbued with only one designation—loyal subjects.

Martyrdom is nothing new. We find a good example in Christianity's early history. Vibia Perpetua was a twenty-two-year-old wife and mother. She became a celebrated martyr from Christian lore in the second century. A well-educated resident of Roman-ruled Carthage, Vibia ignored an edict from Septimus Severus prohibiting conversion to Christianity.[65] Her family beseeched her to rescind her religion for the family's sake. She refused.[66] All she had to do in order to avoid the highest of penalties was to make a sacrifice for the safety of the emperors. With that simple gesture, the authorities would have released her. Despite this option, she refused and, in so doing, reaffirmed her adherence to her Christian faith. Just before her death, she wrote, "Then the judge passed sentence: we were all condemned to the beasts; and in great joy we went down into the prison."[67] Vibia felt that her faith meant more than her corporeal existence and, in the process of forfeiting her life for her beliefs, brought her "joy." Before her death, she dreamed about the impending fate: "At that moment I awoke. And I perceived that I would not be fighting with beasts but with the devil; but I knew that the victory was mine."[68] Through her death, Vibia, already a member of her society's privileged and educated class, departed the world of ordinary mortals and become a renowned figure in her new religion. Her identity as a Christian meant more to her than her identity as a resident of Carthage or a subject of the Roman Empire.

Sacrificing one's life for the chosen creed is one way to appease divine forces and provide a role model for current and future adherents. It is an example based on articulating faith through action and not just belief or mere words. For zealots, self-sacrifice is an unambiguous way to satisfy a deep longing for fulfilling a vital mission undertaken in the name of their community.[69] Such a quest reinstates honor, if any was previously lost or tarnished. Furthermore, it earns the volunteer great pride. This peculiar kind of activity works in two directions. Internally, it fulfills one's sense of self-esteem; it is partly inward looking. Furthermore, the same action instills praise within one's community. Thus, it also looks externally. Counterintuitive as it might seem, combatants who intentionally sacrifice their lives are behaving as rationally as the organizations that endorse their actions and provide them with logistical support up until the final moments. Mia Bloom commented, "Suicide bombing should be disaggregated into two levels of analysis—the individual bombers who blow themselves up and the organizations that send them. To varying degrees, both parties (individuals and organizations) are acting rationally in the strictest sense of the term since they are pursuing goals consistent with picking the option they think is best suited to achieve their goals."[70]

Let us continue our assessment of nationalist martyrdom in a region that overlaps considerably with the Mediterranean. As one regional expert underscored, in order to understand the allure of the national and religious appeal in the Middle East, one must appreciate the emotional dimension: "The appeal of nationalism, just as of religious fundamentalism, in the Middle East is thus to a large extent a reflection of the crisis of dignity, that is, of individuals' sense of self-worth, honor, and esteem."[71] Anne Oliver and Paul Steinberg's six-year journey in Palestinian communities focused on Hamas and the production of sacropolitical messages. Their research provides us with some important insights into the thoughts of the martyr and the would-be martyr.

Arguably, Hamas shaped the intifada's ideological course more than Fatah or any other Palestinian nationalist organization. In Arabic, the word *hamas* means "zeal." But this deliberate play on words is also the acronym for the *Harakat al-Muqawama al-Islamiyya,* or Islamic Resistance Movement.[72] Hamas was born in the tumult emanating out of the first intifada in 1987 by religious and secular Palestinian elites affiliated with the Muslim Brotherhood.[73] This organization's goal was no less than the creation of a state encompassing all Muslims and guided only by the Quran and other key Islamic religious texts.[74] The Muslim Brotherhood was founded in Egypt in 1928 and thereafter spread to other Arab countries. The Brotherhood established connections among its Palestinian brethren as early as 1935. From Egypt, the Brotherhood's point of origin, came the writings of Seyyid Qutb, who wrote *Milestones,* among other influential works. Executed in 1966, his vision of Islamic action was exceedingly active and rejected compromise with secular Arab regimes and non-Muslim foreign powers.[75]

Qutb claimed that the global system based on Western dominance was on its last legs as an inevitable result of its depraved non-Islamic values.[76] Deriding non-Muslim cultures, he said, "The Islamic society is, by its very nature, the only civilized society, and the *jahili* [non-Islamic] societies, in all their various forms, are backward societies."[77] Among the *jahili* societies, he singled out Jewish and Christian communities, which were "unIslamic and illegal."[78] Islam, he insisted, needed to be restored to its former glory so as to fill the void created by the West's decline.[79] Restoration was an active verb. Qutb rejected out of hand the premise that Islam was a "defensive movement."[80] Struggling against the West and nonbelievers was not a temporary stage—it was a perennial state.[81] His mission required offensive collective action, and the name for that action was "*Jihaad,*" or Holy War.[82] Only this kind of holy war could liberate people from the enslavement of other human beings so that they may serve God.[83] At least at an intuitive level, Qutb understood that the believer committed to collective action had to value social and spiritual aspirations more than their material wants. He asserted, "Before a Muslim steps into the battlefield, he has already fought a great battle within himself against Satan—against his own desires and ambitions, his personal interests and inclinations, the interests of his family and of his nation."[84] In *Milestones* Qutb clearly separated a saintly *us* from a demonic *them,* called the faithful to collective action, and he revealed that those who identified with his cause would not make the sacrifices he demanded until they saw beyond their tangible needs. His statement, the one insisting that activists forget their familial and national interests, was not correct. Islam was his new *nation* and Qutb understood that the true believers would think about their families, not in terms of material needs but in regard to family honor.

Inspired by Qutb, along with others in the Muslim Brotherhood, Hamas started employing suicide bombings in 1994. It was in response to Hamas' attempt to grab the mantle of the *true* Palestinian nationalist organization that Fatah's Aqsa Brigades began carrying out suicide bombings during the second Intifada, at which point they became an essential facet of Palestinian resistance to the Israeli occupation.[85] Suicide bombings became an important dividing line distinguishing their absolutist stance against compromising with Israel in juxtaposition to the Palestinian Liberation Organization's (PLO) willingness to negotiate.[86] In a manner of speaking, Hamas exploited suicide bombing not only to inflict pain on their Israeli foes but also to make a point within Palestinian circles. They juxtaposed their direct action with Fatah's *inaction* in a bid to grab the mantle of *authentic* Palestinian liberation movement.[87] With the start of the first Intifada, Hamas and other Palestinian Islamists employed different rhetorical styles in a bid to build up a distinct nation-affirming narrative.[88] Oliver and Steinberg contended, "The Islamist ideal was neither peasant nor shepherd but rather the hajj, the religious pilgrim who relinquishes his earthly possessions in order to fulfill the commands of God."[89] Ideally, dedicated soldiers—those prepared to carry out the will of the nation or the dictates of the divine—are ready to cast aside their fear and willing to go to any lengths in fulfillment of national liberation and glory.

At least in the beginning, it was not a matter of merely soliciting young and inexperienced people to take up the call to arms in order to become suicide bombers. Future martyrs had to prove their dedication. Grandstanding would not suffice. Through action, one earned praise, an acclaim that was disseminated throughout the community. Future suicide bombers had to prove themselves in battle by killing a collaborator or an Israeli. The lone Palestinian fighter was cast as David appearing alongside Goliath, in this case, Israel. As Oliver and Steinberg noted, "one of the most important fantasies involved in Hamas' fearful tableaux is a reversal of power, the bringing down to size of the enemy. Hamas mujahidun are commonly portrayed in the movement's media as massive Herculean figures towering above dwarflike Israelis."[90] Yes, such combatants would have to flee from Israeli authorities, but they were now admired by their community members for standing up to their adversary. Ordinary citizens provided these defenders with provisions and popularized their exploits. They would even produce and disseminate cards with the militant's pictures as a kind of souvenir.[91] Among the combatant ranks were found adults, adolescents, and even children.[92] As Oliver and Steinberg noted, "You will never understand anything about the lure of martyrdom, the center-piece of intifada cosmology, until you realize that someone who has decided to take the path as his own sees himself not only as an avenging Ninja, but also as something of a movie star, maybe even a sex symbol—a romantic figure at the very least, larger than life."[93]

Suicide bombers knew their lofty status would endure long after they were gone. That status befell martyrs and their families. Suhail al-Hindi discussed one of these combatants, his younger brother Muhammad. Suhail felt that the Hamas-produced martyr videos were a major influence on Muhammad's decision to take his life in a paramilitary operation.[94] After Muhammad's death, the family's home was inundated with visitors from throughout the country, eager to offer their condolences. Thousands of martyr cards with his likeness were printed.[95] Public praise and glorification were the martyr's reward. At the times of their deaths, they were aware that these adulations befell them and their family—the hero's relatives. Condemnation and possibly an extremely excruciating demise was the communally inflicted sentence for collaborators. Some of the Hamas videotapes recorded interrogations of collaborators and their admissions of guilt.[96] Town squares became prime spots to view thieves beaten in public for their misdeeds. Accused collaborators were dealt with publicly. Oliver and Steinberg commented, "Whereas person accused of lesser crimes like thievery might simply be beaten in town squares as public spectacles, collaborators were often tortured to death, their mutilated bodies left on the street as warnings."[97] Collaborators faced the ultimate communal wrath. Without the full panoply of state powers, Hamas was able, through its agents, to appraise turncoats and distribute selective punishment for their disobedience.

Suicide bombers knew that, in all likelihood, their lives would end. As a result of faulty wiring, a small number of would-be bombers survived. These irregular soldiers were encouraged, cajoled, and pressured into partaking in a suicide run. In the final analysis, they opted to perform the task. Their existence would end, violently, gruesomely, and quite painfully. Such ultimate soldiers also knew that their standing within their respective communities was secured and done so at the highest level. Their images would enter the pantheon of the greatest of national heroes—the martyrs. Functionally, their images would play a similar role to the tombs of unknown soldiers. They represent the highest of nationalist paradigms—the perfect or near-perfect activist. Although most nationalist movements have survived, indeed flourished, without suicide bombers, there is also no question that nationalist movements could not have succeeded without a satisfactory number of group members willing to become ardent activists and amenable to forfeiting their personal material needs for the sake of the collectivity.

SPECIAL UNIT FORCE

In the opening months of 1942, there was a great deal to celebrate in Japan. The Imperial Navy successfully assailed and devastated the American military complex at Pearl Harbor. Although the United States still had numerous bases on its Atlantic coast, it would be quite a long time before the country's Pacific military naval strength would be restored to pre-December 7, 1941, levels. At about the same time, the Japanese Imperial Navy began invading the Philippines, Indonesia, and parts of continental Southeast Asia. The late 1941 attacks culminated an expansion into China begun years earlier. Annexing Manchuria and other parts of mainland Asia was a logical extension—in military and economic terms—of the country's earlier appropriation of the Korean peninsula. With a wounded U.S. Navy, Japan's forces could claim, at least for a brief period, that they constituted the Pacific's undisputed superpower.

War is a fickle endeavor and, in less than a couple dozen months, the tide turned against the aspirations of Japan's military leaders. Western forces converted Australia into a staging point for a series of battles progressively pushing back Japan's island-hopping conquests. By 1944, General Douglas MacArthur landed in the Philippines. Imperial military forces were losing their grip on its recently territorial acquisitions throughout mainland Asia and on numerous islands. American political leaders made it clear that they intended to do more than restore the colonial *status quo ante*. They were bent on seeing their soldiers stand on the main islands of Japan themselves. With the specter of defeat looming ever-closer, Japanese Navy Vice-Admiral Ōnishi Takijirō developed a special strategy designed to thwart the Allied advance. He dubbed it *Tokkōtai*, or "Special Unit Force." Most of the world is more familiar with another designation for this strategy—the *kamikaze*, or "Divine Wind."[98] Long before these soldiers committed to their missions, the imperial state had already indoctrinated—into millions of young people—the conviction that all citizens, particularly soldiers, had to be ready to make the ultimate sacrifice.[99] Naval pilots called up on a *Tokkōtai* mission were ordered to fly their aircraft directly into American naval vessels. Their one-way missions were designed to create a corpus of Japanese martyrs and, in so doing, turn back the ever approaching American military tide.

These young combatants from more than half a century ago share an important feature with today's suicide bombers. They deliberately forfeited their lives in an act projected to inflict physical and psychological harm on their adversaries. Not only were these soldiers taught to kill, they were also instructed on how to take their lives—a supposedly better fate than being taken alive.[100] To lose one's own life, particularly while taking down one's enemy, was consecrated as badge of honor. On the other hand, to be taken alive and made a prisoner of war was judged a most loathsome disgrace on one's dignity and that of one's family. Indeed, one only need mention the word *kamikaze* in order to conjure up stereotypical images of Japanese young men eager to surrender their lives for the glory of their emperor and his earthly domain. For decades, these World War II-era pilots epitomized the unqualified icon of passion-filled soldiers willing to give up their worldly existence for personal glory, national pride, and a government's imperial designs. In the West, the *kamikaze* pilots represented the clichéd image of a zealous, chauvinistic, fanatical, and deceitful people. Emiko Ohnuki-Tierney insists that this imagery is false, as are comparisons between the events of December 7, 1941, and September 11, 2001.[101]

Out of approximately four thousand *Tokkōtai* pilots, around three thousand were "boy pilots." These were very young and newly conscripted soldiers. Most of the remainder was made up of "student soldiers"—college students the state tapped for suicide missions.[102] Emiko Ohnuki-Tierney studied these self-sacrificing soldiers through their diaries, most of which were written by the student soldiers. As college students or university graduates, these were young and talented men with much to look forward to and were otherwise implausible volunteers for *Tokkōtai* missions. Not all were diehard right-wing conformists. Many will be surprised to learn that some of these combatants were ideologically leftists.[103] High-ranking military leaders may have disseminated the myth that all *Tokkōtai* soldiers were enthusiastic volunteers.[104] But intimidation from above was supplemented with peer pressure from one's fellow soldiers.[105] It is at the grassroots of society where elite mythmakers find their most effective informants and norm enforcers. All the while, the sons of important military, economic, and political leaders were assured that their *volunteering* sons would never be selected for these one-way operations.[106] Ohnuki-Tierney's assessment underscores the multifaceted nature of these students who may have rejected some facets of the state's official ideology, all the while refusing to challenge others.[107] Regardless of their subtle and complex thought processes, in the end they were faced with a dichotomous decision—to serve on a suicide mission or not.

Sasaki Hachirō was one of these student soldiers. An economics major at the Imperial University of Tokyo, Hachirō volunteered to become a *Tokkōtai* pilot in February 1945. While he may have been pressured into volunteering for this mission by his peers, his family would have nothing to do with it. In fact, his father fervidly tried to dissuade Hachirō from taking on this mission. When he did so anyway, his father stopped speaking to him. Sasaki Taizō, Hachirō's brother, speculated that their father's opposition to his brother's decision to join the army was based on their father's experiences in Northern China. Taizō believed that while conducting business there, their father may have witnessed war atrocities.[108] Their father's nation was clearly not a perfect one, or at least its leaders were not. Not quite two months later, this twenty-three-year-old son of an upper-middle class family died on a *Tokkōtai* mission.[109] Interestingly, despite his willingness to join the military, Hachirō was not an ardent militarist. To the contrary, he explicitly and paradoxically noted his opposition to war. While still in college, one week after the attack on Pearl Harbor, he wrote: "Being able to live well in this emperor's state under his benevolence, I would not refuse to be drafted if it is his order. I am not so weak as to be crushed by the war. However, I resolutely declare my anti-war stance. I will attempt to eliminate wars."[110]

In the defense of his homeland, Hachirō viewed himself as a small player in a much larger game of national survival. In this competition, his individual existence was insignificant compared to the perpetuation of his community, his nation, and the monarch he revered. Just before he joined the Imperial Navy, Hachirō commented, "We must now be the shield to protect the eternal life of our nation by going to the front to prevent the enemy's advance as much as possible.…Even if I fall, society does not rely on one individual."[111] In the end, he felt strongly that if he had to sacrifice his life, he should do so with dignity. In April 1940, he wrote, "If one must die, one wishes to die beautifully."[112] Perhaps ironically, his diary entries showed that the closer he came to the time of his impending death, the less patriotic he became.[113] To have willingly forfeited his life, his level of group solidarity was quite high, but had it been equal to one, the endpoint, he would have never compared his national commitment with his antiwar ideology. This and other cases reveal that soldiers in the national militia, whether it is an irregular army or a state-organized army, do not have to be uncompromising fanatics in order to commit horrific acts of violence.

Sasaki Hachirō, a self-described war opponent, obeyed orders and gave up his life for his cause. It is perhaps more remarkable to realize that some of the *Tokkōtai* pilots were not just pacifists but also radicals. Hayashi Tadao's plane was shot down by American forces in late July 1945. At the time, he was twenty-four years old.[114] A member of an economically comfortable family, he was a student of at the prestigious Third Higher School and, later, the Imperial University—both in Kyoto. Both he and his elder brother, Hayashi Katsuya, were Marxists.[115] Tadao's intellectual pursuits included a great enthusiasm for studying foreign languages.[116] Like many of his comrades in arms, this was a young man with a lot to live for were it not for the tragic conditions of time and place. Ortega y Gasset claimed, "Man reaches his full capacity when he acquires complete consciousness of his circumstances."[117] Despite our wishes, we cannot divorce ourselves from our environment. Ortega y Gasset said, "I am myself plus my circumstance" and Tadao could not immunize himself from his perilous situation.[118]

Still, as a college student, Tadao was filled with nationalistic feelings. Tradition was an important lesson emphasized in his household. In point of fact, Tadao's mother taught his elder brother, Hayashi Katsuya, to commit *seppuku*, ritual suicide.[119] But over time, his fervent patriotism diminished. He said, "I have no more passion. The military kills passion and transforms people, making them indifferent, turning them into cogs that turn a wheel mechanically."[120] Even so, he accepted his obligations by fighting in this war and paying with his life in the process.[121] If nationalistic passions were not prompting his actions, what was? As a social being, he felt ensnared less by the power of the state than the social pressures from his society and peers. His friends and family imposed nationalist norms upon him. Now he had to live up to them or face being shunned by his immediate social circle.

One of the most fascinating diaries belonged to Hayashi Ichizō. Both of his parents were educators. His father, who passed away when Ichizō was a toddler, was a professor in the Department of Agriculture at the University of Tokyo. His mother taught elementary school.[122] A graduate of the University of Kyoto, Ichizō was drafted as a student soldier in November 1943. He died on April 12, 1945 off the coast of Okinawa.[123] He was aware of the contradictory ways in which his family and members of his society at large would interpret his death. An instantaneous tragedy for his immediate family might, nonetheless, bring honor to the Hayashi family. Ichizō's diaries illustrate a young man facing his imminent end who waffled over the degree to which he wanted to give his life for the imperial cause.[124] Indeed, in an eleventh-hour attempt to console his mother, he wrote to her, "Mother, please don't feel lonely after I die. This is an honorable death, fighting for the glory of the imperial nation."[125]

Hayashi Ichizō's story may sound similar to those of his fellow *Tokkōtai* pilots and student draftees. He is far from an unconditional nationalist; yet in the end he was determined, or resigned, to die for the glorious national cause. He wrote, "I can't bear the thought of our nation being stampeded by the dirty enemy. I must avenge [it] with my own life."[126] He paused, contemplated the consequences, and, at times, questioned his doom. One important factor does separate him from Hayashi Tadao and Sasaki Hachirō. The emperor was the living symbol of his national affiliation but this monarch was not the object of his spiritual adoration. Ichizō was Christian. His religious convictions did not dampen his emotional attachment to the Japanese national myth. Then again, neither did they blind him to his destiny. Ichizō claimed, "I will die with dignity as a soldier. We are Christians. Nevertheless, Mother, I am sad."[127] As a Christian, he knew that suicide was morally reprehensible. As a proud Japanese soldier, he felt an obligation to defend his country regardless of the personal costs.

Although a minority in Japan, there were some Christian suicide pilots— young men who relinquished their earthly existence for an emperor they did not regard as divine. In the context of the Islamist suicide bombers previously discussed, one could point to an internalized notion—one reinforced in certain parts of Islamic societies—that the combatant was a martyr in a celestial cause. Their future reward was paradise, not just the adulation of their contemporaries. In the Japan of the 1930s and early 1940s, a parallel state-sponsored ideology venerated the young *kamikazes*. They were supposed to blindly follow the emperor's wishes. Ohnuki-Tierney noted that none of Japan's major religions stressed an afterlife: "The supreme reward that the Japanese military government offered to soldiers for loyal sacrifice was metamorphosis into cherry blossoms at the Yasukuni National Shrine, which none of them believed in."[128] Thus, for Christian or non-Christian Japanese *Tokkōtai* pilots, their primary rewards came from the comfort that they would be venerated in their nation and bringing honor to their families. With or without the promise of a hereafter, some nationalist movements succeed in mobilizing their followers to perform the most extreme manifestations of collective action.

Conclusion

Over the course of the past half century, nationalism studies have undergone numerous upheavals. The first chapter outlined some of the fluctuating theoretical trends in the field. There has also been a willingness to expand the geographic parameters of earlier studies. Many of the works on this topic published in the aftermath of World War II focused on nationalism in developing countries—the societies suffering the growing pains of modernization and decolonization. Much of the scholarship from that era assumed that nationalism was associated with disgruntled minority groups challenging the central state. Such a perception is understandable. After all, many regimes justify their policies in ethnic-neutral terms. Their rhetoric, nevertheless, should not dissuade us from examining them as any other case. This book will conclude by looking at one last example of nationalism that could easily have been overlooked. It points out that nationalism is alive and well, even in technologically advanced societies. George W. Bush's mid-September 2001 speech delivered at the vestiges of the World Trade Center highlights many of the classic elements employed in an attempt to mobilize nationalist collective action.

Surrounded by heaps of twisted debris, the chief executive expressed his gratitude to the multitude of civil servants and volunteers who were still frantically searching for any survivors. On behalf of the U.S. government and the American nation, Bush promised to avenge the devastation of these soaring structures, these national landmarks, and the lives of the thousands who perished on what started out as a sunny September day. There he uttered the following: "This nation stands with the good people of New York City, and New Jersey and Connecticut, as we mourn the loss of thousands of citizens....I can hear you. The rest of the world hears you. And the people who knocked down these buildings will hear all of us soon.... The nation sends its love and compassion to everybody who is here. Thank you for your hard work. Thank you for making the nation proud. And may God bless America."[1] Washington claimed that this pledge was fulfilled with the overthrow of Afghanistan's Taliban regime, Hamid Karzai's installation as his country's new president, and the capture of some of the militants affiliated with al Qaeda. Subsequently, the events of that fateful day were used by the same administration to convince many in the United States that the Iraqi government also shared responsibility in this assault and that, as a result, it should suffer Afghanistan's fate.

Not all New Yorkers were thrilled to see the president that day. Some city residents quickly drew parallels between an unpopular Bush and his well-liked predecessor.[2] Still, several volunteers commended Bush for his appearance. One ash-covered volunteer, Kevin Davis, asserted that the president's presence was meaningful. Acknowledging Bush's role as the country's commander in chief, Mr. Davis commented, "Even if some people don't respect the person, you have to respect the position."[3] Similar sentiments were expressed by Miguel Mercado, a welder who had been working at Ground Zero for a couple of days, slicing through one fallen steel beam after another. Mercado said, "It makes you feel good the most important person in our country is here with us. It sure helps me want to get back in there."[4] This speech, and its subsequent reception, highlights many of the dynamics involved in the propagation of nationalist identities, their dissemination, and how elites employ them in a quest to generate large-scale collective action.

While only a small percentage of the entire population witnessed the immediate repercussions of these attacks, there was a strong sentiment stretching out to the country's Pacific shores that the assault of September 11 was just as much theirs as it was to those who suffered through premeditated plane crashes in Washington and New York City. The tragedy plaguing New Yorkers and residents of surrounding areas was metaphorically transformed into a wound inflicted on the entire nation. Bush, the leader, invoked the right to speak on behalf of the entire nation. Speaking on behalf of the nation is not the sole purview of the paramount leader. Many figures of eminent and modest rank claim to express the sentiments of the national community. City mayors often inaugurate patriotic celebrations on significant anniversaries. Then again, a child may be asked to lead a group in the recitation of a pledge of allegiance or the singing of an anthem. At those moments they act as agents of the nation. Nonetheless, the words of the leader more convincingly carry the weight of the entire nation than the expressions of any ordinary group member.

Bush's statement also obeyed the first rule of nationalist discourse—drawing a sharp line between *us* and *them*. Bush's rhetorical skills often were found wanting. He was rarely, if ever, commended for an ability to delve into the intricacies of policy issues and political dilemmas. But on this occasion he kept matters quite simple. No sharper line could be draw than one separating an injured party from a villain. Traumatic events—the basic elements in any *victimology*—make such boundary drawing an easier task. Likewise, historic catastrophes from the past are also useful tools in this process, particularly where the fundamental fact patterns of the episode in question are not in doubt. The first-person plural was made up of the dead, the wounded, and their families. Opposite the injured party was the third-person plural—those who committed the misdeed.

Throughout this "war on terror," White House spokespersons had to be careful to avoid what would have been more forthcoming in previous historic episodes, namely, affixing ethnic labels to *them*. In this enduring conflict, the United States needed the cooperation of several foreign allies—among them, Arab and Muslim states. Not surprisingly, most government officials avoiding using the term *crusade* when describing the state's future response for precisely this reason. Both internally and abroad it would be hypocritical to champion the defense of liberty and equality where suspected ethnic groups are openly persecuted. Japanese Americans forcibly relocated to internment camps during World War II can attest to this experience.

Officially, the rationale for this brief mid-September visit was to show appreciation for the myriad of civil servants and civilian volunteers working at Ground Zero. Thousands worked night and day in a rescue and recovery effort without the expectation of any monetary compensation. Even for those who were on salary, in all likelihood there was not going to be much recompense for the pain and suffering associated with their labors. How could Bush compensate these people? In what way could *the nation* reimburse them for their efforts? The leader did it with praise—by telling these folks he was proud of them. This is not to say that these individuals did not have any material or financial aspirations. But all leaders recognize that we all have cravings for social rewards—the kind that only come from direct participation in collective action. It is one thing to be praised for helping out one's neighborhood. Official recognition for actions undertaken in the name of the sacrosanct nation is of a different order entirely.

The chief executive's message not only impacted the rescue crews in Lower Manhattan but also hundreds of young people who, soon afterward, enlisted in the armed forces to retaliate against Osama bin Laden. Volunteering for military service meant they would have to part from their families for an extended period of time. In the course of their duties, these soldiers knew that they risked being injured or even killed. Even a regular paycheck cannot camouflage the acute risks to life and limb taken by soldiers. A call to duty has no impact on individuals lacking in emotive connections to a collectivity. But it is exceedingly logical for the conventional *Homo sociologicus* to make such choices despite the real physical dangers.

For committed group members, there is no irrationality and there is no paradox, free rider or otherwise, when engaged in collective action. Satisfying their social payoff will come only when they have agreed to engage in the collective struggle heeding their leader's call to action. This logic does not depend on the nature of the national identity. The fundamental dynamics are the same whether the committee group members are partaking in a state-sponsored venture, such as volunteering in the government's militia, or whether these advocates are pursuing the creation of a new state. Although there is a significant difference in the degree of commitment, the enthusiastic soldier and the faithful suicide bomber share the same fundamental logic. They have both opted to evaluate social rewards above and beyond their material counterparts. Hence, it is illogical to judge the rationality of socially driven individuals on the basis of financial or other material rewards.

When politicians make patriotic appeals to national pride and duty, they know precisely what they are doing. It is unnecessary to promise each and every individual an excludable material reward in exchange for their services. One might question their moral authority and even the ethics of their requests, particularly in times of war, but leaders are clear in their goals of attempting to elicit the emotional motivations necessary to galvanize collective action. Their choice of rhetoric and tone is not accidental. Office holders and those who seek their jobs are attempting to assuage a basic need or craving in all of us. Although we may question our leaders' intellectual prowess, their exceedingly calculated actions do more than give the impression that, at an instinctive level, they understand Bentham's core premise. Individual human beings strive to maximize pleasure and minimize pain. Both delight and suffering come in tangible and emotional varieties. The realization of those social desires cannot be divorced from the degree to which an individual feels an emotive bond or dependency on the group in question—national or otherwise.

No leader will ever command sufficient material rewards to compensate all participants directly and individually. This insufficiency sat at the epicenter of the *free-rider paradox*. Social rewards and sanctions, on the other hand, are much more easily produced. That does not mean that they are any easier to earn. Rewards of this kind are handed out strictly on a performance basis. Nonparticipants cannot expect to receive any. States, and even our neighbors, willingly account for who voted and who did not. After all, those who consecrate the righteous and revile the wicked pass judgment to the degree they feel worthy to do so. Alternatively, their eagerness to arbitrate may be impacted less by their assured virtue than their ambition to convince others of their rectitude. Our fellow community members recall who joined the march and who opted to stay at home. Monuments and legends recollect who made the ultimate sacrifice and lament those who did not.

Beyond the parameters of studies in nationalism, this book has another goal. Hopefully this will serve as a wake-up call for adherents to the rational choice approach. For too long the vast majority of these scholars have been stuck in a myopic frame of mind. They have assumed that rational beings operate solely within *Homo economicus* parameters. To a certain degree, this orientation is understandable. After all, without the technology to accurately quantify someone's emotions we cannot hope to achieve the same precision found in studies of tangibles. Craving to be more *scientific* is a reasonable desire and it is one that haunts many social scientists. But by focusing only on the material side, these scholars miss the other half the equation. Thinkers such as Machiavelli, Bentham, and La Rochefoucauld figured this out centuries ago. Fortunately, a new generation of scholarship is pointing out some of the ways in which individuals generate all sorts of social rewards.

A true blue believer delights in contributing to the cause because it is only through active participation that they can generate a payoff. Such a payoff is quietly internalized through pride but social payoffs are also engendered publicly through communal adoration. The same holds true for the reverse side of the coin—the negative payoffs of guilt and shame. Participation in the collective quest will depend on the degree to which an individual feels an emotive attachment to that collective identity. Without solidarity, individual participation will depend on the availability of tangible rewards or sanctions. Those imbued with the maximum levels will not hesitate to sacrifice life and limb for the sacrosanct cause.

The social sciences could benefit by learning from other disciplines that have discovered that material-maximizing plotting and emotional thought processes are not divorced as was previously assumed. Thus, the elites who partake in the great national cause in the anticipation of future measurable rewards are no less rational than the rank-and-file activist joining and making sacrifices for the movement. Ultimately, it is not a matter of logic versus irrationality but individuals at different stations within a movement, each seeking a different end. We all have diverse objective—social as well as material—but they are fulfilled in different manners. While the nation may be comprised of thousands and millions of souls, ultimately all individual group members have to decide for themselves how far they are willing to go to satisfy their national identity. In the meanwhile, ethnic elites will continue to make emotional appeals. Feelings matter, particularly in the study of nationalism, because, ultimately, we are bound by them. Nationalism is all about the *passions that bind*.

Notes

INTRODUCTION

1. Horace *Odes*, iii 2.13–16, translated by Robert Hass (Horace 2002: 162–63).
2. Anderson 1991, 9.
3. Ibid.
4. In an ironic twist of historic fate, the name Tel Hai means "the *hill of life*."
5. Zerubavel 1995, 41.
6. Ibid. [אין דבר, כדאי למות בעד הארץ].
7. Ibid. [טוב למות בעד ארצנו].

CHAPTER 1

1. Chilcote 1994, 179.
2. Almond 1956, 392–93.
3. Almond and Verba 1963, 14–15.
4. Almond 1956, 396.
5. Ross 1997, 45.
6. Geertz 1973, 89.
7. Ross 1997, 42.
8. The *civic* systems were believed to be homogeneous, secular, and its actors internalized the importance of defending freedom, promoting mass welfare, and coveting public security. Their civic cultures harmonized with their political structures. In contrast, the continental European states exhibited other types of political culture. The newly decolonizing states, such as India, exhibited hybrid political cultures blending incompatible elements of "traditional" and Western systems. This incongruity provided fertile terrain for the development of political cultures exhibiting "charismatic nationalism." The civic culture thesis assumed that, eventually, developing societies will follow the path of the Western *homogeneous* and *secular* state. This supposes that the emulation of Western norms is the ultimate goal (Almond 1956, 398–401; Almond and Verba 1963, 8, 31).
9. Geertz 1973, 48–49.
10. Ridley 1996, 69–84.
11. Shils 1957, 131.
12. Shaw and Wong 1987; Van den Berghe 1981; Vanhanen 1999; Whitmeyer 1997.
13. Van den Berghe 1978, 404.
14. Huntington 2004, 63.
15. Huntington 1996, 20.

16. In a universe of exclusive national identities, Huntington identified two significant destabilizing forces in the United States—multiculturalism, an internal danger, and Latin American immigration, an external menace (Huntington 2004, 18). In an attempt to inoculate himself from allegations of ethnic chauvinism, Huntington clarified that he was emphasizing the importance of Anglo-American *culture* and not Anglo-American people (Ibid., xvii).

17. Laponce 1987, 3–4. In response, Pattanayak and Bayer (1987, 261) charged Laponce with "pleading the cause of linguistic apartheid."

18. Huntington 1996, 43.

19. Stalin 1935, 8.

20. Huntington 1996, 43.

21. King, Keohane, and Verba 1994, 109.

22. Ross 1997, 61.

23. Eriksen 1993, 99.

24. Geary 2002, 37.

25. Ibid., 38–39.

26. Ibid., 155.

27. Anderson 1991.

28. Until the last three centuries, European aristocrats recurrently lauded their foreign origins (Davis 1967; Geary 2002; Higonnet 1990; Walicki 2001).

29. This emphasis on an Orthodox faith over national identities, centered on common folk languages, was encouraged by ecclesiastical authorities with the blessings of the Ottoman court (Kitromilides 1994).

30. There is debate over when nationalism first emerged. For Elie Kedourie (1993, 1), it was crafted at the beginning of the nineteenth century. Greenfeld (1992) posited that nationalism went back several hundred years. For instance, she claimed that the roots of English nationalism could be found in the sixteenth century (Ibid., 6, 47). French national identity also dated back centuries (Ibid., 92). Her English proto-nationalism certainly represented an expansion of the elite from the entrenched aristocracy to the emerging merchant middle class. Still, those early cultural identities lacked a myth of common ancestry uniting elite and mass in a shared collective identity. In point of fact, even she noted that "English nationalism at this time certainly was not defined in ethnic terms" (Ibid., 65). Regarding France, a true sense of French national identity did not emerge, Bell (2001, 6) and Kohn (1962, 5) contended, until around the time of the 1789 revolution. Supporters of the revolution replaced a society of subjects divided by privilege with citizens united by a common nationality (Kates 1990, 112). This notion spread at diverse rates in different regions and was not consolidated on the French mainland until the end of the nineteenth century (Weber 1976, 114).

31. Kitromilides 1994, XII 12. The Greek state's claim to Hellenic exclusivity has strained its relations with the government in Skopje. The disintegration of the Yugoslav federation in the 1990s produced an independent state named Macedonia. Greece has challenged its neighbor's use of that name, with great passion,

on the grounds the regime in Athens is the only one entitled to employ names or symbols from the ancient Great past (Danforth 1995, 32).

32. This island is known by the Greek name, Prinkipo.

33. Trotsky 1978.

34. Most nineteenth-century proposals converged on relocating the country's black inhabitants to Central America, the Caribbean, or East Africa (Robinson 2001, 10–11, 19). In the early twentieth century, Jamaican-born Marcus Garvey envisaged resettling black Americans in West Africa. Interestingly, his scheme involved a selective, rather than wholesale, repatriation (Ibid., 25). In the 1960s, the Republic of New Africa movement aspired to set up a black homeland in five southern states running from Louisiana to South Carolina (Ibid., 61).

35. Trotsky 1978, 24.

36. Eriksen 1993, 105.

37. All biblical quotations in this book are taken from the *New American Bible* published by World Bible Publishers.

38. Genesis 35:9–15.

39. Exodus 3:8.

40. Many Christians with Zionist leanings share the same interpretation of those biblical passages. Western biblical scholarship, particularly among some Protestant denominations, supported the Zionist project by portraying a regional history centered on its Jewish past, omitting or downplaying its Canaanite and successive Arab historic legacies (Whitelam 1996). This particular interpretation targeted European and North American Christians (Lieven 2004, 188). For some Christians, the establishment of the State of Israel signaled the realization of biblical prophecy (Robertson 2003). It had less of an impact among Eastern Orthodox and Roman Catholics who already invested a great deal of symbolic capital in their holy cities of Constantinople and Rome, respectively.

41. Zionism was not the only political movement to draw on the same biblical narratives for nation-building purposes. In its symbolic and theological conflict with Catholic Europe, Protestant England reimagined itself as a new promised land (O'Brien 1988, 27–28). England passed this legacy onto the New World by way if its New England colonists (Ibid.). New England Puritans referred to their new home as New Canaan or a promised land (Kaufmann 1999, 441–42). In a sermon delivered in the midst of the American Revolutionary War, the Reverend Nicholas Street compared the rebel cause with the ancient Israelites and their exodus from Pharaoh's kingdom: "We in this land are, as it were, led out of Egypt by the hand of Moses. And now we are in the wilderness, i.e., in a state of trouble and difficulty, Egyptians pursuing us, to overtake us and reduce us" (in Cherry 1998, 69). Almost ninety years later, another cleric—Benjamin Palmer, a Presbyterian minister in New Orleans—employed the same metaphor to endorse the secession of the Confederate states from the North (Ibid., 184). In South Africa, the descendants of Dutch colonists described themselves as an anointed people (Cauthen 1997, 111–12). Under the influence of a Christian missionary, Zulu history was cast in the outline of an exodus narrative—a people wandering to their promised land (Geary 2002, 158–65). Thus, long

before Herzl and Ben Gurion, there were non-Jewish political actors strategically employing some of the same biblical narratives for their own political rationales and nationalist ambitions.

42. Katz 1996, 37–39.

43. Klier 1997; Katz 1996. A rather interesting figure, Mordecai Manuael Noah, envisioned establishing a Jewish sanctuary in Grand Island in western New York State, just north of Buffalo. Noah was born in Philadelphia less than a decade after the American Revolution. He christened his refuge in the Niagara River "Ararat" (Noah 1999, 108). Still, this scheme did not imply that Jews should abandon their dream of eventually returning to Palestine (Ibid., 112).

44. Hertzberg 1997, 103.

45. Ibid., 105.

46. Ibid., 110, 111.

47. Klier 1997, 181.

48. Hess later broke with Marx over his ethical approach to socialism rather than Marx's materialistic determinism (Hertzberg 1997, 117–18).

49. Ibid., 103. During the *Damascus affair,* sixteen members of the city's Jewish community were found guilty of murdering Père Thomas, a French Catholic missionary, and his servant, Ibrahim Amara. It was alleged that the killings were carried out to extract their blood, which allegedly would have been used to make Matzot (plural of Matah) for Passover. Although Thomas and Amara disappeared in Damascus's Jewish quarter, their bodies were never found (Wilson 2002, 63–65). Wilson contends that the trial was manipulated by France to extend its reach into the Ottoman Empire.

50. Hertzberg 1997, 139.

51. Kimmerling 2001, 4, 189.

52. A. Smith 1997, 41.

53. Miles 1998, 11.

54. Denitch 1994, 84.

55. Herzl 1988, 69.

56. Ben Gurion 1954, 112. Although Jewish communities existed outside the parameters of the "Promised Land" prior to the Temple's devastation, its demolition in the first century, followed by the Bar Kokhba uprising in the second century, marked the beginning of the great Diaspora.

57. Ortega y Gasset 2000, 48.

58. Marx 1963, 17.

59. Goetze and Patrick 2004.

60. Ibid., 146.

61. For example, Juka (1984, 21–27) attempted to invoke a glorious past for Albanians by asserting that they were the true descendants of the ancient Illyrians. Albania's Balkan heritage, Juka insisted, could be traced at least as far as the Roman era, unlike the Slavs, who migrated to the area centuries later (Ibid., 27).

62. Harvey 2000, 42–44.

63. Ortega y Gasset 1960, 166.

64. Lichbach and Zuckerman 1997, 5.

65. DeVotta (2004) contended that the Official Language Act of 1956, the statute establishing Sinhala as the country's sole official language, served as a catalyst for other discriminatory policies against the Tamil minority. In the wake of anti-Tamil riots in 1983, the country erupted into civil war.

66. As Anderson (1991, 84–85) noted, the replacement of Latin with German as the language of bureaucratic administration in the Austro-Hungarian Empire elevated the status of German speakers and laid the groundwork for a nationalist backlash by others, starting with the Hungarians. Likewise, Turkification policies in the Ottoman Empire backfired and inspired Arab nationalists, who responded with the establishment of Arab revival societies (Suleiman 2003, 88).

67. Connor 1994, 196.

68. Bulag 1998, 35.

69. Adherents to the *civic culture* thesis within the political culture approach shared this belief in the inherent superiority of the West.

70. Eisenstadt 1964, 577.

71. Apter 1965.

72. Chilcote 1994, 222.

73. Weber posited three types of political authority: the first is rational-legal authority, which he associated with modern Western societies; the second is traditional authority, which is based on a person's "status" and not an "office"; and the third is "charismatic" authority, which is inherently *ad hoc* and thus cannot be transformed into a routine organization of authority (Parsons 1942, 64–69).

74. Rustow 1990, 5.

75. Apter 1972, 4–7; Huntington 1968, 34; Levy 1969, 54.

76. Rustow 1990, 151.

77. Geddes 2003, 8.

78. Morris 1995, 73–74, 82; Rivera 1996, 54; Trías Monge 1997, 183.

79. Some scholars have questioned whether support for Welsh and Scottish nationalism is an accurate gage of quasi separatist sentiment or simply an expression of regional protest (MacIver 1982; Williams 1982). Even if many supporters view this as a protest of some kind, it is interesting, nonetheless, that they choose to channel that anger in the form of nationalism. Not all nationalist movements are separatist. The majority of nationalist movements are committed to cultural autonomy in one guise or another.

80. Geddes 2003, 10.

81. Ibid., 12.

82. Hechter 1975.

83. Ibid., 9–10.

84. McRoberts 1979, 296.

85. Vallières 1971, 35.

86. The links between the Catholic Church and the Quebec's French-speaking society were reinforced by shared class bonds. Whereas many Catholic clerics, particularly the upper clergy, hailed from middle- and upper-class backgrounds, the same did not hold true in Quebec, where priests were recruited from all sectors of society (Quinn 1979, 11).

87. Durham 1905, 11, 14, 17, 43.
88. Dufour 1990, 32; Sheppard 1971, 22, 34–35.
89. Dufour 1990, 35.
90. McRoberts 1984, 72, 73.
91. W. Coleman 1984, 131–32.
92. McRoberts 1979, 305.
93. Ironically, the political figure most associated with fomenting the conditions for the *Révolution Tranquille* was a non-nationalist—Quebec premier Jean Lesage (Clift 1982, 18; Levine 1990, 163). Lesage sought to undermine the socially conservative moderate-nationalists in the Union Nationale party by diminishing the role of churches in public education and promoting secular postsecondary education. While the church attempted to preserve an adherence to the principles of *Ancien Régime*, France's aristocratic old order, this newly emerging elite adhered to secular ideals associated with the anticlerical, revolutionary France (Rioux 1971, 45). In time, Lesage's reforms helped to generate a significant pool of well-educated French speakers who later found restricted access to professional employment commensurate with their training.
94. The most noteworthy of these new public companies was the world's largest producer of hydroelectric power, Hydro-Québec (Levine 1990, 46–47).
95. W. Coleman 1984, 143. By the 1980s, the Francophone business class employed in the private sector displaced their counterparts in the public sector as the "dominant group" in Quebec (Levine 1990, 220).
96. Levine 1990, 44.
97. Woolard 1989.
98. Connor 1994, 47, 161.
99. Herrera 2005, 12.
100. Ibid., 94.
101. Hechter 1986, 265.
102. Barker 2001, 33.
103. Hobsbawm 1990, 8.
104. Edwards 1985, 37.
105. Marx and Engels 1982, 28.
106. Downs 1957, 6.
107. Levi 1997, 20.
108. Aristotle 1988, 1.
109. Machiavelli 1980, 84.
110. Ibid., 89.
111. Bentham 1988, 29. In *The Ethics*, Baruch Spinoza made a similar argument about pleasure maximization and pain minimization (in Descartes, Spinoza, and Leibniz 1974, 281).
112. Levi 1997, 21.
113. It is important to underscore that many structuralists also start with the assumption that national identities are not natural phenomena.
114. Anderson 1991.
115. Gellner 1983, 7.

116. Sahlins 1976, 13; Searle-White 2001, 59.
117. Hardin 1995b, 37.
118. Herzfeld 1997, 67.
119. Rudé 1995, 4.
120. Hardin 2002, 6.
121. Pareto 1991, 36.
122. Tönnies 2001.
123. Eriksen 1993, 18.
124. Motyl 2001, 59.
125. Foster 1991, 242.
126. Handler 1988, 13–15.
127. Barth 1969, 38. As Steinberg (1989, 42) noted in the case of African Americans in the United States, the amalgamation of common cultural elements—such as the sharing of a common language, religion, folk customs, and norms—is no guarantee of ethnic amalgamation.
128. As Barany (2002, 289) contended, the poorly articulated nature of Gypsy/Rom identity has retarded collective organization and mobilization.
129. Chai 1996, 291.
130. Barreto 2001b; Weinstein 1983, 12.
131. In his classic work *Orientalism*, Edward Said (1979) contended that long before the advent of World War I and the imposition of direct British and French rule over vast portions of the Arabian Peninsula, popular culture in the West had already drawn a portrait of the East. In that imagery, the indigenous inhabitants of the East were judged exotic and backward, thus laying an ideological justification for the subordination of colonial peoples.
132. Maldonado-Denis 1972, 22; Quintero Rivera 1986, 2. Among European newcomers to the Americas, even those of humble origin, there was a common feeling of social and cultural superiority vis-à-vis their neighbors on the western side of the Atlantic (Brading 1991, 296). That sense of dominance applied even to the hemisphere's Creoles, or white, American-born inhabitants.
133. Given a shared language, religion, and many other cultural attributes, nineteenth-century Puerto Rican nationalists exalted the *jíbaro*, or the white highland peasant, as the prototypical islander who stood in contrast with European-born Spaniards (Guerra 1998; Janer 1998; Scarano 1996).
134. Meléndez Vélez 1998, 189; Torres González 2002, 121.
135. Rivera Ramos 2001, 200.
136. Barreto 2002, 84; Berríos Martínez 1983, 185; Díaz Quiñones 2000, 88, 95; Mari Bras 1984, 91; Rodríguez-Morazzani 1998, 38.
137. Álvarez Curbelo 1993, 27; Ribes Tovar 1975, 137.
138. Álvarez Curbelo 1993, 87–88.
139. Rodó 1988, 71, 77.
140. Historians have speculated that Albizu Campos's experiences in the Boston area—while a student at Harvard University in the 1910s—led him to draw parallels between Puerto Rico's situation, *vis-à-vis* the United States, with Ireland's relationship with the United Kingdom (Ferrao 1990, 268; Ribes Tovar 1975, 45, 48).

141. The exception during this period was Bishop George Joseph Carvana. He was born in Malta. For a list of the Bishops of the Diocese (later Archdiocese) of San Juan, Puerto Rico see, the webpage of the Archdiocese of San Juan: Archdiocese of San Juan. "Archdiocese of San Juan de Puerto Rico / Archidioecesis Sancti Joannis Portoricensis." http://www.catholic-hierarchy.org/diocese/dsjpr.html (accessed March 26, 2009).

142. Ribes Tovar 1975, 142–43.

143. Barreto 2001a.

144. Connor 1994, 161.

145. Breton 1964.

146. Olson 1971, 105.

147. Furtado and Hechter 1992, 173–74.

148. Popkin 1979, 251.

149. Rousseau 1993, 172.

150. Hobbes 1962, 129.

151. Hechter 1987, 102–3.

152. Hardin 1995b, 20.

153. Hechter 1987, 50–51; 1995, 59.

154. Hechter 1987, 52.

155. Green and Shapiro 1994, 78.

156. Hechter 1987, 133.

157. Green and Shapiro 1994, 16. The paradox does not hold in small groups wherein group leaders can monitor the participation, or defection, of the rank and file.

158. Elster 1985a, 141.

159. Hardin 1995b, 14.

160. Malešević 2002, 193.

CHAPTER 2

1. John von Neumann and Oskar Morgenstern's noteworthy tome *Theory of Games and Economic Behavior* (1980), originally published in 1944, introduced the mathematically based game theoretic branch of the rational choice approach into the social sciences.

2. Not all economists focused exclusively on tangible goods. For example, Thorstein Veblen's (1973) work from over a century ago, *The Theory of the Leisure Class*, combined tangible and emotional elements. He accepted the premise that individuals are strategic and goal- oriented (Ibid., 29). Classic entrepreneurs are wealth maximizers. And yet, through the accumulation of capital, these individuals also acquired honor (Ibid., 35). Veblen wrote, "The possession of wealth, which was at the outset valued simply as an evidence of efficiency, becomes, in popular apprehension, itself a meritorious act" (Ibid., 37). In time, wealth that was acquired passively through inheritance was bestowed with greater honors that wealth earned directly through one's labor (Ibid., 37, 44). Notions of honor,

worthy, and dignity were a direct result of the creation of socioeconomic classes (Ibid., 29).
3. Morrow 1994, 16.
4. Riker and Ordeshook 1973, 46.
5. Downs 1957, 6.
6. This desire for quantification also satisfied the penchant of many social scientists who try to emulate the natural sciences (Handler 1988, 14).
7. Barker 2001, 62–63.
8. Breton 1964, 379, 381.
9. Durkheim 1973, 150–51.
10. Connor 1994, 204.
11. Damasio 1994, 247–48.
12. Ibid., 251.
13. Descartes in Descartes, Spinoza, and Leibnitz 1994, 68.
14. Descartes 1989, 44.
15. LeDoux 1996, 24.
16. Proverbs 14:29–30.
17. 2 Timothy 2:22.
18. McDermott 2004, 699.
19. Barker 2001, 114.
20. Westen 2007, 62.
21. Bentham 1988, 2. In the *Ethics*, Spinoza made a similar argument about pleasure maximization and pain minimization (in Descartes, Spinoza, and Leibniz 1974, 281).
22. Bentham 1988, 24.
23. Ibid., 25.
24. Ibid., 33.
25. Ibid., 33–34.
26. McDermott 2004, 699.
27. Mill 1993, 93.
28. Ibid., 33.
29. Rousseau 1984, 89.
30. Alford and Hibbing 2004, 711.
31. The three parts of the human brain where emotions and rational thought interact are the ventromedial prefrontal cortices, the somatosensory cortices in the right hemisphere, and areas in the prefrontal cortices beyond the ventromedial sector (Damasio 1994, 70).
32. Ibid.
33. Turner 2000.
34. Frean 1996, 554.
35. Semendeferi, *et al.* 1998, 153.
36. Ibid., 143.
37. Boesch 1994.
38. Frank 1988, 69 (emphasis in original).

39. In Robert Axelrod's (1984) now famous computer tournament invited game theorists to submit computer program entries. The winning program was Tit For Tat—a game of perfect reciprocity. But it worked best when it occasionally made allowances for transgressions.
40. Sen 1990, 31.
41. Kollock 1993, 769.
42. Axelrod 1984, 182.
43. Hardin 1990, 359–60.
44. Shaw and Wong 1987.
45. Alford and Hibbing 2004, 707.
46. Ibid., 709.
47. Arnhart 1994, 466.
48. Ibid.
49. Masters 1990, 202.
50. Ibid.
51. Kecmanović 1996, 10
52. Balibar in Balibar and Wallerstein 1991, 94 (emphasis in original).
53. Kollock 1994.
54. Chong 2000; Chwe 2001; Opp 1990.
55. Arnhart 1994, 469.
56. Anderson 1991, 6 (emphasis in original).
57. Hardin 1995a, 7.
58. Hardin 1995b, 24.
59. Recurring rhetoric of common familial bonds never touches upon a logical by-product from this thesis. If everyone in an ethnic community is related, then in-group marriage implies that one has wed a relative. By implication, the *pure* ethnic community is also an inbred grouping.
60. Rogers Brubaker (2004) warned scholars to be careful in assuming that employing the discourse of ethnicity, particularly in conflicts, was objective evidence that the situation was inherently *ethnic*. Protagonists seeking to justify their actions, members of the media, or even agents of the state all may categorize a condition as *ethnic* for strategic reasons (Ibid., 16). Ultimately, the focus of this particular project is not on the objectivity of the ethnic classification of a conflict or state of cooperation. Neither is it on the sincerity of the elites calling their followers to take up to vote, to demonstrate, or even to take up arms. Rather, the spotlight is on the rank-and-file individuals who deem themselves group members, buy into the nationalist myth, and partake in collective action.
61. Trask 1993, 248 (emphasis in original).
62. Kecmanovicć 1996, 11.
63. Although their role in nationalism is crucial, intellectuals represent but one of several sets of societal elites. Bottomore (1993, 52) contended that in the past century, three particular elite subgroups have inherited the mantle of earlier ruling classes. They are intellectuals, captains of industry, and high-ranking government officials.

64. Mosse 1975, 7–8. Tilly (2008) contended that these political public performances, ranging from demonstrations to parades, are regimented by a prevailing repertoire of accepted behavior. In a manner of speaking, organizers and their followers follow a "script" designating the parameters of their actions within particular periods.
65. Mosse 1975, 8–9.
66. Ibid.
67. Schöpflin 1997, 21.
68. J. Coleman 1995, 10; Guss 2000. For example, colonial authorities in Rwanda painted a portrait whereby pastoral groups, such as the Tutsis, were romanticized as noble warriors in opposition to the Hutu majority—a group comprised largely of cultivators. Ethnic segregation was built on a socioeconomic division separating two groups that shared the same language, religion, and most perceptible cultural traits. Economic roles were translated into ethnic division and began a chain of events that delivered, to the Tutsi minority, the upper hand in the postcolonial state. Virulent accusations of discrimination and marginalization served as the backdrop for the 1994 genocide (Nasong'o 2003, 58).
69. Kecmanović 1996, 44.
70. Gramsci insinuated that there is also an intellectual impediment, of sorts. He contended that due to the lack of a formal education among the ordinary folk, as opposed to intellectuals, "philosophy can only be experienced as a faith" (Gramsci 1971, 339).
71. Ibid., 14.
72. Michels 1959, 88.
73. Challenges by rival elites, including upstart elites, represent an exception to this general pattern (Pareto 1991, 36).
74. Rudé 1995, 4.
75. Herzfeld 1997, 68.
76. For example, political elites in many parts of postcolonial Africa successfully maintained one-party regimes for years by presenting the ruling party as the "personification of nationalism." These were the institutions that spearheaded the drive for independence. Rhetorically, they depicted their opponents as antinationalist, pro-European, and colonalist sympathizers (Nasong'o 2005, 30).
77. Gramsci 1971, 340.
78. Lustick 1993.
79. Gramsci 1971, 12.
80. Kuhn 1970.
81. Consuelo Cruz's (2000) study of political discourse in Costa Rica and Nicaragua highlighted how administrators employed rival strategies during the colonial era in a bid to secure greater resources from the Spanish Crown. Costa Rican elites emphasized cooperation; their Nicaraguan counterparts stressed conflict. Their disparate tactics led to the institutionalization of the presumed permanent of particular national characteristics. David Laitin's (1986) study provides another fascinating example. Nigerian society is divided along several cleavages including religion—primarily the Christian-Muslim divide. Most of

the country's major ethnic groups associate themselves with one confession or the other, except the Yorbuas, who center their identities on their birthplace. The seeds of this identity were planted during British colonial rule when colonial policies prescribing the distribution of public funds through territorially centered chiefs rather than religious authorities.

82. Riker and Ordeshook 1973, 60.
83. Pagano 1995, 190 (emphasis in original).
84. Schuessler 2000, 17.
85. Mill 1993, 29.
86. Ibid., 42.
87. Elster 1990, 884.
88. Rousseau 1993, 162.
89. Hume 1992, 277.
90. Hobbes 1962, 131.
91. Rousseau 1984, 167.
92. Maslow 1999, 39.
93. Wintrobe 2002, 27.
94. Searle-White 2001, 66.
95. Ibid., 85.
96. Understanding resentment is an important part of comprehending ethnic violence. Roger Petersen (2002: 40) commented, "Resentment stems from the perception that one's group is located in an unwarranted subordinate position on a status hierarchy. The concept hinges on the linkage between group status and individual esteem."
97. Durkheim 1973, 83, and Hardin 2002, 15.
98. Hobbes 1962, 81.
99. Chong 1992, 174.
100. Aristotle 1987, 287.
101. Pitt-Rivers 1966, 27.
102. Kecmanović 1996, 122.
103. Breton and Dalmazzone 2002, 53.
104. Heckathorn 1990, 373.
105. Tula 1994, 125.
106. Ibid., 126.
107. Ibid.
108. Elster 1979, 21–22.
109. Breton and Dalmazzone 2002, 53.
110. Hechter 1987, 157.
111. Ibid., 158.
112. Heckathorn 1990, 369.
113. Lancaster 1988, 53 (emphasis in original).
114. La Rochefoucauld 1959, 42.
115. Chong 1991.
116. M. Taylor 1982, 19.
117. Elster 1999, 154.

118. Fine and Turner 2001, 54–55.

119. Hechter 1987, 156.

120. Scott 1985, 25.

121. Renan 1990, 19.

122. Kaplan 2006; Lindholm 2008, 99.

123. Kaplan 2003, 403 (emphasis in original).

124. Lafaye 1976, 29.

125. Rohter 1988.

126. Ibid.

127. García Cancilini 2001, 164.

128. Woods 1995, 1114.

129. Luke 2002, 219.

130. Ibid., 16. Still, García Canclini felt there were some advantages to a museum's entertainment dimension. He noted that increasing attendance rates in many European museums—contrasted with a decline in theater and movie attendance—holds out the possibility of a greater democratization of culture (García Canclini 2001, 165).

131. Red, white, black, and green were featured in the Arab Revolt Flag from the 1910s and were subsequently incorporated into the flags of Egypt, Jordan, Libya, Kuwait, the Palestinian Authority, Sudan, Syria, the United Arab Emirates, and Yemen (Flag Research Center 1985; Flag Research Center 1991; W. Smith 1975, 154–55). In 1963, Iraq adopted a new flag based the Pan-Arab colors—before the start of Saddam Hussein's autocratic rule. Hussein added the *Takbir* to the Iraqi flag in 1991, days before the United States militarily responded to Iraq's annexation of Kuwait.

132. Crescent moons are prominently featured on the flags of Algeria, Azerbaijan, Iran, Maldives, Malaysia, Mauritania, Pakistan, Tunisia, Turkey, Turkmenistan, and Uzbekistan.

133. Hobsbawm 1990, 73.

134. Cambanis 2004, A12.

135. Blumer 1969, 71.

136. Hansen 1999, 118 (brackets and italics in original).

137. Ortega y Gasset 2000, 45.

138. La Rochefoucauld 1959, 41.

139. Ibid., 56.

140. Elster 1999, 204.

141. Ibid., 203 (emphasis in original).

142. Durkheim 1973, 83.

143. Ibid., 83, 84.

144. Elster 1979, 146.

145. Mill 1993, 17.

146. Elster 1979, 84–85.

147. La Rochefoucauld 1959, 58.

148. Ibid., 119.

CHAPTER 3

1. As abridged representations of a given process, models help us to understand a phenomenon by narrowing our focus on the most essential elements in our study (Geddes 2003, 32).
2. Michels 1959, 41.
3. Downs 1957, 28.
4. Ibid., 102.
5. Haleem's (2001) study of women's legal rights in Pakistan showed that some of the same Downsian principles could be applied to nonelected regimes. Even military rulers try to appeal to curry favor with the popular will. When political elites—whether they were selected via the ballot box or coup—perceived public support favoring secular policies, they liberalized women's legal rights. To the contrary, when they sensed that the public supported a more socially conservative agenda, they restricted women's legal rights.
6. An important exception to the rule is found in multiparty parliamentary systems. Up to a certain point, vote losses for party A can be inconsequential if voters instead went with B—one of A's predictable coalition partners.
7. It is conceivable that a political society is divided to such an extent that various segments of the electorate align themselves along more than one dimension. Parties can attempt to become "catch-all" institutions. Alternatively, this situation could become fertile terrain for the proliferation of highly specialized and polarized parties. The number of political parties in a system is associated with the mechanisms of selecting lawmakers (see Duverger 1990).
8. Barreto 2001a.
9. Scholars have, long ago, put to rest the *modernizationist* thesis that nationalist movements, and hence nationalist parties, were a manifestation of disgruntled minorities in opposition to an ethnically neutral state. Nationalist parties may espouse the agendas of either dominant or subordinate ethnic communities. In order to assess politics in these societies, the theorist must learn to yield to area studies experts who are in a better position to point out that a party is espousing a *de facto* nationalist agenda while it publicly denies this is part of their legislative or regulatory program.
10. Trías Monge 1997.
11. While the 1952 Commonwealth constitution was drafted by a constitutional convention in Puerto Rico, it was amended and then approved by Congress. In terms of the day-to-day operations of the territorial administration, it functions, in most significant ways, like a state government minus voting representation in Washington, D.C. As a territory, it has no presidential electors, no federal senators, and only a single nonvoting delegate in the House of Representatives.
12. Starting in 1899, the U.S. federal government actively promoted a policy of forced cultural assimilation with a focus on encouraging a language shift toward English. *Americanization* remained an official government policy until the advent of the Commonwealth era. Reconciled to the futility of compulsory assimilation, the Truman administration gave up on Americanization in 1949

(Barreto 2009). In 1902, the island's American-appointed governor signed into law a statute mandating that English and Spanish were the island's two co-official languages. This bill was passed at a time when less than 10 percent of the territorial population could speak English (see Barreto 2001a).

13. Ibid.

14. The Commonwealth government, its agencies, and Puerto Rico's seventy-eight municipalities conduct the overwhelming majority of their business in Spanish. But its jurisdiction does not extend to U.S. federal operations or institutions on the island. Federal offices on the island, including the Federal District Court in San Juan, operate in English.

15. Puerto Rico's largest minorities are comprised of Dominicans—both documented and illegal—and Cubans. Both are Spanish-speaking peoples. Anglophones comprise the largest group of non-Spanish speakers. They can be divided into two groups: American expatriates who live mostly in English-speaking pockets and ethnic Puerto Ricans who were raised on the U.S. mainland.

16. Rivera 1996; Trías Monge 1997, 183.

17. Lichtman (2008) argued that an uncompromising and exclusive fidelity to the English language was an integral part of American nationalism. Indeed, former New York Senator Moynihan (1993, 73–75) pointed out that long ago, Congress established the precedent that statehood applicants had to be English-speaking territories or that they committed themselves to language shift toward English. Rafael Hernández-Colón (1986, 50), the governor who signed this unilingual bill in 1991, was aware of that connection.

18. PPD leaders were genuinely worried about possible congressional retaliation. In a bid to allay any federal anger, Resident Commissioner Jaime Fuster, a PPD member and the island's nonvoting delegate to the House of Representatives, explained the bill's significance on the floor of the House (Barreto 2001a). As Fuster noted, the law was a culturally significant and symbolic piece of legislation with no impact on federal-territorial relations or individual rights and liberties.

19. Wittman 1983; 1990.

20. Page, Kollman, and Miller 1993, 162.

21. Barreto 2001a, 73.

22. This strategy may have worked better than the PPD expected. The party was out of power from 1993 until 2000. During that time, the governing PNP assertively lobbied on behalf of its statehood agenda in the halls of Congress. In spite of such efforts, federal lawmakers reminded representatives of the Puerto Rican government of the moves of the previous administration and wondered aloud whether a future administration might not attempt to resuscitate such a nationalist agenda (Ibid., 127–29).

23. Tsebelis 1990, 7.

24. Batty and Danilović 1997, 95.

25. A core assumption within the rational choice school is that political parties and their leaders are strategic actors. Likewise, scholars employing this approach assume that individual voters are also strategic players in the political process. As is the case

with the *free-rider paradox*, the best interest of individual voters and political parties do not always mesh. Tsebelis (1990, 120) noted an interesting paradox. Some Labour Party activists in the United Kingdom were casting for the Conservative Party. Given the strong leftist leanings of these activists, this action seems illogical until one understands that they were inflicting ideological retribution on their own party. Tsebelis contended that, at times, Labour activists *punished* their own political party, in a manner of speaking, for appointing moderate candidates to vie their constituency's parliamentary seat. In other cases, voters may deny their preferred party their vote in a general election if they deem the party's chances of winning to be low. This is more likely to occur if voter preference for the second party over the third is much stronger than the preference for the first party over the second (Blais and Nadeau 1996, 45). A similar principle would apply to voters deciding among their options in a multicandidate primary. Thus, we need to differentiate between voters' attitudes, or ideological preferences, and the strategy they employ to decide between candidates (Brams 1985, 28).

26. Lijphart 1968, 17. In principle, ethnicity might also constitute a prime fissure in a consociational society.

27. Lijphart 1969, 213. Other examples include Lebanon and Canada. In pre-civil war Lebanon, for example, the President was a Maronite Christian; the Prime Minister, a Sunni Muslim; and the Speaker of the Parliament, a Shi'ite Muslim. There was a ratio of Christian to Muslim in the Chamber of Deputies. Traditionally, government ministries in Canada were divided both linguistically (English versus French) and regionally (Maritime Provinces, Central Canada, Western Canada). Lusztig (1994) contended that the failure to find a thoroughly acceptable compromise to Canada's constitutional disputes—the degree of centralization in Ottawa and the country's binational or multicultural character—is due to the collapse of old consociational compromise.

28. Tsebelis 1990, 164–65.

29. Ibid., 160.

30. The notion of a nested game is useful metaphor to study the ways in which national identities are oftentimes articulated. At times, there is a significant disconnect between popular notions of a national identity and the way in which it is publicly presented. While the government has embraced multiculturalism as a defining feature of national identity, Lee (2007, 2003) countered that older notions of *White Australia* endure and permeate many strata of Australian society.

31. Barreto 2001a, 104.

32. Tsebelis 1990, 167–68.

33. Payoff when k is equal to 1:

$$PO_i = kPO_{ei} + (1-k)PO_{pi}$$
$$PO_i = (1)PO_{ei} + (1-1)PO_{pi}$$
$$PO_i = PO_{ei} + (0)PO_{pi}$$
$$PO_i = PO_{ei} + 0$$
$$PO_i = PO_{ei}$$

Payoff when k is equal to 0:

$\mathrm{PO}i = k\mathrm{PO}ei + (1\text{-}k)\mathrm{PO}pi$
$\mathrm{PO}i = (0)\mathrm{PO}ei + (1\text{-}0)\mathrm{PO}pi$
$\mathrm{PO}i = 0 + (1)\mathrm{PO}pi$
$\quad \mathrm{PO}i = \mathrm{PO}pi$

34. Heckathorn (1984, 152) suggested a nested games solution to problems of social exchange.
35. Muller and Opp 1986.
36. Rambo (1999) interpreted this social dimension almost like a sociopsychological market in which individuals pursue a goal of maximizing sociocultural capital.
37. Passy 2003, 26.
38. Elster 1999, 369.
39. Dawes, van de Kragt, and Orbell 1990, 99.
40. Kelly and Kelly's (1994) study of union members found that the level of personal identification with a labor organization was strongly and positively associated with their willingness to engage in collective action. Furthermore, it turned out that this variable was the most significant predictor of individuals' willingness to contribute to labor union activities.
41. Freud 1959, 78.
42. Payoff when j is equal to 1:

$\mathrm{PO}i = (1\text{-}j)\mathrm{PO}mi + j\mathrm{PO}si$
$\mathrm{PO}i = (1\text{-}1)\mathrm{PO}mi + (1)\mathrm{PO}si$
$\mathrm{PO}i = (0)\mathrm{PO}mi + \mathrm{PO}si$
$\mathrm{PO}i = 0 + \mathrm{PO}si$
$\quad \mathrm{PO}i = \mathrm{PO}si$

Payoff when j is equal to 0:

$\mathrm{PO}i = (1\text{-}j)\mathrm{PO}mi + j\mathrm{PO}si$
$\mathrm{PO}i = (1\text{-}0)\mathrm{PO}mi + (0)\mathrm{PO}si$
$\mathrm{PO}i = (1)\mathrm{PO}mi + 0$
$\quad \mathrm{PO}i = \mathrm{PO}mi$

43. The United States, for example, adheres to a national narrative that claims to absorb newcomers. Accommodating outsiders is rooted in the motto *E Pluribus Unum*—"one from many." Over two centuries of immigration history have revealed that this inclusion has been more effective with European Christian groups than with others (Omi and Winant 1994; Steinberg 1989). Since the civil rights era, African Americans have been gradually included within the parameters of the official national identity (Kook 1998). Still, old-stock Anglo-Irish families, and names, are still perceived as *authentically* American. Particularly in times of crisis, such as around the two world wars, some families sought

to *indigenize* themselves by altering their surnames to last names that sounded more "American" (Waters 1990). In so doing, these individuals and their families completely invented new ancestral pasts to ones that fit better within the existing national saga.

44. Michels 1959, 50–56.

45. Individuals with a high level of group solidarity, or who have an extremely strong emotional attachment to a particular national identity, partake in collective action as a means of generating a selective social payoff. This thesis centers the focus of scholarly attention on the individual, in keeping with the fundamental premises of rational choice analysis. The argument presented here differs significantly from others such as Gupta's (2005) thesis. His conceptualization blended an individual's cost-benefit calculus with their group's strategy. He argued that if the size of the group's net benefit were large enough, an individual would weight collective action above personal needs. Tempting as it might appear, the way in which this hypothesis is framed still leaves us with the classic free-rider paradox and we are still left asking the great question, despite the tremendous value to our community, why should *I* go out and make the sacrifice rather than wait for someone else to do it?

46. Machiavelli 1980, 78.

47. Bloom 2005, 30.

48. Regarding the association between death and a particular cause, we must carefully differentiate between those soldiers who died in battle by misfortune and those who intentionally charged into battle knowing they were going to perish. The end result was the same in both cases, and few would seriously question their overall commitment to the group. While valiant soldiers seek honor and glory they ultimately want to live long enough to enjoy the fruits of their emotion-drenched labor. Martyrs, contrarily, intentionally lay down their lives for their cause and they come closest to the pure *Homo sociologicus*—the individual with an emotional attachment to the collectivity (*j*) at or near 1.

49. Ortega y Gasset 2000, 149.

50. A. Smith 1989, 357.

51. As Hobsbawm (1990, 117) noted, it was the "socially modest but educated middle strata" of society that tenaciously clung to the dissemination of standardized vernaculars in the developmental stages of late eighteenth- and early nineteenth-century nationalist movements. Both the livelihoods and social status of these intellectuals were tied up in the new ideology of nationalism that cast aside the old sacred languages, such as Latin—for bureaucratic purposes—in favor of an artificially regulated vernacular. Their inability to find gainful employment commensurate with their qualifications bred resentment that could be easily swayed by the discourse of resentment toward a dominant ethnic group (A. Smith 1982, 30–32).

52. The first chapter introduced the connection between ethnicity and nationalism. Both share a myth of common ancestry. But nationalism takes this narrative one step further by insisting upon the coincidence of ethnocultural and administrative borders. While it is quite possible for someone to adhere to an ethnic

sentiment, the existence of that belief does not mean, *ipso facto*, that this person deems this a *politically* salient identity.

53. Nationalist movements may employ essential nongroup members such as public relations firms or advertising agencies, campaign managers, or publishers—to help promote their cause. Interestingly, private enterprises have also engaged some of the same outside experts in a bid to make nationalist appeals. Foreign firms have employed local advertising agencies and have sponsored national festivals and other public events in a bid to symbolically *indigenize* or *nationalize* themselves (Dávila 1997; Guss 2000).

54. These share much in common with Pareto's "new elite" that champions the cause of the downtrodden, but does so only for their selfish ends (Pareto 1991, 36).

55. Margolis 1990; Lichbach 1994, 26.

56. Kollock, Blumstein, and Swartz 1994.

57. Maslow 1999, 168–69, 190.

58. Ibid., 39.

59. Ibid., 40.

60. Banton 1994, 6.

61. Harsanyi 1969, 523. Standard rational choice analyses continue resisting the idea that different motivations underlie behavior in different spheres of life (Varshney 2003, 87).

62. States and other political entities punish criminal offences through the judiciary. Law enforcement and armed forces have their own means of internally sanctioning noncompliance. But most states leave social punishments to nonstate actors.

63. Zerubavel 1995, 6 (emphasis in original).

64. Ibid.

65. Elster 1985a, 153; Elster 1985b, 265.

66. Nozick 1974, 243.

67. Hogan 2001, 49.

68. Aristotle 1987, 15.

69. If the value of the payoff is associated with the rank of the adjudicator, then does commendation from the Secretary General of the United Nations surpass the praise of a national leader? The answer to that question is "yes" for those who strongly identified with that particular organization or those hold a universal, rather than a national, identity. Outside religious identification, so-called *universal* identities do not invigorate individuals' passions to the same degree as ethnic or national classifications. Furthermore, someone could downplay the value of an honor coming from what some believe to be a weak organization.

70. Aristotle 1987, 270.

71. Elster 1985a, 154.

72. Hume 1992, 596.

73. Elster 1999, 170; Hume 1992, 377.

74. La Rochefoucauld (1959, 60) suggested in his 179th maxim that our willingness to criticize others, particularly those close to us, may be a veiled attempt to deflect attention from our own deficiencies.

75. Hume 1992, 320.
76. La Rochefoucauld 1959, 92.
77. Ibid., 55.
78. Ibid.
79. In the weeks and months following the tragic events of September 11, 2001, many observed an astonishing proliferation of American flags throughout the United States in residences, places of business, and displayed in cars. On a personal note, I recall hearing several individuals question the loyalty of those who did not participate in this patriotic ritual, particularly if the homeowners or business people were immigrants. Years after that calamity, I tend to see rather prominent and reverent American flag displays in many of the neighborhood shops, gasoline stations, and in taxis in the Boston area. It may be a coincidence, but a significant number of these mom-and-pop businesses are owned or operated by Arabs and South Asians. Apparently, immigrants' outsider status, particularly in the case of Muslims or Sikhs (who may be confused with Muslims because of their turbans), has imposed on them a greater burden to perform their Americanness with greater zeal, frequency, and pageantry.

CHAPTER 4

1. Laclau and Mouffe 2001, 152–53.
2. Scott 1985.
3. Barker 2001.
4. Regarding linguistically *defined* identities, the central issue is not always the language that is spoken. In Vanuatu, for example, the division between Anglophones and Francophones is not based on vernaculars. The vast majority of this archipelago's population speaks neither English nor French, but Bislama; this is not an indigenous Melanesian language but a pidgin (Miles 1998, 142–43). Like other pidgins, or language blends, in the Pacific and parts of West Africa, Bislama is based largely on English (Aitchison 1991, 181). These identities as Anglophones and Francophones emerged under the colonial period and they have endured despite the country's independence.
5. Laponce 1980, 158.
6. Judge 2000, 73.
7. Due to the costs associated with communicative efficiency, languages have a propensity to organize themselves in territorially compact niches juxtaposed to one another (Laponce 1993, 26). Hence, disparate language speakers have a propensity to self-segregate.
8. Edwards 1985, 23–25.
9. Fichte 1922, 223–24.
10. Tocqueville 1969, 33.
11. Schmidt 2006, 97.
12. Suleiman 2004, 15.
13. Ibid., 9.

14. When counting the number of Hebrew speakers in Israel, one must include hundreds of thousands of Israeli Arabs and Palestinian legal residents of East Jerusalem. They tend to lead diglossic lives relegating public uses of Arabic to their neighborhoods (Ibid., 144). Hebrew is compulsory in Arab schools in Israel (Ibid., 150).

15. The partitioning of languages and ethnic identities in Israel is further complicated by the arrival of many Jewish immigrants from Middle Eastern countries. Many of these so-called Oriental Jews, or Mizrahim, were native Arabic speakers (Ibid., 153).

16. Attempts to impose Turkish in the empire's Arab provinces fueled resentment toward Istanbul and Pan-Arab nationalism rather than foment a sense of common Ottoman identity (Suleiman 2003, 79).

17. Karlins and Petersen 1993, 607.

18. Aitchison 1991, 75.

19. Bilaniuk 2005, 104. As one might expect from a nonstandardized form of speech, *surzhyk* is not one discrete language but a constellation of linguistic forms blending different Russian and Ukrainian elements. This author identified five major variants that range from the urbanized-peasant *surzhyk* that blends Russian elements into Ukrainian to the *surzhyk* spoken by native Russophones who add Ukrainian elements into their Russian (Ibid., 125–34).

20. Both Ukrainian and Russian share a common Slavic heritage. As is the case with most forms of speech, geography plays a significant role in their evolution. Situated closer to the center of Europe, Ukrainian and Belorussian exhibit influences from German and Polish while Russian tends to borrow more heavily from Church Slavonic (Carmichael 2000, 272).

21. Bilaniuk 2005, 72.

22. Urciuoli's (1998) research into the social, cultural, and linguistic experiences of Puerto Ricans in inner-city enclaves in the United States underscores that even when these migrants to the U.S. mainland learn to speak English fluently, their speech is stigmatized and *racialized* as "broken" or "mixed" in sharp contrast to "good English." The point of contention has less to do with dialect or even accent then the socioeconomic stigma attached to the variety of English they learn. Absorbing this new language in urban settings, Puerto Ricans are most likely to come into contact and adopt a variety of English associated with working-class African Americans (Flores 1993, 164).

23. Bilaniuk 2005, 192.

24. Suleiman 2003, 28.

25. Bilaniuk 2005, 74.

26. Ibid., 15.

27. Ibid., 79, 85.

28. Carmichael 2000, 270.

29. Bilaniuk 2005, 16–17.

30. The Ukrainian language, and concurrently the nationalism associated with this tongue, was stronger in the West than in eastern Ukraine. That geographic divided corresponded, roughly, with a historic-administrative divide. For

centuries, western Ukrainians lived under Austro-Hungarian, Lithuanian, and Polish sovereignty whereas their eastern co-ethnics lived under Russian rule. As a result of this administrative divide, the eastern regions of the Ukrainian Republic had a much larger ethnic Russian presence. While major urban areas in the republic's west were somewhat Russified, public life in the cities of the East was conducted almost solely in the Russian language (Ibid., 40).

31. Ibid., 14–15.
32. Ibid., 93–94.
33. Ibid., 19.
34. García Canclini 2001.
35. Bulag 1998, 2002.
36. Bilaniuk 2005, 117–18.
37. Ibid., 22.
38. Ibid., 55.
39. Ibid.
40. Ibid., 57.
41. Ibid., 58.
42. Chatterjee 1993.
43. Bilaniuk 2005, 55.
44. Chatterjee 1993, 126.
45. Kandiyoti 1991, 433.
46. Chatterjee 1993, 116.
47. Bilaniuk 2005, 60.
48. Ibid., 56.
49. Ibid., 61.
50. Levine 1990.
51. Bilaniuk 2005, 58.
52. Ibid., 61.
53. Sternhell 1998.
54. Hobsbawm 1983b, 279.
55. Lipset 1990, 26. We should not uncritically accept claims to universalism and ethnic neutrality (Carrión 1993, 12). This kind of civic nationalism frequently masks deeply entrenched ethnocentrism (Pabón 2002, 325; Said 1994, 8–9).
56. Lee 2007; Lee 2003; Moran 2002.
57. Özyürek 2005, 12–13.
58. Lewis 1999, 27.
59. Ibid., 8. For Turkish nationalists eradicating Arabic and Persian loan words from their language represented a symbolic decolonization "freeing Turkish from the yoke of foreign languages" (Ibid., 67). In more recent decades, this policy has not prevented the introduction of English loan words into Turkish, thus developing a Turkish-English patois, or *Türkilizce* (Ibid., 133–38).
60. Ibid., 14–18, 28. As privileged members of the intelligentsia, these languages reformers logically sought to exalt their speech patterns. Therefore, the new Turkish archetype was centered on the Istanbul dialect (Ibid., 33).

114. Ibid., 37.
115. Ibid., 9.
116. Ibid., 111.
117. Ibid., 44.
118. Ibid., 62.
119. Ibid., 225.

CHAPTER 5

1. MacArthur 1962.
2. While the ANC was larger than the PAC, most of its leadership was either imprisoned or exiled by the early 1960s (Wood 2000, 124). Following the 1976 Soweto Uprising, thousands of activists in the black townships fled South Africa to join the struggle in exile (Ibid., 135).
3. Mphahlele 2002, 14.
4. Ibid., 45.
5. Fredrickson 2000, 39.
6. Mphahlele 2002, 46.
7. Goodwin and Schiff 1995, 263. Some of the Afrikaners interviewed for this project said that they did not understand why blacks would oppose classroom instructions in Afrikaans since, after all, these youngsters "have to compete in the white man's language in the end" (Ibid.).
8. Mphahlele 2002, 46–47.
9. Ibid., 62.
10. Ibid., 59.
11. Ibid., 69.
12. Ibid., 211.
13. Ibid., 113.
14. Ibid., 123.
15. Ibid., 125.
16. Ibid., 126.
17. Ibid., 127.
18. Ibid.
19. Ibid., 136.
20. Ibid., 144.
21. Ibid., 145.
22. Ibid., 146.
23. Kulin 2005, 17.
24. Ibid., 9, 14.
25. Petersen 2002, 238–40.
26. Kulin 2005, 19.
27. Milošević 1989.
28. Kulin 2005, 20.
29. Ibid., 21.
30. Ibid., 20.

31. Yugoslavia's demise also heralded the downfall of Serbo-Croatian as a unified, standard language. Despite the linguistic heterogeneity in the former Yugoslavia, political elites at the republican level took advantage of the federation's break up to establish their capital's regional dialect as the new standard for distinct Serbian, Croatian, and Bosnian languages (Dragojević 2005; Greenberg 1994; 1996). The new Croatian state, for example, embarked on a policy of eradicating presumed Serbian influences from its vernacular, replacing some of these previously customary words with new ones derived from obscure nineteenth-century dictionaries (Greenberg 1999, 148). This bid to break from the past is reminiscent of the Turkey republic's policy of *purifying* its language of foreign influences.

32. Kulin 2005, 40.

33. Ibid., 40–41.

34. Roosens 1989, 161.

35. Kulin 2005, 42.

36. Ibid., 74.

37. Ibid., 78.

38. Ibid., 92.

39. Ibid.

40. Ibid., 45.

41. Ibid., 145–46.

42. Ibid., 146.

43. Boyce (1982, 82) and O'Brien (1988, 39) noted the great historical irony of Irish nationalism's origins and how it is perceived today. While contemporary Irish nationalism is associated with the struggle of Irish Catholics against a Protestant Great Britain and North Ireland Protestants, the movement originated with Irish Protestants who, in their pursuit of greater autonomy vis-à-vis London, promoted a sense of Irish islanders versus British islanders.

44. P. Taylor 1997, 37.

45. Ibid., 43.

46. Ibid., 46.

47. Ibid., 52–53.

48. Ibid., 17.

49. Ibid., 60.

50. Ibid., 61.

51. Ibid., 68–69.

52. Ibid., 70.

53. Ibid., 105.

54. Throughout his tenure, U.S. President Ronald Reagan was often referred to as "the *great communicator*." A great example of his rhetorical skills was his successful framing of the 1980s war in Nicaragua as an extension of the cold war. He repeatedly referred to the anti-Sandinista forces as "freedom fighters." Without an effective counternarrative from his Democratic opposition, the label largely stuck in the minds of many American citizens (Westen 2007, 94).

55. Horgan 2005, 45.

56. P. Taylor 1997, 124.

57. Ibid., 88–89.
58. Ibid., 89.
59. O'Brien 1988, 40.
60. P. Taylor 1997, 294.
61. Borrowing a concept from Durkheim, Pape (2005, 173–80) differentiated between *egoistic* suicide and *altruistic* suicide. The egoistic variety is a private act. On the other hand, its altruistic counterpart is exceedingly public.
62. Ibid., 82.
63. Ibid., 90.
64. Anderson 1991, 9.
65. Chenu, *et al.*, 1990, 61.
66. Ibid., 64.
67. Ibid., 65.
68. Ibid., 67.
69. The question of what conditions promote fertile terrain for would-be martyrs lies outside the parameters of this book. Some have questioned the mental state of martyrs-in-the-making and wonder whether models of rational behavior apply to mentally unstable individuals. Post (2005, 55) noted, "Terrorists as individuals for the most part do not demonstrate serious psychopathology." Extreme conditions of poverty, humiliation, and deprivation may provide fertile ground for suicide bombers to seek revenge (Ahmed 2005, 97). Still, these individuals remain instrumentally rational. Their actions are deliberate and calculated to fulfill their goals.
70. Bloom 2005, 84.
71. Razi 1990, 82.
72. Abu-Amr 1993, 11.
73. Ibid., 10.
74. Ibid., 6.
75. Ibid.
76. Qutb, 8.
77. Ibid., 94; emphasis in original.
78. Ibid., 80–84.
79. Ibid., 9.
80. Ibid., 61–62.
81. Ibid., 65.
82. Ibid., 63.
83. Ibid., 70.
84. Ibid., 71.
85. Meital 2006, 106–7; Oliver and Steinberg 2005, xxi.
86. Ibid., xxii.
87. Meital 2006, 107.
88. Oliver and Steinberg 2005, 64.
89. Ibid., 65.
90. Ibid., 78. The term "mujahidun" in Arabic is the plural of *mujahid*, or holy warrior (Ibid., 186).

91. Ibid. 73.
92. Ibid., 83.
93. Ibid., 72–73.
94. Ibid., 163.
95. Ibid., 159.
96. Ibid., 96.
97. Ibid., 95.
98. Ohnuki-Tierney 2006, 1.
99. Ibid., xiii.
100. Ibid., 4.
101. Ibid., xiv–xv.
102. Ibid., 1–2.
103. Ibid., 2.
104. Ibid., 6–7.
105. Ibid., 7.
106. Ibid., 8.
107. Ibid., 29.
108. Ibid., 41.
109. Ibid., 39–40.
110. Ibid., 55.
111. Ibid., 60.
112. Ibid., 62.
113. Ibid., 67.
114. Ibid., 71–72.
115. Ibid., 74.
116. Ibid., 87.
117. Ortega y Gasset 2000, 41.
118. Ibid., 45.
119. Ohnuki-Tierney 2006, 73.
120. Ibid., 85.
121. Ibid., 79.
122. Ibid., 164.
123. Ibid., 163.
124. Ibid., 163, 170–71.
125. Ibid., 175.
126. Ibid., 170; brackets in original.
127. Ibid., 174.
128. Ibid., 35.

CONCLUSION

1. Bush 2001, 1110.
2. Murphy 2001.
3. Ibid.
4. Ibid.

BIBLIOGRAPHY

Abu-Amr, Ziad. 1993. "Hamas: A historical and political background." *Journal of Palestine Studies* 22 (4): 5–19.

Ahmed, Hisham H. 2005. "Palestinian resistance and 'suicide bombing': Causes and consequences." In *Root causes of terrorism: Myths, reality and ways forward*, ed. Tore Bjørjo, 87–102. London: Routledge.

Aitchison, Jean. 1991. *Language change or decay?* 2nd ed. Cambridge: Cambridge University Press.

Alford, John R., and John R. Hibbings. 2004. "The origins of politics: An evolutionary theory of political behavior." *Perspectives on Politics* 2 (4): 707–23.

Almond, Gabriel A. 1956. "Comparative political systems." *Journal of Politics* 18 (3): 391–409.

Almond, Gabriel A., and Sidney Verba. 1963. *The civic culture: Political attitudes and democracy in five nations*. Princeton, NJ: Princeton University Press.

Álvarez Curbelo, Silvia. 1993. "El discurso populista de Luis Muñoz Marín: Condiciones de posibilidad y mitos fundacionales en el período 1932–1936." In *Del nacionalismo al populismo: Cultura y política en Puerto Rico* [From Nationalism to Populism: Culture and Politics in Puerto Rico], ed. Silvia Álvarez Curbelo and María E. Rodríguez Castro, 13–35. Río Piedras, PR: Ediciones Huracán.

Anderson, Benedict. 1991. *Imagined communities: Reflections on the origin and spread of nationalism*. Rev. ed. London: Verso.

Apter, David E. 1972. *Ghana in transition*. Princeton, NJ: Princeton University Press. (Orig. pub. 1955.)

———. 1965. *The politics of modernization*. Chicago: University of Chicago Press.

Archdiocese of San Juan. "Archdiocese of San Juan de Puerto Rico / Archidioecesis Sancti Joannis Portoricensis." http://www.catholic-hierarchy.org/diocese/dsjpr.html (accessed March 26, 2009).

Aristotle. 1988. *The politics*. Cambridge: Cambridge University Press. (Orig. pub. 350 BCE)

———. 1987. *The Nicomachean Ethics*. Trans. J. E. Welldon. Amherst, NY: Prometheus. (Orig. pub. 350 BCE)

Arnhart, Larry. 1994. "The Darwinian biology of Aristotle's political animals." *American Journal of Political Science* 38 (2): 464–85.

Axelrod, Robert M. 1984. *The evolution of cooperation*. New York: Basic Books.

Balibar, Etienne, and Immanuel Wallerstein. 1991. *Race, nation, class: Ambiguous identities*. Trans. Chris Turner. London: Verso.

Banton, Michael. 1994. "Modeling ethnic and national relations." *Ethnic and Racial Studies* 17 (1): 1–19.

Barany, Zoltan. 2002. "Ethnic mobilization without prerequisites: The East European gypsies." *World Politics* 54 (3): 277–307.

Barker, Rodney. 2001. *Legitimating identities: The self-presentations of rulers and subjects.* Cambridge: Cambridge University Press.

Barreto, Amílcar A. 2009. "Enlightened tolerance or cultural capitulation? Contesting notions of American identity." In *Colonial crucible: Empire in the making of the modern U.S. state,* ed. Francisco Scarano and Alfred McCoy, 145–50. Madison: University of Wisconsin Press.

———. 2005. "Toward a theoretical explanation of political extremism." In *Democratic development and political terrorism: The global perspective,* ed. William Crotty, 17–31. Boston: Northeastern University Press.

———. 2002. *Vieques, the Navy, and Puerto Rican politics.* Gainesville: University Press of Florida.

———. 2001a. *The politics of language in Puerto Rico.* Gainesville: University Press of Florida.

———. 2001b. "Constructing identities: Ethnic boundaries and elite preferences in Puerto Rico." *Nationalism & Ethnic Politics* 7 (1): 21–40.

Barrington, Lowell W., Erik S. Herron, and Brian D. Silver. 2003. "The motherland is calling: Views of homeland among Russians in the near abroad." *World Politics* 55: 290–313.

Barth, Fredrik. 1969. "Introduction." In *Ethnic groups and boundaries: The social organization of culture difference,* ed. Fredrik Barth, 9–38. Boston: Little, Brown & Company.

Batty, Susan E., and Vesna Danilović. 1997. "Gorbachev's strategy of political centrism: A game-theoretic interpretation." *Journal of Theoretical Politics* 9 (1): 89–106.

Bell, David A. 2001. *The cult of the nation in France: Inventing nationalism, 1680–1800.* Cambridge, MA: Harvard University Press.

Ben Gurion, David. 1954. *Rebirth and destiny of Israel.* Trans. and ed. Mordekhai Nurock. New York: Philosophical Library.

Bentham, Jeremy. 1988. *The principles of morals and legislation.* Amherst, NY: Prometheus Books. (Orig. pub. 1781.)

Berkowitz, Michael. 1996. *Zionist culture and West European Jewry before the First World War.* Chapel Hill: University of North Carolina Press. (Orig. pub. 1993)

Berríos Martínez, Rubén. 1983. *La independencia de Puerto Rico: Razón y lucha* [The independence of Puerto Rico: Reason and struggle]. México, DF: Editorial Línea.

Bilaniuk, Laada. 2005. *Contested tongues: Language politics and cultural correction in Ukraine.* Ithaca, NY: Cornell University Press.

Blais, André, and Richard Nadeau. 1996. "Measuring strategic voting: A two-step procedure." *Electoral Studies* 15 (1): 39–52.

Bloom, Mia. 2005. *Dying to kill: The allure of suicide terror.* New York: Columbia University Press.

Blumer, Herbert. 1969. *Symbolic interactionism: Perspective and method.* Berkeley: University of California Press.

Boesch, Christophe. 1994. "Cooperative hunting in wild chimpanzees." *Animal Behaviour* 48 (3): 653–67.

Bosque-Pérez, Ramón, and José Javier Colón Morera, eds. 2006. *Puerto Rico under colonial rule: Political persecution and the quest for human rights.* Albany: State University of New York Press.

Bottomore, Tom. 1993. *Elites and society.* 2nd ed. London: Routledge.

Boyce, D. G. 1982. "Separatism and the Irish national tradition." In *National separatism,* ed. Colin H. Williams, 75–103. Cardiff: University of Wales Press.

Brading, David A. 1991. *The first America: The Spanish monarchy, Creole patriots, and the liberal state, 1492–1867.* Cambridge: Cambridge University Press.

Brams, Steven J. 1985. *Rational politics: Decisions, games, and strategy.* Boston: Academic Press.

Breton, Albert. 1964. "The economics of nationalism." *Journal of Political Economy* 72 (4): 376–86.

Breton, Albert, and Silvana Dalmazzone. 2002. "Information control, loss of autonomy, and the emergence of political extremism." In *Political extremism and rationality,* ed. Albert Breton, Gianluggi Galeotti, Pierre Salmon, and Ronald Wintrobe, 44–66. Cambridge: Cambridge University Press.

Brubaker, Rogers. 2004. *Ethnicity without groups.* Cambridge, MA: Harvard University Press.

Bulag, Uradyn E. 1998. *Nationalism and hybridity in Mongolia.* Oxford: Clarendon Press.

Bush, George W. 2003. *Public papers of the presidents of the United States: George W. Bush.* Vol. 2. Washington, DC: Government Printing Office.

Cambanis, Thanassis. 2004. "Flap over flag design prompts changes." *Boston Globe,* May 1, A12.

Carmichael, Cathie. 2000. "Coming to terms with the past: Language and nationalism in Russia and its neighbours." In *Language and nationalism in Europe,* ed. Stephen Barbour and Cathie Carmichael, 264–79. Oxford: Oxford University Press.

Carrión, Juan M. 1993. "Etnia, raza y nacionalidad puertorriqueña." In *La nación puertorriqueña: Ensayos en torno a Pedro Albizu Campos* [The Puerto Rican nation: Essays on Pedro Ablizu Campos], ed. Juan M. Carrión, Teresa C. Gracia Ruiz, and Carlos Rodríguez Fraticelli, 3–18. Río Piedras, PR: Editorial de la Universidad de Puerto Rico.

Cauthen, Bruce. 1997. "The myth of divine election and Afrikaner ethnogenesis." In *Myths and nationhood,* ed. Geoffrey Hosking and George Schöpflin, 107–31. New York: Routledge.

Chai, Sun-Ki. 1996. "A theory of ethnic group boundaries." *Nations and Nationalism* 2 (2): 281–307.

Chatterjee, Partha. 1993. *The nation and its fragments: Colonial and postcolonial histories.* Princeton, NJ: Princeton University Press.

Chenu, Bruno, Claude Prud'homme, France Qúeré, and Jean-Claude Thomas. 1990. *The book of Christian martyrs.* Trans. John Bowden. New York: Crossroad Publishing.

Cherry, Conrad, ed. 1998. *God's new Israel: Religious interpretations of American destiny*. Rev. ed. Chapel Hill: University of North Carolina Press.

Chilcote, Ronald H. 1994. *Theories of comparative politics: The search for a paradigm reconsidered*. 2nd ed. Boulder, CO: Westview.

Chong, Dennis. 2000. *Rational lives: Norms and values in politics and society*. Chicago: University of Chicago Press.

————. 1992. "Social incentives and the preservation of reputation in public-spirited collective action." *International Political Science Review* 13 (2): 171–98.

————. 1991. *Collective action and the civil rights movement*. Chicago: University of Chicago Press.

Chwe, Michael S. 2001. *Rational ritual: Culture, coordination, and common knowledge*. Princeton, NJ: Princeton University Press.

Clift, Dominique. 1982. *Quebec nationalism in crisis*. Kingston, Ontario: McGill-Queen's University Press.

Coleman, James S. 1995. "Rights, rationality, and nationality." In *Nationalism and rationality*, ed. Albert Breton, Gianluggi Galeotti, Pierre Salmon, and Ronald Wintrobe, 1–13. Cambridge: Cambridge University Press.

Coleman, William D. 1984. "Social class and language politics in Quebec." In *Conflict and language planning in Quebec*, ed. Richard Y. Bourhis, 130–47. Clevedon, UK: Multilingual Matters.

Connor, Walker. 1994. *Ethnonationalism: The quest for understanding*. Princeton, NJ: Princeton University Press.

Cruz, Consuelo. 2000. "Identity and persuasion: How nations remember their pasts and make their futures." *World Politics* 52 (3): 275–312.

Damasio, Anthony R. 1994. *Descartes' error: Emotion, reason and the human brain*. New York: Putnam.

Danforth, Loring M. 1995. *The Macedonian conflict: Ethnic Nationalism in a transnational world*. Princeton, NJ: Princeton University Press.

Dávila, Arlene. 1997. *Sponsored identities: Cultural politics in Puerto Rico*. Philadelphia: Temple University Press.

Davis, Horace B. 1967. *Nationalism and socialism: Marxist and labor theories of nationalism to 1917*. New York: Monthly Review Press.

Dawes, Robyn M., Alphons J. C. van de Kragt, and John M. Orbell. 1990. "Cooperation for the benefit of us—Not me, or my conscience." In *Beyond self-interest*, ed. Jane J. Mansbridge, 97–110. Chicago: University of Chicago Press.

Denitch, Bogdan. 1994. *Ethnic nationalism: The tragic death of Yugoslavia*. Minneapolis: University of Minnesota Press.

Descartes, René. 1989. *The passions of the soul*. Trans. Stephen Voss. Indianapolis: Hackett Publishing. (Orig. pub. 1649.)

Descartes, René, Benedict de Spinoza, and Gottfried W. F. Leibniz. 1974. *The rationalists*. New York: Anchor Books.

DeVotta, Neil. 2004. *Blowback: Linguistic nationalism, institutional decay, and ethnic conflict in Sri Lanka*. Stanford, CA: Stanford University Press.

Díaz Quiñones, Arcadio. 2000. *El arte de bregar: Ensayos* [The art of dealing: Essays]. San Juan, PR: Ediciones Callejón.

Downs, Anthony. 1957. *An economic theory of democracy.* New York: Harper & Row.

Dragojević, Mila. 2005. "Competing institutions in national identity construction: The Croatian sase." *Nationalism and Ethnic Politics* 11 (1): 61–87.

Dufour, Christian. 1990. *A Canadian challenge—Le défi québécois.* Halifax, NS: Institute for Research on Public Policy.

Durham, John. 1905. *The report of the Earl of Durham, her majesty's high commissioner and governor-general of British North America.* 2nd ed. London: Methuen & Co.

Durkheim, Emile. 1973. *On morality and society.* Ed. Robert N. Bellah. Chicago: University of Chicago Press.

Duverger, Maurice. 1990. "The two party system and the multiparty system." In *The West European party system*, ed. Peter Mair, 84–95. Oxford: Oxford University Press.

Edwards, John. 1985. *Language, society and identity.* Oxford: Basil Blackwell.

Eisenstadt, S. N. 1964. "Modernization and conditions of sustained growth." *World Politics* 16 (4): 576–94.

Elster, Jon. 1999. *Alchemies of the mind: Rationality and the emotions.* Cambridge: Cambridge University Press.

———. 1990. "Norms of revenge." *Ethics* 100 (4): 862–85.

———. 1985a. "Rationality, morality, and collective action." *Ethics* 96 (1): 136–55.

———. 1985b. "Weakness of will and the free-rider problem." *Economics and Philosophy* 1:231–65.

———. 1979. *Ulysses and the sirens: Studies in rationality and irrationality.* Cambridge: Cambridge University Press.

Encyclopedia Judaica. 2007. "Pittsburgh Platform." 2nd ed. Vol. 16. Jerusalem: Keter Publishing House. 190-191.

Eriksen, Thomas H. 1993. *Ethnicity and nationalism: Anthropological perspectives.* London: Pluto Press.

Ferrao, Luis A. 1990. *Pedro Albizu Campos y el nacionalismo puertorriqueño, 1930–1939* [Pedro Albizu Campos and Puerto Rican nationalism, 1930–1939]. Río Piedras, PR: Editorial Cultural.

Fichte, Johann G. 1922. *Address to the German nation.* Trans. R. F. Jones and G. H. Turnbull. Chicago: Open Court Publishing Company.

Fine, Gary A., and Patricia A. Turner. 2001. *Whispers on the color line: Rumor and race in America.* Berkeley: University of California Press.

Flag Research Center. 1985. "New Flags: Arab Republic of Egypt." *The Flag Bulletin.* 110:39–44.

Flag Research Center. 1991. "New Flags: Republic of Iraq." 1991. *The Flag Bulletin.* 140:42–49.

Flores, Juan. 1993. *Divided borders: Essays on Puerto Rican identity.* Houston: Arte Público Press.

Foster, Robert J. 1991. "Making national cultures in the global ecumene." *Annual Review of Anthropology* 20:235–60.

Frank, Robert H. 1988. *Passions within reason: The strategic role of the emotions.* New York: W. W. Norton.

Frean, Marcus. 1996. "The evolution of degrees of cooperation." *Journal of Theoretical Biology* 182 (4): 549–59.

Fredrickson, George M. 2000. *The comparative imagination: On the history of racism, nationalism, and social movements.* Berkeley: University of California Press.

Freud, Sigmund. 1959. *Group psychology and the analysis of the ego.* Trans. James Strachey. New York: W. W. Norton. (Orig. pub. 1922.)

Furtado, Charles F., and Michael Hechter. 1992. "The emergence of nationalist politics in the USSR: A comparison of Estonia and the Ukraine." In *Thinking theoretically about Soviet nationalities: Histories and comparison in the study of the USSR*, ed. Alexander J. Motyl, 169–204. New York: Columbia University Press.

García Canclini, Néstor. 2001. *Culturas híbridas: Estratégias para entrar y salir de la modernidad* [Hybrid cultures: Strategies for entering and exiting Modernity]. Buenos Aires: Editorial Paidós.

Geary, Patrick J. 2002. *The myth of nations: The medieval origins of Europe.* Princeton, NJ: Princeton University Press.

Geddes, Barbara. 2003. *Paradigms and sand castles: Theory building and research design in comparative politics.* Ann Arbor: University of Michigan Press.

Geertz, Clifford. 1973. *The interpretation of cultures.* New York: Basic Books.

Gellner, Ernest. 1983. *Nations and nationalism.* Ithaca, NY: Cornell University Press.

Goetze, David B., and James Patrick. 2004. "Evolutionary psychology and the explanation of ethnic phenomenon." *Evolutionary Psychology* 2:142–59, http:// human-nature.com/ep/articles/ep02142159.html (accessed June 3, 2006).

Goodwin, June, and Ben Schiff. 1995. *Heart of whiteness: Afrikaners face black rule in the new South Africa.* New York: Scribner.

Gordon, Aaron David. 1973. *Selected essays.* New York: Arno Press. (Orig. pub. 1938.)

Gramsci, Antonio. 1971. *Selections from the prison notebooks.* Trans. and ed. Quintin Hoare and Geoffrey N. Smith. New York: International Publishers.

Green, Donald P., and Ian Shapiro. 1994. *Pathologies of rational choice theory: A critique of applications in political science.* New Haven: Yale University Press.

Greenberg, Robert D. 1999. "In the aftermath of Yugoslavia's collapse: The politics of language death and language birth." *International Politics* 36:141–58.

———. 1996. "The politics of dialects among Serbs, Croats, and Muslims in the former Yugoslavia." *East European Politics and Societies* 10 (3): 393–415.

———. 1994. "Southwest Balkan linguistic contacts: Evidence from appellative language." *Journal of Slavic Linguistics* 2 (2): 273–81.

Greenfeld, Liah. 1992. *Nationalism: Five roads to modernity.* Cambridge, MA: Harvard University Press.

Guerra, Lillian. 1998. *Popular expression and national identity in Puerto Rico: The struggle for self, community, and nation.* Gainesville: University Press of Florida.

Gupta, Dipak K. 2005. "Exploring roots of terrorism." In *Root causes of terrorism: Myths, reality and ways forward*, ed. Tore Bjørjo, 16–32. London: Routledge.

Guss, David M. 2000. *The festive state: Race, ethnicity, and nationalism as cultural performance.* Berkeley: University of California Press.

Haleem, Irm. 2001. Women's legal rights, military regimes, and political legitimacy in Pakistan. PhD diss., Boston University.

Handler, Richard. 1988. *Nationalism and the politics of culture in Quebec*. Madison: University of Wisconsin Press.

Hansen, Thomas B. 1999. *The saffron wave: Democracy and Hindu nationalism in modern India*. Princeton, NJ: Princeton University Press.

Hardin, Russell. 2002. "The crippled epistemology of extremism." In *Political extremism and rationality*, ed. Albert Breton, Gianluggi Galeotti, Pierre Salmon, and Ronald Wintrobe, 3–22. Cambridge: Cambridge University Press.

———. 1995a. *One for all: The logic of group conflict*. Princeton, NJ: Princeton University Press.

———. 1995b. "Self-interest, group identity." In *Nationalism and rationality*, ed. Albert Breton, Gianluggi Galeotti, Pierre Salmon, and Ronald Wintrobe, 14–42. Cambridge: Cambridge University Press.

———. 1990. "The social evolution of cooperation." In *The limits of rationality*, ed. Karen Schweers Cook, and Margaret Levi, 358–82. Chicago: University of Chicago Press.

Harsanyi, John C. 1969. "Rational-choice models of political science vs. functionalist and conformist theories." *World Politics* 21 (4): 513–38.

Harvey, Frank P. 2000. "Primordialism, evolutionary theory and ethnic violence in the Balkans: Opportunities and constraints for theory and policy." *Canadian Journal of Political Science* 33 (1): 37–65.

Hechter, Michael. 1987. *Principles of group solidarity*. Berkeley: University of California Press.

———. 1986. "Rational choice theory and the study of race and ethnic relations." In *Theories of race and ethnic relations*, ed. John Rex and David Mason, 264–79. Cambridge: Cambridge University Press.

———. 1975. *Internal colonialism: The Celtic fringe in British national development, 1536–1966*. Berkeley: University of California Press.

Heckathorn, Douglas D. 1990. "Collective sanctions and compliance norms." *American Sociological Review* 55 (3): 366–84.

———. 1984. "A formal theory of social exchange: Process and outcome." *Current Perspectives in Social Theory* 5: 145–80.

Hernández Colón, Rafael. 1986. *La nueva tesis* [The new thesis]. Río Piedras, PR: Editorial Edil.

Herrera, Yoshiko M. 2005. *Imagined economies: The sources of Russian regionalism*. New York: Cambridge University Press.

Hertzberg, Arthur, ed. 1997. *The Zionist idea: A historic analysis and reader*. Philadelphia: Jewish Publication Society.

Herzfeld, Michael. 1997. *Cultural intimacy: Social poetics in the nation-state*. New York: Routledge.

Herzl, Theodor. 1988. *The Jewish state*. New York: Dover Publications. (Orig. pub. 1896.)

Higonnet, Patrice. 1990. "Cultural upheaval and class formation during the French Revolution." In *The French Revolution and the birth of modernity*, ed. Ferenc Fehér, 69–102. Berkeley: University of California Press.

Hobbes, Thomas. 1962. *Leviathan. Or the Matter, forme, and power of a commonwealth ecclesiasticall and civil.* Ed. Michael Oakshott. New York: Collier Books. (Orig. pub. 1651.)

Hobsbawm, Eric J. 1990. *Nations and nationalism since 1780: Programme, myth, reality.* 2nd ed. Cambridge: Cambridge University Press.

———. 1983a. "Introduction: Inventing traditions." In *The invention of tradition*, ed. Eric Hobsbawm and Terence Ranger, 1–14. Cambridge: Cambridge University Press.

———. 1983b. "Mass-producing traditions: Europe, 1870–1914." In *The invention of tradition*, ed. Eric Hobsbawm and Terence Ranger, 263–307. Cambridge: Cambridge University Press.

Hogan, Patrick C. 2001. *The culture of conformism: Understanding social consent.* Durham, NC: Duke University Press.

Horace. 2002. *The odes: New translations by contemporary poets.* Ed. J. D. McClatchy. Princeton, NJ: Princeton University Press.

Horgan, John. 2005. "The social and psychological characteristics of terrorism and terrorists." In *Root causes of terrorism: Myths, reality and ways forward*, ed. Tore Bjørjo, 44–53. London: Routledge.

Hume, David. 1992. *A treatise of human nature.* Amherst, NY: Prometheus Books. (Orig. pub. 1739.)

Huntington, Samuel P. 2004. "The Hispanic challenge." *Foreign Policy* 141: 30–45.

———. 1996. *The clash of civilizations: Remaking of world order.* New York: Simon & Schuster.

———. 1968. *Political order in changing societies.* New Haven, CT: Yale University Press.

Janer, Zilkia. 1998. Colonial nationalism: The nation building literary field and subaltern intellectuals in Puerto Rico (1948–1952). PhD diss., Duke University.

Judge, Anne. 2000. "France: 'One state, one nation, one language'?" In *Language and nationalism in Europe*, ed. Stephen Barbour and Cathie Carmichael, 44–82. Oxford: Oxford University Press.

Juka, Safete S. 1984. *Kosova: The Albanians in Yugoslavia in light of historical documents—An essay.* New York: Waldon Press.

Kandiyoti, Deniz. 1991. "Identity and its discontents: Women and the nation." *Millennium* 20 (3): 429–43.

Kaplan, Sam. 2006. *The pedagogical state: Education and the politics of national culture in post-1980 Turkey.* Stanford, CA: Stanford University Press.

———. 2003. "Nuriye's dilemma: Turkish lessons of democracy and the gendered state." *American Ethnologist* 30 (3): 401–17.

Karlins, Rasma, and Roger Petersen. 1993. "Decision calculus of protestors and regimes: Eastern Europe 1989." *Journal of Politics* 55 (3): 588–614.

Kates, Gary. 1990. "Jews into Frenchmen: Nationalism and representation in revolutionary France." In *The French Revolution and the birth of modernity,* ed. Ferenc Fehér, 103–16. Berkeley: University of California Press.

Katz, Jacob. 1996. "The forerunners of Zionism." In *Essential papers of Zionism,* ed. Jehuda Reinharz and Anita Shapira, 33–45. New York: New York University Press.

Kaufmann, Eric. 1999. "American exceptionalism reconsidered: Anglo-Saxon ethnogenesis in the 'universal' nation, 1776–1850." *Journal of American Studies* 33 (3): 437–57.

———. 1998. "'Naturalizing the nation': The rise of naturalistic nationalism in the United States and Canada." *Comparative Studies in Society and History* 40 (1): 666–95.

Kecmanović, Dušan. 1996. *The mass psychology of ethnonationalism.* New York: Plenum Press.

Kedourie, Elie. 1993. *Nationalism.* 4th ed. Oxford: Blackwell. (Orig. pub. 1960.)

Kelly, Caroline, and John Kelly. 1994. "Who gets involved in collective action? Social psychological determinants of individual participation in Trade Unions." *Human Relations* 47 (1): 63–88.

Kimmerling, Baruch. 2001. *The invention and decline of Israeliness: State, society, and the military.* Berkeley: University of California Press.

King, Gary, Robert O. Keohane, and Sidney Verba. 1994. *Designing social inquiry: Scientific inference in qualitative research.* Princeton, NJ: Princeton University Press.

Kitromilides, Paschalis M. 1994. *Enlightenment, nationalism, orthodoxy: Studies in culture and political thought of south-eastern Europe.* Aldershot, UK: Ashgate.

Klier, John D. 1997. "The myth of Zion among East European Jewry." In *Myths and nationhood,* ed. Geoffrey Hosking and George Schöpflin, 170–81. New York: Routledge.

Kohn, Hans. 1962. *The age of Nationalism: The first era of global history.* New York: Harper & Brothers.

Kollock, Peter. 1994. "The emergence of exchange structures: An experimental study of uncertainty, commitment, and trust." *American Journal of Sociology* 100 (2): 313–45.

———. 1993. "'An eye for an eye leaves everyone blind': Cooperation and accounting systems." *American Sociological Review* 58 (6): 768–86.

Kollock, Peter, Philip Blumstein, and Pepper Swartz. 1994. "The judgment of equity in intimate relationships." *Social Psychology Quarterly* 57 (4): 340–51.

Kook, Rebecca. 1998. "The shifting status of African Americans in the American collective identity." *Journal of Black Studies* 29 (2): 154–78.

Kuhn, Thomas S. 1970. *The structure of scientific revolutions.* 2nd ed. Chicago: University of Chicago Press.

Kulin, Elvir. 2005. *In a Bosnian trench: A wartime memoir of a Bosnian soldier.* Victoria, BC: Trafford.

Laclau, Ernesto, and Chantal Mouffe. 2001. *Hegemony and socialist strategy: Towards a radical democratic politics.* 2nd ed. London: Verso.

Lafaye, Jacques. 1976. *Quetzalcóatl and Guadalupe: The formation of Mexican national consciousness, 1531–1813*. Chicago: University of Chicago Press.

Laitin, David D. 1986. *Hegemony and culture: Politics and religious change among the Yoruba*. Chicago: University of Chicago Press.

Lancaster, Roger. 1988. *Thanks to God and the revolution: Popular religion and class consciousness in the new Nicaragua*. New York: Columbia University Press.

Laponce, Jean A. 1993. "The case for ethnic federalism in multilingual societies: Canada's regional imperative." *Regional Politics & Policy* 3 (1): 23–43.

———. 1987. *Languages and their territories*. Trans. Anthony Martin-Sperry. Toronto: University of Toronto Press.

———. 1980. "The city centre as conflictual space in the bilingual city: The case of Montreal." In *Centre and periphery*, ed. Jean Gottman, 149–62. Beverly Hills, CA: Sage Publications.

La Rochefoucauld, François. 1959. *Maxims*. Trans. Leonard Tancock. London: Penguin Books. (Orig. pub. 1665.)

LeDoux, Joseph. 1996. *The emotional brain: The mysterious underpinnings of emotional life*. New York: Touchstone.

Lee, Michelle A. 2007. *A fair go: Race politics and public discourse in Australia*. Saarbrücken, Germany: VDM Verlag Dr. Müller.

———. 2003. "Multiculturalism as nationalism: A discussion of nationalism in pluralistic nations." *Canadian Review of Studies in Nationalism* 30 (1–2): 103–23.

Levi, Margaret. 1997. "A model, a method, and a map: Rational choice in comparative and historical analysis." In *Comparative politics: Rationality, culture, and structure*, ed. Mark I. Lichbach and Alan S. Zuckerman, 19–41. Cambridge: Cambridge University Press.

Levine, Marc V. 1990. *The reconquest of Montreal: Language policy and social change in a bilingual city*. Philadelphia: Temple University Press.

Levy, Marion J. 1969. *Modernization and the structure of societies: A setting for international affairs*. Princeton, NJ: Princeton University Press.

Lewis, Geoffrey. 1999. *The Turkish language reform: A catastrophic success*. Oxford: Oxford University Press.

Lichbach, Mark I. 1994. "Rethinking rationality and rebellion: Theories of collective action and problems of collective dissent." *Rationality and Society* 6 (1): 8–39.

Lichbach, Mark I., and Alan S. Zuckerman. 1997. "Research traditions and theory in comparative politics: An introduction." In *Comparative politics: Rationality, culture, and structure*, ed. Mark I. Lichbach and Alan S. Zuckerman, 3–16. Cambridge: Cambridge University Press.

Lichtman, Allan J. 2008. *White protestant nation: The rise of the American conservative movement*. New York: Atlantic Monthly Press.

Lieven, Anatol. 2004. *America right or wrong: An anatomy of American nationalism*. New York: Oxford University Press.

Lijphart, Arend. 1969. "Consociational democracy." *World Politics* 21 (2): 207–25.

———. 1968. *The politics of accommodation: Pluralism and democracy in the Netherlands*. Berkeley: University of California Press.

Lindholm, Charles. 2008. *Culture and authenticity*. Malden, MA: Blackwell.

Lipset, Seymour M. 1990. *Continental divide: The values and institutions of the United States and Canada*. London: Routledge.

Luke, Timothy W. 2002. *Museum politics: Power plays at the exhibition*. Minneapolis: University of Minnesota Press.

Lustick, Ian S. 1993. *Unsettled states, disputed lands: Britain and Ireland, France and Algeria, Israel and West Bank-Gaza*. Ithaca, NY: Cornell University Press.

Lusztig, Michael. 1994. "Constitutional paralysis: Why Canadian constitutional initiatives are doomed to fail." *Canadian Journal of Political Science* 27 (4): 747–71.

MacArthur, Douglas. 1962. Duty, honor, country. May 12, http://www.americanrhetoric.com/speeches/douglasmacarthurthayeraward.html (accessed June 18, 2008).

Machiavelli, Niccolò. 1980. *The prince*. New York: New American Library. (Orig. pub. 1532.)

MacIver, Donald N. 1982. "The paradox of nationalism in Scotland." In *National separatism*, ed. Colin H. Williams, 105–44. Cardiff: University of Wales Press.

Maldonado-Denis, Manuel. 1972. *Puerto Rico: A socio-historic interpretation*. Trans. Elena Vialo. New York: Vintage Books.

Malešević, Siniša. 2002. "Rational choice theory and the sociology of ethnic relations: A critique." *Ethnic and Racial Studies* 25 (2): 193–212.

Margolis, Howard. 1990. "Dual utilities and rational choice." In *Beyond self-interest*, ed. Jane J. Mansbridge, 239–53. Chicago: University of Chicago Press.

Mari Bras, Juan. 1984. *El independentismo en Puerto Rico: Su pasado, su presente y su porvenir* [Independentism in Puerto Rico: Its past, its present and its future]. San Juan, PR: Editorial CEPA.

Márquez, Alberto L. 2006. "Puerto Rican independentistas: Subversives or subverted?" In *Puerto Rico under colonial rule: Political persecution and the quest for human rights*, ed. Ramón Bosque-Pérez and José J. Colón Morera, 139–49. Albany: State University of New York Press.

Marx, Karl. 1963. *The eighteenth Brumaire of Louis Bonaparte*. Ed. C. P. Dutt. New York: International Publishers. (Orig. pub. 1869.)

Marx, Karl, and Frederick Engels. 1982. *Manifesto of the Communist party*. New York: International Publishers. (Orig. pub. 1848.)

Maslow, Abraham H. 1999. *Toward a psychology of being*. 3rd ed. New York: John Wiley. (Orig. pub. 1968.)

Massad, Joseph. 1995. "Conceiving the masculine: Gender and Palestinian nationalism." *Middle East Journal* 49 (3): 467–83.

Masters, Roger D. 1990. "Evolutionary biology and political theory." *American Political Science Review* 84 (1): 195–210.

McDermott, Rose. 2004. "The feeling of rationality: The meaning of neuroscientific advances for political science." *Perspectives on Politics* 2 (4): 691–706.

McRoberts, Kenneth. 1984. "The sources of neo-nationalism in Quebec." *Ethnic and Racial Studies* 7 (1): 55–85.

———. 1979. "Internal colonialism: The case of Quebec." *Ethnic and Racial Studies* 2 (3): 293–318.

Meital, Yoram. 2006. *Peace in tatters: Israel, Palestine, and the Middle East*. Boulder, CO: Lynne Rienner.

Meléndez Vélez, Edgardo. 1998. *Partidos, política pública y status en Puerto Rico* [Parties, public policy and status in Puerto Rico]. San Juan, PR: Ediciones Nueva Aurora.

Michels, Robert. 1959. *Political parties: A sociological study of the oligarchical tendencies of modern democracy.* New York: Dover Publications. (Orig. pub. 1915.)

Miles, William F. S. 2007. *Zion in the desert: American Jews in Israel's reform kibbutzim.* Albany: State University of New York Press.

———. 1998. *Bridging mental boundaries in a postcolonial microcosm: Identity and development in Vanuatu.* Honolulu: University of Hawai'i Press.

Mill, John S. 1993. *Utilitarianism, On liberty, considerations on representative government.* Ed. Geraint Williams. London: J. M. Dent. (Orig. pub. 1910.)

Milošević, Slobodan. 1989. Kosovo Polje address, June 28. http://www.ocf.berkeley.edu/~bip/docs/kosovo_polje/kosovo_polje.html (accessed January 20, 2009).

Moran, Anthony. 2002. "The psychodynamics of Australian settler-nationalism: Assimilating or reconciling with the aborigines?" *Political Psychology* 23 (4): 667–701.

Morris, Nancy. 1995. *Puerto Rico: Culture, politics, and identity.* Westport, CT: Praeger.

Morrow, James D. 1994. *Game theory for political scientists.* Princeton, NJ: Princeton University Press.

Mosse, George L. 1975. *The nationalization of the masses: Political symbolism and mass movements in Germany from the Napoleonic Wars through the Third Reich.* Ithaca, NY: Cornell University Press.

Motyl, Alexander J. 2001. "Inventing invention: The limits of national identity formation." In *Intellectuals and the articulation of the nation,* ed. Ronald G. Suny and Michael D. Kennedy, 57–75. Ann Arbor: University of Michigan Press.

Moynihan, Daniel P. 1993. *Pandaemonium: Ethnicity in international politics.* Oxford: Oxford University Press.

Mphahlele, Letlapa. 2002. *Child of this soil: My life as a freedom fighter.* Cape Town, SA: Kwela Books.

Muller, Edward N., and Karl-Dieter Opp. 1986. "Rational choice and rebellious collective action." *American Political Science Review* 80 (2): 471–87.

Murphy, Dean E. 2001. "After the attacks: The reaction." *New York Times,* September 15.

Nasong'o, Shadrack W. 2005. *Contending political paradigms in Africa: Rationality and the politics of democratization in Kenya and Zambia.* New York: Routledge.

———. 2003. "Ethnonationalism and state integrity in Africa: Cultural objectification and the Rwandan genocide." *Canadian Review of Studies in Nationalism* 30 (1–2): 53–63.

Noah, Mordecai M. 1999. *The selected writings of Mordecai Noah.* Michael Schuldiner and Daniel J. Kleinfeld, eds. Westport, CT: Greenwood.

Nozick, Robert. 1974. *Anarchy, state, and utopia.* New York: Basic Books.

O'Brien, Connor C. 1988. *God land: Reflections on religion and nationalism.* Cambridge, MA: Harvard University Press.

Ohnuki-Tierney, Emiko. 2006. *Kamikaze diaries: Reflections of Japanese student soldiers*. Chicago: University of Chicago Press.

Oliver, Anne M., and Paul F. Steinberg. 2005. *The road to martyr's square: A journey into the world of the suicide bomber*. New York: Oxford University Press.

Olson, Mancur. 1971. *The logic of collective action: Public goods and the theory of groups*. Cambridge, MA: Harvard University Press. (Orig. pub. 1965.)

Omi, Michael, and Howard Winant. 1994. *Racial formation in the United States: From the 1960s to the 1980s*. 2nd ed. New York: Routledge.

Opp, Karl-Dieter. 1990. "The attenuation of customs." In *Social institutions: Their emergence, maintenance and effects*, ed. Michael Hechter, Karl-Dieter Opp, and Reinhard Wippler, 119–39. New York: Aldine de Gruyer.

Ortega y Gasset, José. 2000. *Meditations on Quixote*. Trans. Evelyn Rugg and Diego Marín. Urbana: University of Illinois Press. (Orig. pub. 1961.)

———. 1960. *The revolt of the masses*. New York: W. W. Norton. (Orig. pub. 1932.)

Özyürek, Esra. 2005. *Nostalgia for the modern: State secularism and everyday politics in Turkey*. Durham, NC: Duke University Press.

Pabón, Carlos. 2002. *Nación postmortem: Ensayos sobre los tiempos de insoportable ambigüedad* [Postmortem Nation: Essays on Times of Unendurable Ambiguity]. San Juan, PR: Ediciones Callejón.

Pagano, Ugo. 1995. "Can economics explain nationalism?" In *Nationalism and rationality*, ed. Albert Breton, Gianluggi Galeotti, Pierre Salmon, and Ronald Wintrobe, 173–203. Cambridge: Cambridge University Press.

Page, Scott E., Ken Kollman, and John H. Miller. 1993. "Adaptive parties and spatial voting theory." In *Information, participation, and choice: An economic theory of democracy in perspective*, ed. Bernard Grofman, 161–77. Ann Arbor: University of Michigan Press.

Pape, Robert A. 2005. *Dying to win: The strategic logic of suicide terrorism*. New York: Random House.

Pareto, Vilfredo. 1991. *The rise and fall of elites: An application of theoretical sociology*. New Brunswick, NJ: Transaction Publishers.

Parsons, Talcott. 1942. "Max Weber and the contemporary political crisis: I. The sociological analysis of power and authority structures." *The Review of Politics* 4 (1): 61–76.

Passy, Florence. 2003. "Social networks matter. But how?" In *Social movements and networks: Relational approaches to collective action*, ed. Mario Diani and Doug McAdam, 21–48. Oxford: Oxford University Press.

Pattanayak, D. P., and J. M. Bayer. 1987. "Laponce's 'The French language in Canada: Tensions between geography and politics'—A rejoinder." *Political Geography Quarterly* 6 (3): 261–63.

Petersen, Roger D. 2002. *Understanding ethnic violence: Fear, hatred, and resentment in twentieth-century Eastern Europe*. Cambridge: Cambridge University Press.

Pinsker, Leon. 1944. *Road to freedom: Writings and addresses*. Introduction by B. Netanyahu. New York: Scopus Publishing.

Pitt-Rivers, Julian. 1966. "Honour and social status." In *Honour and shame: The values of Mediterranean society*, ed. J. G. Peristiany, 19–77. Chicago: University of Chicago Press.

Popkin, Samuel L. 1979. *The rational peasant: The political economy of rural society in Vietnam*. Berkeley: University of California Press.

Post, Jerrold M. 2005. "The socio-cultural underpinnings of terrorist psychology: When hatred is bred in the bone." In *Root causes of terrorism: Myths, reality and ways forward*, ed. Tore Bjørjo, 54–69. London: Routledge.

Quinn, Herbert F. 1979. *The union nationale: Quebec nationalism from Duplessis to Lévesque*. 2nd ed. Toronto: University of Toronto Press.

Quintero Rivera, Ángel G. 1986. *Conflictos de clase y política en Puerto Rico* [Class and political conflicts in Puerto Rico]. 5th ed. Río Piedras, PR: Ediciones Huracán.

Qutb, Seyyid. n.d. *Milestones*. Damascus, Syria: Dar Al-Ilm.

Rambo, Eric H. 1999. "Symbolic interests and meaningful purposes." *Rationality and Society* 11 (3): 317–42.

Ramos-Zayas, Ana Y. 2003. *National performances: The politics of class, race, and space in Puerto Rican Chicago*. Chicago: University of Chicago Press.

Rapport, Nigel. 1998. "Coming home to a dream: A Study of the immigrant discourse of 'Anglo-Saxons' in Israel." In *Migrants of identity: Perceptions of home in a world of movement*, ed. Nigel Rapport and Andrew Dawson, 61–83. Oxford: Berg.

Razi, G. Hossein. 1990. "Legitimacy, religion, and nationalism in the Middle East." *American Political Science Review* 84 (1): 69–91.

Renan, Ernest. 1990. "What is a nation?" In *Nation and narration*, ed. Homi K. Bhabha, 8–22. London: Routledge.

Ribes Tovar, Federico. 1975. *Albizu Campos: El revolucionario* [Albizu Campos: The revolutionary]. New York: Plus Ultra.

Ridley, Matt. 1996. *The origins of virtue: Human instinct and the evolution of cooperation*. New York: Penguin Books.

Riker, William H., and Peter C. Ordeshook. 1973. *An introduction to positive political theory*. Englewood Cliffs, NJ: Prentice-Hall.

Rioux, Marcel. 1971. *Quebec in question*. Trans. James Boake. Toronto: James Lewis & Samuel.

Rivera, Ángel A. 1996. *Puerto Rico: Ficción y mitología en sus alternativas de status* [Puerto Rico: Fiction and mythology in its status alternatives]. San Juan, PR: Nueva Aurora.

Rivera Ramos, Efrén. 2001. *The legal construction of identity: The judicial and social legacy of American colonialism in Puerto Rico*. Washington, DC: American Psychological Association.

Robertson, Tatsha. 2003. "Evangelicals flock to Israel's banner: Christian Zionists see Jewish state bringing Messiah." *Boston Globe*, October 21, A3.

Robinson, Dean E. 2001. *Black nationalism in American politics and thought*. Cambridge, UK: Cambridge University Press.

Rodó, José E. 1988. *Ariel*. Trans. Margaret Sayers Peden. Austin: University of Texas Press. (Orig. pub. 1900.)

Rodríguez-Morazzani, Roberto P. 1998. "Political cultures of the Puerto Rican left in the United States." In *The Puerto Rican movement: Voices from the diaspora*, ed. Andrés Torres and José Velázquez, 25–47. Philadelphia: Temple University Press.

Rohter, Larry. 1988. "Mexico City journal Marilyn and Virgin: Art or sacrilege?" *New York Times*, April 2, 4.

Roosens, Eugeen E. 1989. *Creating ethnicity: The process of ethnogenesis.* Newbury Park, CA: Sage.

Ross, Marc H. 1997. "Culture and identity in comparative political analysis." In *Comparative politics: Rationality, culture, and structure*, ed. Mark I. Lichbach and Alan S. Zuckerman, 42–80. Cambridge: Cambridge University Press.

Rousseau, Jean-J. 1993. *The social contract and discourses.* Trans. G. D. H. Cole. London: J. M. Dent. (Orig. pub. 1762.)

———. 1984. *A discourse on inequality.* Trans. Maurice Cranston. London: Penguin Books. (Orig. pub. 1754.)

Rudé, George. 1995. *Ideology and popular protest.* Chapel Hill: University of North Carolina Press. (Orig. Pub. 1980.)

———. 1959. *The crowd in the French Revolution.* Oxford, UK: Oxford University Press.

Rustow, Walt W. 1990. *The stages of economic growth: A non-Communist manifesto.* 3rd ed. Cambridge: Cambridge University Press.

Sahlins, Marshall. 1976. *The use and abuse of biology: An anthropological critique of sociobiology.* Ann Arbor: University of Michigan Press.

Said, Edward W. 1994. *Culture and imperialism.* New York: Vintage Books.

———. 1979. *Orientalism.* New York: Vintage Books.

Sánchez Korrol, Virginia E. 1994. *From colonia to community: The history of Puerto Ricans in New York City.* Berkeley: University of California Press.

Scarano, Francisco A. 1996. "The Jíbaro masquerade and the subaltern politics of Creole identity formation in Puerto Rico, 1745–1823." *American Historical Review* 101 (5): 1398–1431.

Schmidt, Ronald. 2006. "Political theory and language policy." In *An introduction to language policy: Theory and method*, ed. Thomas Ricento, 95–110. Malden, MA: Blackwell.

Schöpflin, George. 1997. "The function of myth and a taxonomy of myth." In *Myths and nationhood*, ed. Geoffrey Hosking and George Schöpflin, 19–35. New York: Routledge.

Schuessler, Alexander A. 2000. *A logic of expressive choice.* Princeton, NJ: Princeton University Press.

Scott, James C. 1985. *Weapons of the weak: Everyday forms of peasant resistance.* New Haven, CT: Yale University Press.

Searle-White, Joshua. 2001. *The psychology of nationalism.* New York: Palgrave.

Semendeferi, Katrina, Este Armstrong, Axel Schleicher, Kart Zilles, and Gary W. Van Hoesen. 1998. "Limbic frontal cortex in hominids: A comparative study of Area 13." *American Journal of Physical Anthropology* 106 (2): 129–55.

Sen, Amartya K. 1990. "Rational fools: A critique of the behavioral foundations of economic theory." In *Beyond self-interest*, ed. Jane J. Mansbridge, 25–43. Chicago: University of Chicago Press.

Shaw, R. Paul, and Yuwa Wong. 1987. "Ethnic mobilization and the seeds of warfare: An evolutionary perspective." *International Studies Quarterly* 31:5–31.

Sheppard, Claude-Armand. 1971. *The law of languages in Canada*. Ottawa: Studies of the Royal Commission on Bilingualism and Biculturalism.

Shils, Edward. 1957. "Primordial, personal, sacred and civil ties." *British Journal of Sociology* 8 (2): 130–45.

Smith, Anthony D. 1997. "The 'golden age' and national revival." In *Myths and nationhood*, ed. Geoffrey Hosking and George Schöpflin, 36–59. New York: Routledge.

———. 1989. "The origin of nations." *Ethnic and Racial Studies* 12 (3): 340–67.

———. 1982. "Nationalism, ethnic separatism and the intelligentsia." In *National separatism*, ed. Colin H. Williams, 17–41. Cardiff: University of Wales Press.

Smith, Whitney. 1975. *Flags throughout the ages and across the world*. Maidenhead, UK: McGraw-Hill.

Stalin, Joseph. 1935. *Marxism and the national and colonial question*. New York: International Publishers.

Steinberg, Stephen. 1989. *The ethnic myth: Race, ethnicity, and class in America*. Boston: Beacon Press.

Sternhell, Zeev. 1998. *The founding myths of Israel*. Trans. David Maisel. Princeton, NJ: Princeton University Press.

Suleiman, Yasir. 2004. *A war of words: Language and conflict in the Middle East*. Cambridge: Cambridge University Press.

———. 2003. *The Arabic language and national identity*. Washington, DC: Georgetown University Press.

Taylor, Michael. 1982. *Community, anarchy and liberty*. Cambridge: Cambridge University Press.

Taylor, Peter. 1997. *Behind the mask: The IRA and Sinn Fein*. New York: TV Books.

Tilly, Charles. 2008. *Contentious performances*. Cambridge: Cambridge University Press.

Tocqueville, Alexis de. 1969. *Democracy in America*. Trans. George Lawrence. Ed. J. P. Mayer. New York: Harper Perennial. (Orig. Pub. 1835 and 1840.)

Tönnies, Ferdinand. 2001. *Community and civil society*. Trans. José Harris and Margaret Hollis. Ed. José Harris. Cambridge: Cambridge University Press. (Orig. pub. 1887.)

Toksöz, Itır. 2007. "Security dilemmas and threat perceptions: Turkey at the crossroads." PhD diss., Northeastern University, Boston.

Torres, Andrés. 1998. "Introduction: Political radicalism in the diaspora—The Puerto Rican experience." In *The Puerto Rican movement: Voices from the diaspora*, ed. Andrés Torres and José Velázquez, 1–22. Philadelphia: Temple University Press.

Torres González, Roamé. 2002. *Idioma, bilingüismo y nacionalidad: la presencia del inglés en Puerto Rico* [Language, bilingualism and nationality: The presence of English in Puerto Rico]. Río Piedras, PR: Editorial de la Universidad de Puerto Rico.

Trask, Haunai-Kay. 1993. *From a native daughter: Colonialism and sovereignty in Hawai'i*. Monroe, ME: Common Courage Press.

Trías Monge, José. 1997. *Puerto Rico: The trials of the oldest colony in the world*. New Haven: Yale University Press.

Trotsky, Leon. 1978. *Leon Trotsky on black nationalism & self-determination*. Ed. George Breitman. New York: Pathfinder.

Tsebelis, George. 1990. *Nested games: Rational choice in comparative politics*. Berkeley: University of California Press.

Tula, María T. 1994. *Hear my testimony: María Teresa Tula, human rights activist of El Salvador*. Trans. and ed. Lynn Stephen. Boston: South End Press.

Turner, Jonathan H. 2000. *On the origins of human emotions: A sociological inquiry into the evolution of human affect*. Stanford, CA: Stanford University Press.

Urciuoli, Bonnie. 1998. *Exposing prejudice: Puerto Rican experiences of language, race, and Class*. Boulder, CO: Westview.

Vallières, Pierre. 1971. *White niggers of America*. Trans. Joan Pinkham. Toronto: McClelland & Stewart.

Van den Berghe, Pierre L. 1978. "Race and ethnicity: A sociobiological perspective." *Ethnic and Racial Studies* 1 (4): 401–11.

———. 1981. *The ethnic phenomenon*. New York: Elsevier.

Vanhanen, Tatu. 1999. "Domestic ethnic conflict and ethnic nepotism: A comparative analysis." *Journal of Peace Research* 36 (1): 55–73.

Varshney, Ashutosh. 2003. "Nationalism, ethnic conflict, and rationality." *Perspectives on Politics* 1 (1): 85–99.

Veblen, Thorstein. 1973. *The theory of the leisure class*. Boston: Houghton Mifflin. (Orig. pub. 1899.)

Von Neumann, John, and Oskar Morgenstern. 1980. *Theory of games and economic behavior*. Princeton, NJ: Princeton University Press. (Orig. pub. 1944.)

Walicki, Andrzej. 2001. "Intellectual elites and the vicissitudes of 'imagined nation' in Poland." In *Intellectuals and the articulation of the nation*, ed. Ronald G. Suny and Michael D. Kennedy, 259–87. Ann Arbor: University of Michigan Press.

Waters, Mary C. 1990. *Ethnic options: Choosing identities in America*. Berkeley: University of California Press.

Weber, Eugen. 1976. *Peasants into Frenchmen: The modernization of rural France, 1870–1914*. Stanford, CA: Stanford University Press.

Weinstein, Brian. 1983. *The civic tongue: Political consequences of language choice*. New York: Longman.

Westen, Drew. 2007. *The political brain: The role of emotion in deciding the fate of the nation*. New York: Public Affairs.

Whitelam, Keith W. 1996. *The invention of ancient Israel: The silencing of Palestinian history*. New York: Routledge.

Whitmeyer, Joseph M. 1997. "Endogamy as a basis for ethnic behavior." *Sociological Theory* 15 (2): 162–78.

Williams, Colin H. 1982. "Separatism and the mobilization of Welsh national identity." In *National separatism*, ed. Colin H. Williams, 145–201. Cardiff: University of Wales Press.

Wilson, Mary C. 2002. "The Damascus Affair and the beginning of France's empire in the Middle East." In *Histories of the modern Middle East: New directions*, ed. Israel Gershoni, Hakan Erdem, and Ursula Woköck, 63–74. Boulder, CO: Lynne Rienner.

Wintrobe, Ronald. 2002. "Leadership and passion in extremist politics." In *Political extremism and rationality*, ed. Albert Breton, Gianluggi Galeotti, Pierre Salmon, and Ronald Wintrobe, 23–43. Cambridge: Cambridge University Press.

Wittman, Donald. 1983. "Candidate motivation: A synthesis of alternative theories." *American Political Science Review* 77 (1): 142–57.

———. 1990. "Spatial strategies when candidates have policy preferences." In *Advances in the spatial theory of voting*, ed. James M. Enelow and Melvin J. Hinich, 66–98. Cambridge: Cambridge University Press.

Wood, Elisabeth J. 2000. *Forging democracy from below: Insurgent transitions in South Africa and El Salvador*. Cambridge, UK: Cambridge University Press.

Woods, Thomas A. 1995. "Museums and the public: Doing history together." *Journal of American History* 82 (3): 1111–15.

Woolard, Kathryn A. 1989. *Double talk: Bilingualism and the politics of ethnicity in Catalonia*. Berkeley: University of California Press.

World Bible Publishers. 1976. *New American Bible*. Iowa Falls, IA.

Zerubavel, Yael. 1995. *Recovered roots: Collective memory and the making of Israeli national tradition*. Chicago: University of Chicago Press.

INDEX